Jack London

Revised Edition

Twayne's United States Authors Series

Nancy A. Walker, General Editor

Vanderbilt University

TUSAS 230

JACK LONDON
Reproduced by permission of The Huntington Library, San Marino, California

Jack London

Revised Edition

Earle Labor and
Jeanne Campbell Reesman

*Centenary College of Louisiana and the
University of Texas at San Antonio*

Twayne Publishers • New York
Maxwell Macmillan Canada • Toronto
Maxwell Macmillan International • New York Oxford Singapore Sydney

Twayne's United States Authors Series No. 230

Jack London, Revised Edition
Earle Labor and Jeanne Campbell Reesman

Copyright © 1994 by Twayne Publishers

Twayne Publishers   Maxwell Macmillan Canada, Inc.
Macmillan Publishing Company   1200 Eglinton Avenue East
866 Third Avenue   Suite 200
New York, New York 10022   Don Mills, Ontario M3C 3N1

Library of Congress Cataloging-in-Publication Data

Labor, Earle, 1928–
    Jack London / Earle Labor, Jeanne Campbell Reesman.—Rev. ed.
        p.   cm.—(Twayne's United States authors series; TUSAS 230)
    Includes bibliographical references and index.
    ISBN 0-8057-4033-3
    1. London, Jack, 1876–1916—Criticism and interpretation.
    Reesman, Jeanne Campbell. II. Title. III. Series.
PS3523.046Z68   1994
813' .52—dc20   93-49825
                                                                     CIP

The paper used in this publication meets the minimum requirements of American National Standard for Information Sciences—Permanence of Paper for Printed Library Materials. ANSI Z3948–1984. ∞™

10 9 8 7 6 5 4 3 2 1 (hc)

Printed in the United States of America

For
King Hendricks
and
Joseph Evan Campbell, Jr.

Contents

Preface

This new edition is necessitated—and, we hope, justified—for at least two reasons: the considerable amount and quality of scholarship and criticism produced on Jack London during the past 20 years, and our own desire to rectify two general misconceptions about London's work, still widely held, despite this impressive scholarly and critical work.

Apropos of the first reason, our bibliography of secondary sources has been substantially expanded to include what we believe to be the most important works of London scholarship to appear since the early 1970s. Among these, especially noteworthy are the half-dozen or so books that have significantly enhanced our understanding of London's complex genius and character. Thanks to the efforts of Russ Kingman, whose *Pictorial Life of Jack London* (1979) combines the sympathetic understanding and the biographical integrity so long needed in the various publications about London's life, we at last have a reliable account of the major factors that shaped London's legendary career. More recently, the publication of Kingman's *Jack London: A Definitive Chronology* (1992) has been hailed as a milestone in London scholarship. And thanks to James I. McClintock and Charles N. Watson, Jr., we have substantial book-length critical studies of the two major facets of London's literary work: his short stories (McClintock's *White Logic,* 1975) and his novels (Watson's *The Novels of Jack London: A Reappraisal,* 1983).

The centennial of London's birth, 1976, was, of course, a banner year for London studies: three major scholarly journals in America—*Modern Fiction Studies, Western American Literature,* and *The Pacific Historian*—published special Jack London issues, as did the Paris-based journal *Europe.* A score of first-rate essays appeared in these publications. Subsequently, Joan Sherman's *Jack London: A Reference Guide* (1977), Jacqueline Tavernier-Courbin's *Critical Essays on Jack London* (1983), and David Mike Hamilton's *"The Tools of My Trade": Annotated Books in Jack London's Library* (1986), have complemented the work of Hensley Woodbridge and Dale Walker in providing the London scholar with useful resource materials. Reliable texts of many of London's most important works are appearing with increasing frequency from major publishing houses. Beyond these contributions, articles on London have appeared regularly in the scholarly journals during the past 20 years, providing valuable insights into London's works as well as giving him academic respectability. In 1991, for example, *American Literary Realism* presented a special issue with new essays by major scholars, and in 1992 *Thalia: Studies in Literary Humor* devoted a special issue to London. The continuing interest in London among foreign scholars—in China, Japan, and India, as well as in Europe—confirms his status as a significant figure in world literature, and *The Call of the Wild*—now translated into more than 80 different languages—is America's best claim to a great world novel.

Concerning the second reason for undertaking a new edition of this book, we particularly wish to correct two serious misconceptions about London's work: first, that London's greatest literary strength lay in his ability (indeed, in his compulsion) to produce formulaic hackwork for the literary marketplace—that it was essentially the demands of the literary marketplace that dictated what he produced, and, second, that his creative energies declined sharply during the last decade of his life. Both of these assumptions are demonstrably invalid, as any careful reading of London's works will attest. The problem is—and always has been—that the critics who make such assumptions have not taken the trouble to read London. We have therefore discussed at some length four important neglected stories in a new chapter 5—and have commented briefly on a dozen others. But we have only scratched the surface; much work remains to be done on London's lesser-known creations, the scope of which is truly astonishing.

Before he was an American hero, political figure, or war adventurer, Jack London was a *writer.* As newer approaches to his narrative style and structure have developed, their application to London's works has been richly rewarding. For example, notwithstanding critical acknowledgment of the philosophical challenge to his individualism posed by his Socialism, London is coming to be seen less and less as strictly a "Naturalist" writer in the traditional sense of dwelling upon individual survival and power within a (usually) hostile environment. We trace throughout his works a number of competing emphases, especially his recurring insistence that survival is a matter of relying on comradeship within the society one occupies as well as achieving a sense of connectedness to all humanity through psychic integration of what is sometimes called the collective unconscious. As an artist Jack London is complex and conflicted, driven to search for meaning within and without, driven to "make it new" *and* to make it public. His career enacts again and again the urge to connect self and "other." In this regard, for example, we have found particularly illuminating the application of gender studies to London's works, which reveals radical patterns of thought regarding masculinity and femininity (especially in his late fiction) that generate new narrative forms, dialogic and polyphonic. Other such unexpected facets of his writing are also explored in these pages.

For their guidance and encouragement in writing the first edition, Professor Labor wishes again to acknowledge his substantial debts to P. B. Lindsey, who introduced him in his college years to *Martin Eden;* to A. P. Palmer of Carol's Book Shop in Shreveport, Louisiana, who helped him begin collecting London books; to Harry Hayden Clark, who directed his dissertation on London's literary artistry at the University of Wisconsin; to such friends as Sam Baskett, Steven Dhondt, Lilian Furst, Wilfred Guerin, Howard Lachtman, Lee Morgan, Diane Price, James Sisson, Dick Weiderman, and John Willingham, who periodically revived his scholarly morale; and to the editors who allowed him to quote from his previously published works, including Hensley Woodbridge (*Jack London Newsletter*), Harwood Hinton (*Arizona and the West*), G. B. Tennyson (*Nineteenth Century Fiction*), Harrietta Burford (University of California Press), Rochelle Girson and Roberta Craig (*Saturday Review*), Frank L. Hoskins, Jr. (*Studies in Short Fiction*), and Elisabeth Jakab (Harper & Row). He remains grateful for the grants he received from Adrian College, Centenary College, the Henry E. Huntington Library, and the National Endowment for the Humanities; for the expert advice of Tony Bubka, Russ Kingman, and Sal Noto; for the generous friendship of Irving Shepard and King Hendricks; and for the gracious assistance of the directors and staffs of the Huntington Library and the Merrill Library at Utah State University. Above all, he is forever indebted to the late Betty Labor for her many years of loving support.

For their helpful suggestions in the preparation of this new edition, we wish to express our gratitude especially to Russ Kingman; Howard Lachtman; Charles N. Watson, Jr.; Earl J. Wilcox; Hensley Woodbridge; Andrew Furer; Liz Traynor Fowler; Lawrence I. Berkove; Robert C. Leitz, III; David Nordloh, and Nancy A. Walker. Our only regret is that we could not incorporate all their thoughtful advice into the limited compass of this volume. For his unwavering support and warm generosity we are grateful to I. Milo Shepard. At Centenary College, we thank former President Donald A. Webb, the Faculty Personnel and Economic Policy Committee, and Mr. and Mrs. Edwin C. Harbuck for financial assistance that has furthered the progress of this work. At the University of Texas at San Antonio, we are grateful to Provost Raymond T. Garza, Dean William F. Lee III, and

Division Director Alan E. Craven for their support. We deeply appreci-
ate the unfailing assistance of Alan Jutzi, Virginia Renner, Sara S.
Hodson, Janet Hawkins, and Barbara Quinn at the Huntington Library.
We thank Gary Scharnhorst, James Barbour, and Robert Fleming, edi-
tors of *American Literary Realism,* for permission to use sections of Jeanne
Campbell Reesman's 1992 article, "Jack London's New Woman in a
New World: Saxon Brown Roberts' Journey into the Valley of the
Moon," and Thomas J. Lyon, editor of *Western American Literature,* for
permission to use material from Earle Labor's essay on "Jack London's
Agrarian Vision," which originally appeared in the London Centennial
Number of that journal, and from Jeanne Campbell Reesman's 1988
"The Problem of Knowledge in 'The Water Baby.'" For help in preparing
our manuscript we are indebted to Patty Roberts, Thom Wood, Mark
Juelg, Gail Jones, and Amanda Bunt. We warmly thank Therese Myers,
Mark Zadrozny, and Lesley Poliner at Twayne Publishers for their careful
attention to the preparation of this volume.

Earle Labor
Centenary College of Louisiana
Jeanne Campbell Reesman
University of Texas at San Antonio

From the Preface to the First Edition

Jack London was the most flamboyant literary representative of the Strenuous Age in America. At the height of that era his name was a byword for rugged individualism and romantic adventure, and his private life was front-page copy for every major newspaper in the country.[1] In the decade preceding World War I, London dominated the public imagination—and the literary marketplace—as few authors have done, before or since. His fabulous career meshed with the Golden Era of the Magazine (his success was, in large measure, predicated on the popularity of the magazine), and he commanded top dollar in the best: the *Atlantic, Century, Harper's, Collier's, Cosmopolitan, Saturday Evening Post.* Virtually everything he wrote, he sold—and he wrote 1,000 words each day for 17 years. During the years from 1900 until his death in 1916, he produced more than 50 books with a an astonishing range of subjects: agronomy, architecture, astral projection, boating, ecology, gold-hunting, hoboing, loving, penal reform, prizefighting, Socialism, warfare. He became one of the world's most translated, most widely read, authors.[2] Today, persistent neglect by the academic critics notwithstanding, more than 80 editions of his works are listed in *Books in Print.*

Because of the scope of London's work, I must in this brief introduction be suggestive rather than exhaustive. My aim is to provide the reader with a reasonably accurate guide to the literary world of Jack London, much of which has remained a dark continent for the critics. Most are vaguely aware of *The Sea-Wolf* and of a handful of the Klondike stories because these may still be encountered in junior high school anthologies and in the old "B" movies on television late shows. But few realize that London pioneered in the apocalyptic novel and dystopian fiction, that a major segment of his work deals with the American Dream and the Myth of Success, that parts of his *People of the Abyss* compare favorably with William Blake's treatises on the poor of industrial England, that his indictments of the white man's exploitation of the South Seas are as incisive as Herman Melville's, and that his fictional use of Freud and Jung anticipated the new literature of the 1920s. Most of the critics do not know these things because they have not read him.

While dealing individually with London's more than 500 separately published items within the limits of this book is impossible, I do indicate the extent of the London canon and have selected for specific analysis works that represent his major thematic concerns as well as his distinctive stylistic and temperamental characteristics. I can only hope that more readers will be encouraged to discover these treasures for themselves.

In addition to pointing out the extent of London's work, I also attempt to probe the mystery of his remarkable creative genius. On one level the animation of that genius was the direct result of the dynamics of his cultural mythology: Jack London was a self-made man who drove himself to spectacular heights because his social conscience whispered that in America "getting ahead" was not merely possible but expected. In other words, he was motivated by the same cultural imperative that has driven the American hero ever since Benjamin Franklin demonstrated that the Puritan work ethic could be pleasurable as well as profitable. Success, in its peculiar American version, is a key factor in London's career; and because of his overwhelming commitment to the American Dream, much of what he wrote speaks forcefully to our own era.

But the tension produced by the individual ego working to assert its mastery over the phenomenal world is not the deepest source of London's creative energy. That source is deeper than the American culture, and to give it a label I must resort to Carl Gustav Jung, who used such terms as *the collective unconscious* and *primordial vision*. As I suggest in analyzing several of London's works, not only was he a dedicated professional craftsman, but he often wrote better than he knew. Ironically, although he considered himself supremely rational—a scientific thinker and a "materialistic monist"—his most enduring work was generated from psychological depths beyond his logical understanding. *The Call of the Wild* is an outstanding case in point, but it is only one of many such instances. We cannot fully comprehend London's artistic significance until we have plumbed those psychic depths.

When I say that Jack London merits recognition as a "major figure" in American literature, I use the term advisedly. His status as a great writer or as a major American author is yet to be established. I am personally convinced he deserves serious consideration for both offices, but I cannot confer such honors—they must be won by fair election at the critical polls. My primary aim is to place London's name on the ballot.

Earle Labor
Centenary College of Louisiana

Chronology

1876   Jack London born in San Francisco, California, 12 January, the only child of Flora Wellman, who names as the father William Henry Chaney, an astrologer and public lecturer she lived with during 1874–75. She names the child John Griffith Chaney. On 7 September 1876 she marries John London, a widower with two daughters, Eliza and Ida. The baby is now named John Griffith London.

1891   After living on several farms and ranches in California, London completes grammar school in Oakland. Works in cannery. Purchases sloop, the *Razzle-Dazzle,* with $300 loaned by his former wet nurse, "Aunt Jenny" Prentiss. Raids oyster beds; then joins the California Fish Patrol.

1893   Seven-month voyage aboard the sealing schooner *Sophia Sutherland.* Wins first prize in contest for "best descriptive article" in San Francisco *Morning Call* for "Story of a Typhoon off the Coast of Japan."

1894   Works as coal-heaver in electric railway power plant; leaves this for tramping experiences, later recounted in *The Road* (1907).

1895   Resumes public-school education at Oakland High School, where he writes sketches for student magazine, *The High School Aegis.* Falls in love with Mabel Applegarth, the Ruth Morse of *Martin Eden.*

1896   Joins Socialist Labor Party. Attends the University of California for one semester.

1897   Joins Klondike gold rush and spends winter in the Yukon Territory. John London dies.

1898   Returns from the Yukon and undertakes writing as a profession.

1899   Publishes his first story, "To the Man on Trail," and other Northland stories in the *Overland Monthly;* begins selling other items to magazines and newspapers.

1900   Publishes "An Odyssey of the North" in the *Atlantic Monthly*. Marries Bessie Maddern. *The Son of the Wolf* is published.

1901   First daughter, Joan, born 15 January. Runs unsuccessfully for mayor of Oakland on the Socialist ticket.

1902   Lives for six weeks in East End of London, England, collecting materials for *The People of the Abyss* (1903). Second daughter, Becky, born 20 October. First novel, *A Daughter of the Snows,* is published by J. B. Lippincott.

1903   *The Call of the Wild* brings him worldwide acclaim. Falls in love with Charmian Kittredge; separates from Bessie.

1904   Hearst correspondent for Russo-Japanese War. Divorce proceedings are initiated by Bessie. *The Sea-Wolf* is published.

1905   Marries Charmian Kittredge. Purchases ranch in Glen Ellen, California. Another unsuccessful mayoral race. Lectures throughout East on Socialism, including stop at Harvard. Publishes the first prizefight novel, *The Game*.

1906   Lectures at Yale, Carnegie Hall, and throughout the Midwest. Reports on San Francisco earthquake for *Collier's*. Begins building famous sailboat, the *Snark*. Publishes *White Fang*.

1907   Sails from Oakland on the *Snark* 23 April; visits Hawaii, the Marquesas, and Tahiti. Is publicly accused of "nature faking" by President Theodore Roosevelt.

1908   After brief return home aboard the steamship *Mariposa* to straighten out financial affairs, continues *Snark* voyage: to Samoa, Figi, New Hebrides, and the Solomons. Answers President Roosevelt's nature-faking charge in article "The Other Animals" (*Collier's,* 5 September). *The Iron Heel* is published.

1909   Is hospitalized in Sydney, Australia, with multiple tropical ailments. Abandons plans for sailing *Snark* around the world: returns home via Ecuador, Panama, New Orleans, and Grand Canyon. *Martin Eden* is published.

1910   Devotes energies to building Beauty Ranch; starts construction of Wolf House, his massive stone-and-redwood lodge built to last for centuries. Daughter Joy is born and dies. Publishes *Burning Daylight,* his first Sonoma ranching novel.

1911   Drives four-horse carriage with Charmian and manservant Nakata through Northern California and Oregon.

1912   Sails around Cape Horn aboard the *Dirigo.* Charmian's second baby is lost (miscarriage). *The House of Pride,* a collection of Hawaiian stories, is published.

1913   Publishes *The Abysmal Brute* (prizefight novel), *The Night-Born* (miscellaneous stories), *John Barleycorn* (best-selling treatise on alcoholism), and *The Valley of the Moon* (his second Sonoma novel). Wolf House is destroyed by fire, cause unknown.

1914   Reports Mexican Revolution for *Collier's;* is forced to return home by severe case of dysentery. Suffers attacks of rheumatism.

1915   Spends several months in Hawaii, hoping to improve health. *The Star Rover* is published.

1916   His last Sonoma novel, *The Little Lady of the Big House,* is published. Resigns from Socialist Labor Party "because of its lack of fire and fight, and its loss of emphasis on the class struggle." Returns home from Hawaii in late July. Suffers severe bouts of uremia and rheumatism; is warned by his doctors to restrict drinking and diet. Dies 22 November; bulletin is issued by four attending physicians attributing cause of death to "gastro-intestinal type of uraemia." Probable cause of death: stroke and heart failure.

Chapter One

The American Adam

"No great American idol," the historian Dixon Wecter tells us, "has lacked a touch lent by the struggle against odds, or by discouragement and passing failure. He must be a man who fights uphill."[1] Wecter's comment is most useful in helping us to understand the phenomenal career of Jack London, a literary idol who became a national legend before he reached age 30.[2] No major figure in American literature struggled against greater odds, none fought uphill with more spectacular success, and none achieved wider popularity. He was born out of wedlock, reared under the constant threat of hardship, spent much of his adolescence in delinquency, and entered maturity without formal professional training—yet he succeeded in becoming one of the most talented, most widely read, most highly paid authors of his epoch. In reviewing the facts of his life, we can readily appreciate the observation that "the greatest story Jack London ever wrote was the story he lived."[3]

Even in America that story seems incredible. He had returned penniless from adventures in the Klondike gold rush; his adoptive father, John London, had recently died, leaving London with the burden of supporting the family; his frantic efforts to become a professional writer had earned no more than a boxful of rejection slips. But from this adversity came the kind of vital resolution that characterized Jack London throughout his life. "I don't care if the whole present, all I possess, were swept away from me," he declared, "I will build a new present. . . ."[4] Within a year he had achieved success by making his way into the exclusive pages of the *Atlantic Monthly* and by signing his first book contract with a distinguished Boston publishing house. Within five years his sociological crusades and his personal escapades, counterpointing his Northland adventure tales, made his name international newscopy. During the 18 years from his resolution to succeed in 1898 until his death in 1916 he accomplished enough to satisfy a half-dozen normally ambitious men. He managed to support several families from his earnings as a writer. He traveled, lectured, and wrote freely in behalf of the Socialist Labor Party. He risked his life by disappearing into the hellholes of London's East End to gather firsthand material for an impressive soci-

1

ological exposé, *The People of the Abyss.* He worked as a war correspondent
during the Russo-Japanese War of 1904 and the Mexican Revolution of
1914. Moreover, his newspaper articles on professional boxing signaled a
new field of sports writing. He built and sailed his own ship, the fabled
Snark, halfway around the globe. He became a landowner, developing in
Northern California's Valley of the Moon a model ranch, part of which is
now the Jack London State Historical Park. A friend to horticulturalist
Luther Burbank, London pioneered in modern agricultural methods and
livestock breeding. He worked hard to bring about reforms in the
California penal system, giving free room and board to paroled convicts
at his ranch. An eclectic reader, he responded not only to the work of
such established literary figures as Robert Louis Stevenson, Rudyard
Kipling, and Joseph Conrad, but also to the radical new extraliterary
concepts of Sigmund Freud and C. G. Jung. At the same time he managed somehow to answer countless letters from friends, aspiring writers,
down-and-outers, literary admirers, and editors. In this same 18-year
period, London also produced a half-hundred books.

The Mythic Hero

Born only 14 years before the 1890 census marked the closing of the
frontier, coming of age during that decade called "the watershed of
American history,"[5] and dying less than a year before the United States
entered World War I, London personified crucial transition in his
nation's cultural development. Although America's childhood had been
left behind at Gettysburg and Appomattox, America's maturity was
delayed: it was still the Age of Adolescence, with the manifestations of
tension, instability, extravagance, and contrariness that characterize this
phase in nations as well as in individuals.[6] Aggressively optimistic,
bluntly honest but unselfconscious, dynamic, and extraverted, London
was a child of that experience. Yet he became a man of the twentieth
century: complex, hypersensitive, fragmented, melancholic—at
moments self-destructive and profoundly aware of the darkness within
the human heart.[7]

A combination of apparent inconsistencies, arising perhaps from his
frontier heritage with its paradoxical juxtapositions,[8] has made Jack
London a difficult subject for scholarly analysis. He insisted, especially in
his later years, that he hated writing and that he wrote only for money,
but most of his work departed sharply from the best-seller formulas of
his age, and he was militant in defending his literary sincerity. On the

one hand, he was dedicated to telling the truth as he saw it; on the other, he could not resist a penchant for bardic exaggeration. Despite his reputation as a crude, red-blooded Naturalist, his fictional treatment of sex was embarrassingly genteel. Honest to a fault in his personal relationships, he was a sharp horse trader who was capable of swapping his worst hack writing for hard cash. Big-hearted, generous to the verge of bankruptcy, he also had a remarkable talent for petty squabbling and invective, as many of his letters attest. A humanitarian with profound compassion for the underdog, regardless of color or class, he nevertheless exhibited views typical of his time regarding white, and specifically Anglo-Saxon, superiority.

A tough fighter, relentless when his ego was challenged, he was a warmly sensitive friend and a sentimental lover. He was the manliest of men, yet he never outgrew his weaknesses for childish fun and games, practical jokes, and candy. Despite his love of the outdoors and his reputation as a superman, his medical history is an appalling record of debilitating ailments; physically, he was worn-out by age 40. Self-educated, he considered himself a great thinker, yet he could unblinkingly accommodate to his weltanschauung the disparate philosophical attitudes of Friedrich Nietzsche, Karl Marx, Ernst Haeckel, Herbert Spencer, and Benjamin Kidd,[9] while blandly admitting that metaphysicians such as Ralph Waldo Emerson and Henri Bergson were beyond him. A rugged individualist who preached Socialism, London fought his crusade for World Revolution with a unique mixture of Marxist piety and frontier pep. While he insisted he was a logical positivist and a materialistic monist, his best work is permeated with poetry and myth.

If this image of Jack London confuses us, we should bear in mind that many of these apparent discrepancies were the manifestations of a dynamic personality and a versatile intelligence. His life was a symbolic epitome of the myth of the rugged individual, and not even Walt Whitman, who devoted all his genius to projecting this archetype, could so thoroughly incarnate in his personal identity the traits of the American folk hero.

The Hero as Juvenile

In *The American Adam,* R. W. B. Lewis defined the mythic figure of his title as "a radically new personality, the hero of the new adventure: an individual emancipated from history, happily bereft of ancestry, untouched and undefiled by the usual inheritances of family and race; an individual standing alone, self-reliant and self-propelling, ready to confront whatever awaited him with the aid of his own unique and inherent resources."[10]

The definition might have been personally tailored to suit Jack London, who was born in the poorer district of San Francisco, a "natural" child, literally if not happily bereft of ancestry; for his paternity has never been conclusively established. Several biographers, including London's own daughter Joan, have suggested that the father was William Henry Chaney, a footloose astrologer with whom Flora Wellman, his mother, lived in 1875;[11] it was Chaney whom Flora named as father on the infant's birth certificate. But Chaney had left her in an indignant rage when he learned of her pregnancy; and when, many years later, London wrote to Chaney asking him if he were truly his father, the old man insisted that he had been impotent at the time of the child's conception and could not possibly have been the father. In any case, eight months after the child's birth, Flora Wellman Chaney married John London, a widower who had two daughters and who treated the boy as his own from that time forward.[12]

Aside from the question of London's paternal ancestry, he clearly felt the threat of poverty during his early years. John London was a good father and a conscientious worker, but his vitalities had been sapped by Civil War injuries and by chronic misfortune. The get-rich schemes and the frequent moves instigated by Flora aggravated the family's economic problems. At an early age London was forced by necessity to become a self-propelling individualist confronting circumstances and destiny "with the aid of his own unique and inherent resources." Describing his childhood miseries in a letter to Mabel Applegarth, he wrote:

> . . . I have fought and am fighting my battle alone. . . . Do you know my childhood? When I was seven years old, at the country school of San Pedro, this happened. Meat, I was that hungry for it I once opened a girl's basket and stole a piece of meat—a little piece the size of my two fingers. . . . In those days, like Esau, I would have literally sold my birthright for a mess of pottage, a piece of meat. . . .
> This meat incident is an epitome of my whole life.
> I was eight years old when I put on my first undershirt made at or bought at a store. Duty—at ten years I was on the streets selling newspapers. Every cent was turned over to my people, and I went to school in constant shame of the hats, shoes, clothes I wore. Duty—from then on I had no childhood. Up at three o'clock in the morning to carry papers. When that was finished I did not go home but continued on to school.

School out, my evening papers. Saturday I worked on an ice wagon.
Sunday I went to a bowling alley and set up pins for drunken Dutchmen.
Duty—I turned over every cent and went dressed like a scarecrow.
(*Letters*, 23–24)

Later in a letter to his first publisher, he asserted, ". . . from my ninth
year, with the exception of the hours spent at school (and I earned them
by hard labor), my life has been one of toil" (*Letters*, 149). But, lest it
seem that he was nothing more than a drudge—"a work beast," as he
called himself—it should be pointed out he was able repeatedly to
escape the dull routine of toil.

His first means of escape was through romantic literature. "I always
could read and write," he boasted, "and have no recollection antedating
such a condition. Folks say I simply insisted upon being taught. Was an
omnivorous reader. . . . Remember reading some of Trowbridge's works
for boys at six years of age. At seven I was reading Paul du Chaillu's
Travels, Captain Cook's *Voyages*, and *Life of Garfield*. . . . At eight I was
deep in Ouida and Washington Irving" (*Letters*, 148). For those familiar
only with the Jack London legend and not with the boy behind the legend, it comes as something of a shock to realize that as a youngster he
was regarded by his grade-school classmates as a "bookworm." At age
10, after his family had moved back to the city after five years of living
on farms and ranches, London discovered the Oakland Public Library, a
major event in his life. "It was this world of books, now accessible, that
practically gave me the basis of my education," he later explained: "Not
until I began fighting for a living and making my first successes so that I
was able to buy books for myself did I ever discontinue drawing many
books on many library cards from out of the Oakland free public library"
(*Letters*, 1392).

So desperately did London crave the riches he found in this new world
that for weeks he haunted the library, spending every spare hour with its
treasures. Years afterward he recalled with some humor that he had very
nearly developed a case of St. Vitus dance in his hollow-eyed nervous
exhaustion: "I read mornings, afternoons, and nights. I read in bed, read
at table, I read as I walked to and from school, and I read at recess while
the other boys were playing."[13]

But such bibliomania could not last. Hard work brought him back
into the real world. Shortly after finishing grade school, he went to work
full-time in Hickmott's cannery in West Oakland, where the working
day ranged from 10 to 20 hours. A traumatic experience, the cannery

ordeal indelibly impressed upon young Jack the deadly odium of physical toil. His later story "The Apostate" was emotionally, if not literally,
autobiographical; of Johnny, the boy in the story, London wrote: "There
was no joyousness in life for him. The procession of the days he never
saw. The nights he slept away in twitching unconsciousness. . . . He had
no mental life whatever; yet deep down in the crypts of his mind,
unknown to him, were being weighed and sifted every hour of his toil,
every movement of his hands, every twitch of his muscles, and prepara-
tions were making for a future course of action that would amaze him
and all his little world."[14]

Johnny, the apostate, deserts his role as a "work-beast" by hopping a
freight train. In similar spirit Jack borrowed $300 from his onetime wet
nurse, "Aunt Jennie" Prentiss, bought a sloop, joined the hoodlum gang
on the Oakland waterfront, and became at age 15, "Prince of the Oyster
Pirates." "San Francisco Bay is no mill pond by the way," he wrote about
those irresponsible years. "I was a salmon fisher, an oyster pirate, a
schooner sailor, a fish patrolman, a longshoreman, and a general sort of
bay-faring adventurer—a boy in years and a man amongst men." Yet
even during these adventures he did not lose his craving for books:
"Always a book, and always reading when the rest were asleep; when
they were awake I was one with them, for I was always a good comrade"
(*Letters,* 149). The American Adam, no matter how keen his intellectual
appetite, never allowed books to preempt comradeship.

Reminiscing about his juvenile escapades, London remarked that all
his waterfront colleagues had wound up either dead or behind bars; and
perhaps the greatest miracle of his miraculous career was that he managed to reach manhood at all, for he was a habitual friend to danger as
well as to his fellows. The frequency with which these adventures of
London's youth are used in his writings suggests that he himself saw in
them more than commercial fodder; they represented a spirit of freedom.
He devoted two entire books—*The Cruise of the Dazzler* and *Tales of the
Fish Patrol*—and parts of a half-dozen others to fictionalized projections
of this juvenile persona. In *The Valley of the Moon,* for instance, the heroine, during a stroll along the Bay shore, makes the acquaintance of a 13-
year-old boy named John who tells her his dreams of glory:

> Don't you sometimes feel you'd die if you didn't know what's beyond
> them hills an' what's beyond the other hills behind them hills? An' the
> Golden Gate! There's the Pacific Ocean beyond, and China an' Japan, an'

India, an' . . . an' all the coral islands. You can go anywhere out through
the Golden Gate—to Australia, to Africa, to the seal islands, to the
North Pole, to Cape Horn. Why, all them places are just waitin' for me
to come an' see 'em. I've lived in Oakland all my life, but I'm not going
to live in Oakland the rest of my life, not by a long shot. I'm goin' to get
away . . . away. . . .[15]

London was undoubtedly recalling the far music of his own youthful
dreams. Within a week of his seventeenth birthday, jaded even with his
bay-faring life, he shipped before the mast as an able seaman on the
Sophia Sutherland, a sealing schooner bound for Japan and the Bering Sea.

The Wonderful Boy—Manqué

The seven-month voyage aboard the *"Sophie" Sutherland,* as London
called her, was relatively unspectacular, but it yielded several important
results, including materials that he would profitably use later. Most
immediately, it provided evidence that, with a bit of touching up, the
stuff of raw experience could be crafted into prose and exchanged for
cash. Two months after his ship had docked, the San Francisco *Morning
Call* sponsored a creative-writing contest for young talent. Encouraged
by his mother, London wrote a brief narrative sketch that described a
typhoon he had experienced during his voyage. Simply titled "Story of a
Typhoon off the Coast of Japan," the piece was an unusual accomplishment for a 17-year-old with only a grade-school education. Fresh, vivid,
unpretentious, it still reads well. It reveals, moreover, several of the characteristics that distinguish London's mature work: a natural feel for
graceful syntax and for imagery that evokes multiple sensory response,
particularly through sound symbolism:

> . . . Huge gunies rose slowly, fluttering their wings in the light breeze
> and striking their webbed feet on the surface of the water for over half a
> mile before they could leave it. Hardly had the patter, patter died away
> when a flock of sea quail rose, and with whistling wings flew away to
> windward, where members of a large band of whales were disporting
> themselves, their blowings sounding like the exhaust of steam engines.
> The harsh, discordant cries of a sea-parrot grated unpleasantly on the ear,
> and set half a dozen on the alert in a small band of seals that were ahead
> of us. . . . The boats were soon among the seals, and the bang! bang! of
> the guns could be heard from down to leeward.[16]

The story contains more than good descriptive detail. Added to the narrative suspense as the ship suffers the rising violence of the great storm, and synchronized with it, is the dying agony of one of the crew members, a former bricklayer who has tuberculosis. London's conclusion shows the instinct of the born storyteller to correlate natural phenomenon and human interest: "And so with the storm passed away the bricklayer's soul." Amateur work, obviously, it nevertheless hints of a genuine talent that also impressed the judges of the *Morning Call* contest. They awarded London the $25 first prize over second- and third-place entries by students from Berkeley and Stanford.

With a bit of luck Jack London might have developed then and there into another Thomas Chatterton, the Wonderful Boy. Elated by his victory, he whipped out a half-dozen more short pieces. But the contest was past, and although he had received money for writing, he was still a long way from being a professional.

The Wonderful Year—Manqué

In 1893, in many ways the annus mirabilis of the decade, Frederick Jackson Turner offered his now-famous thesis that "American social development has been continually beginning over again on the frontier. This perennial rebirth, this fluidity of American life, this expansion westward with its new opportunities, its continuous touch with the simplicity of primitive society, furnish the forces dominating American character. . . . And now, four centuries from the discovery of America, at the end of a hundred years of life under the Constitution, the frontier has gone, and with its going has closed the first period of American history." Since the days of Columbus America had been "another name for opportunity," but by Turner's day its incessant tone of expansion had already begun to be replaced with nostalgia for the old days and their "gifts of free land" (Turner, 21).

Eighteen ninety-three was also the year of the great Columbian Exposition in Chicago, and what Henry Adams saw there was a clear if unsettling indication of the new way. "During this last decade everyone talked and seemed to feel *fin-de-siècle*," he wrote in his prophetic autobiography. "Education ran riot at Chicago": the alleged unity of natural force that had for ages anchored the logical faith of the historian was at Chicago unmasked as fond delusion, and the historical mind, hitherto attuned to metaphysical and political causality, was helpless when confronted with mechanical sequence. The ultimate destiny for an America bound to such sequence might be in grave question, but the direction itself was unmistakable: "For a hundred years . . . the American people had hesitated, vacillated, swayed forward and back, between two forces, one simply industrial, the other capitalistic, centralizing, and mechanical. In 1893, the issue came on the single gold standard, and the majority at last declared itself, once for all, in favor of the capitalistic system with all its necessary machinery."[17]

Parts for this necessary machinery were an overseas market for manufactured goods and a huge labor force—preferably with a surplus of laborers—to produce those goods. America found herself in possession of these and the other necessary parts by the end of the nineteenth century. Unfortunately, among the risks of capitalism was that of severe economic recession, and overseas interests enhanced that risk. Eighteen ninety-three was, in consequence, the year of the economic catastrophe known as the Great Panic, and it ushered in what Samuel Eliot Morison and Henry Steele Commager have described as the darkest period in American history since the Civil War.[18] To save the nation, "General" Jacob Coxey, a wealthy quarry owner in Massillon, Ohio, had decided that he would lead an army of unemployed workers in protest to the steps of the Capitol in Washington, D.C.

Meanwhile, Jack London was learning the facts about the new American system as an industrial buck private. His first job after returning from sea had been in the jute mills, where he worked for the same wages that he had received years earlier as a boy worker in the cannery. Deciding that he must learn a trade, he presented himself eagerly to the superintendent at the power plant for the Oakland, San Leandro, and Hayward Street Railway, to whom he offered his muscle power cheaply in return for a chance to become an electrician: ". . . I still believed in the old myths which were the heritage of the American boy when I was a boy. A canal boy could become a President. Any boy, who took employment with any firm, could, by thrift, energy and sobriety, learn the business and rise from position to position until he was taken in as a junior partner. After that the senior partnership was only a matter of time. Very often—so ran the myth—the boy, by reason of his steadiness and application, married his employer's daughter" (*Barleycorn,* 187–88).

London was indeed "taken in," but not in the sense he anticipated, and his reward was not the boss's daughter—it was a two-man job at less than half pay: the alert superintendent, with his eye on profit, hired the eager youth at $30 per month to replace two coal shovelers at $40 each. Instead of making an electrician out of him, London recollected, that superintendent had decided to make $50 a month out of him. For several weeks London endured an agony the like of which he had never imagined, even in the cannery and jute mills; but he was finally rescued by one of the older hands at the plant who risked his own job to tell Jack about the superintendent's shenanigan. "Learning a trade could go hang," London decided when he learned the ruse. "It was a whole lot better to royster and frolic over the world in the way I had previously done. So I headed out on the adventure path again, starting to tramp East by beating my way on the railroads" (*Barleycorn,* 201). At this point his personal destiny meshed with the larger economic forces set in motion during the Critical Year.

Portrait of the Artist as a Road Kid

By "The Road" London meant the railroad. As early as his oyster-pirating days, he had lucked into "a push" of road kids who taught him how to ride the "blinds" over "the hill" (the Sierra Nevada), how to "batter the main stem for light pieces" (to beg for money on the main street), and how to "throw his feet" for handouts. Consequently, the announcement in the Oakland newspapers that, "General" Charles T. Kelly would lead the Western contingent of Coxey's Army of the Unemployed across the nation on flatcars was all the excuse London needed to hit The Road again. "I became a tramp—well, because of the life that was in me, of the wanderlust in my blood that would not let me rest," he wrote. "I went on 'The Road' because I couldn't work all my life on 'one same shift'; because—well, just because it was easier to than not to." As he later looked back on what he learned from this time, London realized that at this stage, he was interested in adventure, not in sociology. "Sociology was merely incidental," he admitted, "it came afterward in the same manner that a wet skin follows a ducking."[19] He spent no more than a month with Kelly's Army, missing its departure on the morning of 6 April 1894; catching up with it in Council Bluffs, Iowa; "hustling chewin's" down the Des Moines River; finally deserting the army and heading out on his own near the end of May from Sam Clemens's home town, Hannibal, Missouri. London wanted to tour the country and see the World's Fairgrounds at Chicago, a much finer prospect than getting arrested for trespassing on the Capitol lawn—the May Day anticlimax for Coxey's dream of reform.

    London saw the Fairgrounds, but he was too late to see the great Exposition and too naive to perceive the deeper significances that had worried Henry Adams. His own philosophical awakening would start abruptly a month later near Niagara Falls. En route, he spent several days at the home of his Aunt Mary Everhard in St. Joseph, Michigan, where he met a cousin whose name—Ernest—sounded eminently usable for the fictionist; and a dozen years later Ernest Everhard became the appropriate name of London's tough, dedicated hero in his most famous sociological novel, *The Iron Heel.* When London rode into Niagara Falls in a "side-door Pullman" (the hobo euphemism for *boxcar*) on the afternoon of 28 June, he went directly to the great falls. So entranced was he that he lingered to watch the rushing water by moonlight until eleven that evening; then after "flopping" in a nearby field, he arose at five the next morning to see the falls at dawn—a sight he was destined never to enjoy.

On his way he was arrested for vagrancy and sentenced without trial to 30 days in the Erie County Penitentiary. Though he had already seen much of the world's underside, he was scarcely prepared for the horrors he witnessed during the following month. "It would take a deep plummet to reach bottom in the Erie County Pen," he reflected, a deeper plummet than even the former Prince of the Oyster Pirates and Sailor Kid was willing to drop. Years later, in *The Road,* he merely skimmed the surface, excising most of the events of this experience as monstrously "unbelievable . . . unprintable . . . unthinkable" (*Road,* 106–7).

But if these events were themselves unthinkable, they made a rugged young individualist pause for meditation about the system that fostered them. He had been momentarily dropped into the Pit, the "submerged tenth" of society; and it gave him a scare he would never forget. The "bath of sociology" he received in the Erie County Pen wet him deeper than the skin. It was, in fact, his philosophical baptism: "I had been reborn, but not renamed, and I was running around to find out what manner of thing I was. I ran back to California and opened the books."[20]

The Books

London's half-year odyssey on The Road produced three important results. First, it sharpened his storytelling ability. "I have often thought that to this training of my tramp days is due much of my success as a story-writer," he said. "In order to get the food whereby I lived, I was compelled to tell tales that rang true. At the back door, out of inexorable necessity, is developed the convincingness and sincerity laid down by all authorities on the art of the short-story. Also, I quite believe it was my tramp-apprenticeship that made a realist out of me. Realism constitutes the only goods one can exchange at the kitchen door for grub" (*Road*, 10). Second, it tempered his naively individualist attitude and started his questioning of the American socioeconomic system: ". . . my joyous individualism was dominated by the orthodox bourgeois ethics. . . . [But] on this new *blond-beast* adventure I found myself looking upon life from a new and totally different angle. I had dropped down from the proletariat into what sociologists love to call the 'submerged tenth,' and I was startled to discover the way in which that submerged tenth was recruited" (*War*, 272–73).

Contrary to his previous misconception, most of the members of this fraternity of social castaways had been men as good as London himself who, by accident and hardship, had been cut loose to drift aimlessly into the hobo jungles, jails, and potters' fields. It therefore became obvious that the man who relied on his physical prowess for his livelihood did so at great peril. And this realization was the third significant result of his tramping excursion: London resolved to use his brain rather than his brawn to make his way in the world. This realization, as much as anything, pushed him to open the books.

His initial step was to resume his formal education. In the fall of 1894, he entered Oakland High School, a man of the world among schoolchildren. He felt foolishly out of place, but the school did provide a chance to try his hand at writing again. His school journal, *The High School Aegis,* welcomed his contributions; and, if he got no pay for his writing, he gained confidence by getting his work printed. All told, the magazine published 10 of his pieces—a sociological essay, two Frisco Kid stories based on his hoboing experiences, and several sketches that show him developing his skills.

But even more significant than the education he was getting at Oakland High School was what he was learning outside the school. He became an active member of the Henry Clay Debating Society, where he began meeting other young intellectuals with whom he could exchange ideas and begin to articulate his growing awareness of the world of thought. He was by now reading widely, not merely books of romance, travel, and fiction, but Charles Darwin's *On the Origin of Species,* Adam Smith's *The Wealth of Nations,* Immanuel Kant's *Critique of Pure Reason,* Benjamin Kidd's *Social Evolution,* and—most important—Herbert Spencer's "Philosophy of Style," to which he subsequently attributed his own mastery of style, and *First Principles,* which he claimed would do more for humankind through the ages than a thousand books like

Dickens's *Nicholas Nickleby* and Harriet Beecher Stowe's *Uncle Tom's Cabin* (*Letters,* 104). Spencer's audacious synthesis of the laws of biology, physics, and sociology; his emphasis on the necessity of progress and the perfectibility of humanity; his survival-of-the-fittest ethic; and his advocacy of the individual over society—these were exactly what London's voracious intellectual appetite had been craving, and to the god who had provided them he would remain faithful for the rest of his life, long after the great Spencerian fad which swept America had declined.

There were, of course, other deities in London's pantheon. Shortly after his return from The Road, he had read *The Communist Manifesto.* From Karl Marx, he learned that he was no longer a rampant individualist with bourgeois ethics: without having known it, he had the makings of a Socialist. An individualist he would remain all his life—but also recognized himself as a member of the proletariat. In April 1896 he joined the Socialist Labor Party. Within a year he had managed to get himself arrested for soapbox oratory and to acquire notoriety as Oakland's "Boy Socialist." For the next 20 years he signed his letters, "Yours for the Revolution."

In 1896 he also decided that he did not have another two years to spend finishing his high school education and that he could move faster on his own. He began cramming at the University Academy in Alameda. Finding the pace too slow, he began studying 19 hours a day at home. In August he passed the entrance examinations for the University of California and began bicycling daily from Oakland to the Berkeley campus. Although he made no headlines as a college student, he did make lasting impressions on some of his fellows: James Hopper, the stocky football star who later became a member of the artists' colony at Carmel, recalled that London "possessed already then a certain vague reputation among us boys as one who had done many things." After they had met, Hopper discovered that, characteristically, London "was full of gigantic plans—just as, indeed, I was to find him always whenever I came upon him later in life. . . . He was going to take all the courses in English, all of them, nothing less. Also, of course, he meant to take most of the courses in the natural sciences, many in history, and bite a respectable chunk out of the philosophies."[21]

Exploiting the elective system in his status as a special student, London began his college career by taking three courses in English and two in history. Unfortunately, his hopes outran the pace of his professors. For one who had confronted reality firsthand, the world offered too much to waste time sitting and taking secondhand notes. Because life was so short—and funds even shorter—he withdrew from college after one semester. Disappointing though it had been, that semester had nevertheless worked as an important catalyst. "I decided immediately to embark on my career," he explained:

> I had four preferences: first, music; second, poetry; third, the writing of philosophic, economic, and political essays; and fourth, and last, and least, fiction writing. I resolutely cut out music as impossible, settled down in my bedroom, and tackled my second, third, and fourth choices simultaneously. Heavens, how I wrote! . . . I wrote everything—ponderous essays, scientific and sociological, short stories, humorous verse, verse of all sorts from triolets and sonnets to blank verse tragedy and elephantine epics in Spenserian stanzas. On occasion I composed steadily, day after day, for fifteen hours a day. At times I forgot to eat, or refused to tear myself away from my passionate outpouring in order to eat. (*Barleycorn,* 220–21)

Without realizing it, London had virtually completed his professional training by the summer of 1897; but he was not yet ready for a successful literary career. He had written too much too soon; he later counseled other aspiring writers, "Take your time; study the stuff of the other fellows who've mastered the trick—study until you can turn the same trick. Take your time; elaborate; omit; draw; develop. Paint—paint pictures and characters and emotions—but paint, paint, draw. And take your time" (*Letters,* 976). London himself had painted and drawn feverishly during the early months of 1897; now he needed to take time—time for taking stock, for maturing. Indeed, he was forced to take it during the coming winter.

The Long, Cold Winter

Like Henry David Thoreau, Jack London was born in the nick of time. Had he been three or four years later, he would have missed the last frontier stampede, which started on 14 July 1897 when the steamship *Excelsior* docked at San Francisco, disembarking 40 miners who lugged a ton of gold down the gangplank. At Seattle three days later a second group carrying more than two tons in gold dust and nuggets debarked from the *Portland.* Both groups had floated down the Yukon River from the Klondike to the ocean port at St. Michaels, and the wealth they brought out seemed to confirm the rumors of a fantastic bonanza in the Far North. Overnight the nation went mad to reach that remote country.

Although there had been richer strikes (the extent of the gold field was grossly overestimated, and most of the bonanza claims would have been taken before the mob arrived), Pierre Berton points out that there had never been such a sudden and dramatic reaction: "The Klondike stampede did not start slowly and build up to a climax, as did so many earlier gold rushes. It started instantly with the arrival of the *Excelsior* and *Portland,* reached a fever pitch at once, and remained at fever pitch until the following spring, when, with the coming of the Spanish-American War, the fever died almost as swiftly as it arose. . . . It was the last and most frenzied of the great international gold rushes."[22] Suddenly and unexpectedly the vast, mysterious Northland held forth one final, splendid opportunity for a return to the paradisal wilderness yearned for by a nation emerging from the economic depression, decadence, and unquiet desperation of the 1890s.

It is not surprising that Jack London was among the first of the stampeders. Two years of schooling and drudgery had passed since he had returned from The Road, and he had little to show for his efforts except rejection slips. On 25 July, along with his brother-in-law, Captain J. H. Shepard, who had mortgaged his home for their stake, London boarded the *Umatilla* for the Klondike. "I had let career go hang," he wrote, "and was on the adventure-path again in quest of fortune" (*Barleycorn,* 231).

Though London complained he brought nothing from the Klondike but scurvy, that year was in many ways the richest investment of his life. His 400-mile trek from Dyea Beach over the rugged Chilkoot Pass, through the dangerous White Horse Rapids, and downriver to the mouth of the Stewart River, where he spent most of the winter, was in itself the adventure of a lifetime—as was the 2,000-mile journey by raft down the great Yukon River the following spring. But these personal experiences were a slim return in comparison with the rich payload he mined during the long Arctic night listening to the tales that passed between the veteran "sourdoughs" and newly arrived *chechaquos.* Many of the stories that passed for fact were undoubtedly fictions and glamorized truths, for—said London—"The Alaskan gold hunter is proverbial, not so much for his unveracity, as for his inability to tell the precise truth. In a country of exaggerations, he likewise is prone to hyperbolic descriptions of things actual. But when it came to [the] Klondike, he could not stretch the truth as fast as the truth itself stretched."[23] As he remarked in "Jack London by Himself," a pamphlet, "It was in the Klondike that I found myself. There you get your perspective. I got mine."

Yet London was never one to be inhibited by the threat of either peril or failure. During the long, dark winter he was not merely collecting the raw materials that would be transmuted into fictional character and narrative; he was absorbing the very atmosphere of the Northland itself. As a result, and contrary to the usual critical assumptions about his work, his best fiction would not rely primarily upon plot but, instead, would derive its impact from what in "The Art of Fiction" Henry James called "truth of detail," "the air of reality," "solidity of specification"—"the merit on which all its other merits . . . helplessly and submissively depend."[24] This special ambiance would be largely responsible for the fact that, out of the more than 100 books written about the Klondike gold rush, London's tales are virtually the only literary survivors nearly a century afterwards.

The physical consequences of the long winter of good comradeship and tale swapping were less salutary. By the spring thaws the lack of exercise—coupled with a lack of fresh vegetables—was taking its toll. London's gums began to swell and bleed, and his teeth started to loosen and rattle in his head: the dread symptoms of "Arctic leprosy"—scurvy. As his condition worsened with aching joints and lameness, he decided that for himself the law of diminishing returns now governed his Klondike adventure. On 8 June 1898, while thousands of new stampeders were beginning to pour into the gold country after the long winter, London with two companions started home aboard a jerrybuilt houseboat on the Yukon River.

We need only look at a map of Alaska to appreciate the scope of this downriver journey. The Yukon is perhaps the world's most indecisive river. Its headwater lakes are located just north of Juneau, almost within a stone's throw of the Pacific Ocean. But, instead of taking the logical short route to the sea, it wanders northward for almost 1,000 miles until it reaches the Arctic Circle, where, meeting the southwest-bound Porcupine, it changes course at an 80° angle and heads toward the Bering Sea. Seven hundred miles later, after moving into Anvik southwest, it turns southwest to Holy Cross, hesitates and then wanders southwest for another 100 miles until it passes Russian Mission. Then, meandering the last 150 miles mostly northward, it oozes in countless channels across the great mud flats into Norton Sound. The Yukon is almost as long as, and in spots wider than, the Mississippi; and the land it traverses is still one of the wildest regions in North America, abundant with myriad forms of wildlife—where mosquitos swarm thickly enough, swear returning travelers, to darken the sky, suffocate pack animals, and drive humans into hysteria.

London kept notebooks about his downriver journey, and he later published his story in the *Illustrated Buffalo Express* under the title "From Dawson to the Sea." A Northland variation of the *Adventures of Huckleberry Finn,* the story is built upon the raft-as-home theme:

> Our boat was home-made, weak-kneed and leaky, but in thorough harmony with the wilderness we were traversing. . . . In the bow was the woodshed, while amidships, built of pine boughs and blankets was the bed chamber. Then came the rower's bench, and, jammed between this and the steersman, was our snug little kitchen. It was a veritable home, and we had little need of going ashore, save out of curiosity or to lay in a fresh supply of firewood.
>
> The three of us had sworn to make of this a pleasure trip, in which all labor was to be performed by gravitation, and all profit reaped by ourselves. And what a profit it was to us who had been accustomed to pack great loads on our backs or drag all day at the sleds for a paltry 25 or 30 miles. We now hunted, played cards, smoked, ate and slept, sure of our six miles an hour, of our 144 a day. (Shepard, 42)[25]

Three weeks of this kind of drifting—punctuated by occasional stops at Indian villages and trading posts ashore—brought the raft and its crew to St. Michaels where London worked as a coal passer aboard a steamer headed for San Francisco. A month later, he was home and was synthesizing the materials that would bring him the success he had resolved so desperately to achieve. By the time *The Call of the Wild* appeared in 1903, $100 million in gold dust and nuggets had been milked from the cold, muddy tributaries of the Yukon, and only a handful of mining engineers and inveterate sourdoughs were left in the ghostly wastelands and deserted boom towns to gather the residual deposits of the precious metal. Within less than a decade America's last frontier became a golden memory. No longer a material reality to excite people to frantic action, it was a rich lode for the writer who could tap its mystic bedrock and incite readers to dream.

Chapter Two
The Literary Frontiersman

Because we have been conditioned by more than three generations of Realism, it is difficult to imagine the kind of fiction that dominated American magazines at the turn of the century. Perhaps the easiest way is to look at a few issues of the prestigious *Atlantic Monthly*. Volumes 84 and 85 (1889 and 1900) disclose a genuine editorial concern for social and political relevance in the publication of such articles as Jacob A. Riis's series on the slums, Frank Norris's "Comida: An Experience in Famine" (an essay on the civilian war victims in Cuba), William James's *Talks to Teachers on Psychology,* and Prince Peter Kropotkin's *The Autobiography of a Revolutionist.* But the fiction in these volumes scarcely suggests such concern. For example, Mary Johnston's *To Have and to Hold*—a serialized historical romance reported to have doubled *Atlantic Monthly*'s circulation in 1900—is set in early seventeenth-century Virginia; the action revolves about the love affair of Captain Ralph Percy and the lovely Jocelyn Leigh as they endure the tribulations of piracy, Indian savagery, and Lord Carnal's lecherous villainy. The following scene describes—in typical fashion—the hero's sentimental reverie as he lies awaiting death at the hands of his savage captors:

> I was no babe to whimper at a sudden darkness, to cry out against a cur-tain that a Hand chose to drop between me and the life I had lived. Death frighted me not, but when I thought of one whom I should leave behind me I feared lest I should go mad. Had this thing come to me a year before, I could have slept the night through; now—now—
>
> I lay, bound to the log, before the open door of the lodge, and, looking through it, saw the pines waving in the night wind and the gleam of the river beneath the stars, and saw her as plainly as though she had stood there under the trees, in a flood of noon sunshine. . . . One of my arms was free; I could take from within my doublet the little purple flower, and drop my face upon the hand that held it. The bloom was quite withered, and scalding tears would not give it life again.[1]

Another generation would pass before American readers were ready to appreciate the restraint of Hemingway.

If William Dean Howell's teacup therapy had not managed to rid the popular novel of such sugar-and-spice Romanticism, the short story—virtually ignored in Realist theory—was worse yet. In the August 1899 issue of the *Atlantic Monthly,* for instance, Elizabeth Stuart Phelps's "Loveliness: A Story" begins typically: "Loveliness sat on an eider-down cushion embroidered with cherry-colored puppies on a pearl satin cover. . . . For Loveliness was a little dog . . . the essence of tenderness; set, soul and body, to one only tune. To love and be beloved—that was his life." And, in the January 1900 issue, Margaret L. Knapp's "Mother" ends just as typically: "Jack, dear heart, it was selfish in me to . . . leave you; but I had to do it,—I had to see my mother. Mother knows."

Such samples, culled from America's foremost literary magazine, help to explain why the period has been called the Mauve Decade. We should remember, in all fairness to the *Atlantic* editors, that this period was the same one in which Leo Tolstoy's *The Awakening* was bowdlerized by the editors of *Cosmopolitan,* Thomas Hardy's *Jude the Obscure* was expurgated in *Harper's* under the fetching title *Hearts Insurgent,* and Theodore Dreiser's *Sister Carrie* was suppressed on grounds of impropriety by Doubleday, Page. Into this literary hothouse Jack London entered as a bracing draft of Arctic air: "Except for the similar sensation caused by the appearance of Mark Twain's mining-camp humor in the midst of Victorian America, nothing more disturbing to the forces of gentility had ever happened in our literature," Kenneth Lynn has written, "and it decisively changed the course of American fiction."[2]

London scarcely saw himself in such a messianic role; he was simply concerned with getting ahead in the world. In *John Barleycorn* London contended, "Some are born to fortune, and some have fortune thrust upon them. But in my case I was clubbed into fortune, and bitter necessity wielded the club" (*Barleycorn,* 237–38). The financial situation at home was acute when he returned from his Klondike trip in the summer of 1898. London had many talents, but no skill or trade; and, though he listed his name with five employment bureaus and advertised in three newspapers, he could get no steady work and was reduced to odd jobs such as mowing lawns, trimming hedges, and beating carpets. He scored high on the civil service examinations for postman, but there were no vacancies. In desperation he turned once again to writing, not this time—or so he thought—as a career, but merely to put bread on the table at home. Figuring that the minimum pay for newspaper articles was $10, he sat down to organize an account of his downriver exodus from the Klondike. "My honest intention in writing that article," he

insisted, "was to earn ten dollars. And that was the limit of my intention. It would help to tide me along until I got steady employment. Had
a vacancy occurred in the post office at that time, I should have jumped
at it" (*Barleycorn*, 238).

In September, he sent the following letter to the editor of the San
Francisco *Bulletin:*

> Dear Sir:
> I have returned from a year's residence in the Clondyke, entering
> the country by way of Dyea and Chilcoot Pass. I left by way of St.
> Michaels, thus making altogether a journey of 2,500 miles on the Yukon
> in a small boat. I have sailed and traveled quite extensively in other parts
> of the world and have learned to seize upon that which is interesting, to
> grasp the true romance of things, and to understand the people I may be
> thrown amongst.
> I have just completed an article of 4,000 words, describing the trip
> from Dawson to St. Michaels in a rowboat. Kindly let me know if there
> would be any demand in your columns for it—of course, thoroughly
> understanding that the acceptance of the manuscript is to depend upon
> its literary and intrinsic value.
>
> Yours very respectfully,
Jack London
(Letters, 18)

In what would seem to have been one of the great blunders of publishing history, the editor returned the letter with a hasty reply scribbled on
the bottom: "Interest in Alaska has subsided in an amazing degree.
Then, again, so much has been written that I do not think it would pay
us to buy your story."[3]

Most important, however, in London's early letter is the disclosure of
three essential factors which account in large measure for his success as a
writer: first, "to seize upon that which is interesting"; second, "to grasp
the true romance of things"; and third, "to understand the people I may
be thrown amongst." Human interest, romantic imagination, sympathetic understanding: these are the major ingredients in his work and—
combined with the forces of luck, talent, and plain "dig"—made him
one of the most popular writers of his generation. Another element,
which he did not mention and of which, indeed, he seemed hardly hardly aware—a genius for myth—made his achievement ultimately something more lasting than popular success.

But during the bleak winter of 1898 such possibilities as success and fame seemed remote. Try as he would, London could not find steady employment. Because he had no viable alternative, he worked between odd jobs at a rented typewriter upon which he ground out articles, poems, jokes, stories—including a 21,000-word serial for *Youth's Companion.* He pawned his bike and winter suit to get stamps for mailing off his manuscripts, which were in turn mailed back with sickening regularity.

But soon he was mulling over a letter from the *Overland Monthly,* the magazine given nationwide prestige a generation earlier by Bret Harte. "We have read your MS.," the letter began, "and are so greatly pleased with it, that, though we have an enormous quantity of accepted and paid-for material on hand, we will at once publish it in the January number, if—aye, if you can content yourself with five dollars."[4] Such acceptance might be a way to fame, but the fee would hardly make one's fortune. At $5 for 3,700 words, he could in fact make more money digging sewers or shoveling coal. Nevertheless, despite his disappointment, he accepted the *Overland Monthly* offer and continued to write. On 25 December 1898—"the loneliest Christmas I ever faced"—he vowed "an entire change of front" for the new year: "I shall forsake my old dogmas, and henceforth, worship the true god. 'There is no God but Chance, and Luck shall be his prophet!' He who stops to think or beget a system is lost. As in other creeds, faith alone atones. Numerous hecatombs and many a fat firstling shall I sacrifice—you just watch my smoke (I beg pardon, I mean incense)" (*Letters,* 31–32).

As his new God would have it, he passed his point of no return three weeks later when the Oakland postmaster telephoned to say there was a vacancy for mail carrier and London could have the job if he were ready to go to work. The starting pay would be $65 a month—with opportunities for regular increases, as well as security and retirement benefits. One month of delivering mail would pay more than he had made from five years of writing—unless he counted the amount promised by the *Black Cat:* the incredible sum of $40 for a mediocre science-fiction tale titled "A Thousand Deaths," the kind of stuff he could write with his eyes shut. Perhaps this sum was indicative of a real change in his luck. Furthermore, his odds would be bettered by the deal offered him by *Overland Monthly* editor James Howard Bridge: If London would continue to produce stories as good as "To the Man on Trail" and "The White Silence," which would be published in the January and February 1899, numbers, he would be given not only $7.50 a sketch but also prime space in the magazine. Although the prestige of the "Gold Coast *Atlantic*" had become slightly tarnished (Ambrose Bierce now referred to it as "The warmed-*Overland Monthly*"), it was still a big-name magazine and, despite its picayune fees, might serve as a springboard for an unknown young writer.

The prospects for literary success had never been more tantalizing; on the other hand, the pressure to accept the certain income and the excellent security of the government job was urgent. London tells in *John Barleycorn* how the dilemma was resolved for him:

> I couldn't decide what to do. And I'll never be able to forgive the post-master of Oakland. I answered the call, and I talked to him like a man. I frankly told him the situation. . . . Now, if he would pass me by and select the next man on the eligible list, and give me a call at the next vacancy—
>
> But he shut me off with: "Then you don't want the position?"
>
> "But I do," I protested. "Don't you see, if you will pass me over this time—"
>
> "If you want it you will take it," he said coldly.
>
> Happily for me, the cursed brutality of the man made me angry.
>
> "Very well," I said. "I won't take it." (*Barleycorn,* 239)

Had Chance decreed a vacancy 10 days earlier, or a more civil postmaster, America might have gained another servant of the public mails, inadvertently relegating the name "Jack London" to the dead letter office. London should not merely have forgiven but should have thanked the postmaster of Oakland for angering him into pursuing his true calling.

Spring—the time of the open road—was approaching again; but this time the only road left open to London led him to success in the world of belles-lettres. That road is charted in two thumb-worn nickel composition books now secured under double lock in Merrill Library at Utah State University and simply labeled:

NO. 1   NO. 2
MAGAZINE SALES   MAGAZINE SALES
FROM 1898 TO MAY 1900   FROM MAY 1900 TO FEB. 1903

These two unpretentious notebooks not only confirm the legend of London's fabulous rise to success, but they also tell, as King Hendricks has pointed out, "a graphic story of feverish work, disappointments and frustrations and of the tenacious determination to succeed."[5]

The first notebook is more noteworthy for its number of failures than its successes. Of the 103 items listed, only 57 were accepted for publication, and of these 57, only 15 were accepted the first time they were submitted. Of the remainder, more than 30 items were permanently "retired" after multiple rejections; four were lost; and another four were rewritten and carried over to the second notebook. The 103 items in the first book garnered more than 400 rejections.

What is most impressive about these entries, in addition to the author's amazing persistence, is their variety: short stories, sonnets, triolets, humorous sketches, jokes, essays on subjects ranging from grammar to economics—anything, in short, that might sell for 50 cents upward. By May 1900, London had found out his strengths and weaknesses. Gone are the crippled verses and lame jokes. More than half of the 72 entries in the second notebook are short stories; the rest are sketches and essays. Of these 72, only two were retired, and one of these was later resurrected for publication in a book of London's essays.

One of the most significant entries in either notebook is the fifty-third item in the first notebook: "An Odyssey of the North," mailed to the *Atlantic Monthly* on 10 June 1899. Two days later London complained to his literary pen pal Cloudesley Johns, "I am groping, groping, groping for my own particular style, for the style which should be mine but which I have not yet found" (*Letters,* 83). Six weeks later the *Atlantic Monthly* returned "An Odyssey of the North" with the note that if he would shorten the manuscript by 3,000 words, the story would be accepted. On 1 August, he sent back the revised story; on 30 October he received a check for $120 along with a complimentary one-year subscription.

Acceptance by America's premier literary monthly signified a major breakthrough. The *Overland Monthly* had provided literary respectability, and the *Black Cat* had given financial reassurance. The *Atlantic Monthly* gave London these things and something even more valuable: self-confidence. Henceforth, there would be no further groping for his own particular style. What was good enough for the *Atlantic Monthly* was surely good enough for the rest. By the winter of 1899, when he signed the contract with Houghton Mifflin for his first book—a collection of the eight Klondike stories that had appeared in the *Overland Monthly,* along with "An Odyssey of the North"—London had abandoned the amateurish frenzy of his early writings and had settled into the steady profes-

sional pace he maintained for the rest of his life. "Am now doing a thousand words per day, six days per week," he wrote to Johns. "Last week I
finished 1,100 words ahead of the required amount" (*Letters,* 117). And
by the time Houghton Mifflin released *The Son of the Wolf* in the spring of
1900, he had set not only the routine but also the style that would
remain essentially unchanged throughout the rest of his career. "Let me
tell you how I write," he explained in a letter to Elwyn Hoffman, another early fan. "In the first place I never begin a thing, but what I finish
before I begin anything else. Further; I type as fast as I write, so that each
day sees the work all upon the final MS. I fold it up and send it off without once going back to see what all the previous pages were like. So, in
fact, when a page is done, that is the last I see of it till it comes out in
print" (*Letters,* 194). This remarkable facility explains in part why it was
that London had so little regard for much of his work and why there is
so little change in his style. The changes had already taken place, for the
most part, in the period of feverish apprenticeship before his first book
appeared on the market. Later, answering the critics who had raised their
eyebrows over the incredible success of his hero in *Martin Eden,* London
asserted, "In three years, from a sailor with a common school education,
I made a successful writer of him. The critics say this is impossible. Yet I
was Martin Eden" (*Barleycorn,* 242).

The Northland Saga

A reading public that had dieted on propriety and pap for more than a
generation and whose appetite for strenuous action had been whetted
by the colorful melodramas of Kipling and by the melodramatics of
Theodore Roosevelt was hungry for the meaty fare of Jack London's
Northland. The opening sentence of "An Odyssey of the North" is the
harbinger of a new kind of American fiction: "The sleds were singing
their eternal lament to the creaking of the harnesses and the tinkling
bells of the leaders; but the men and dogs were tired and made no
sound."[6] Others had already used the Klondike materials for profit,
but their writings lacked the vividness and poetic cadence of London's
style, a style that fused the vigorous and the picturesque. Furthermore,
his was a fresh breed of fictional heroes—not the maudlin gentlemen
who scalded flowers with their tears or who emasculated themselves on
the altars of sentimental caprice—but "a lean and wiry type, with
trail-hardened muscles, and sun-browned faces, and untroubled souls
which gazed frankly forth, clear-eyed and steady" (*Wolf,* 192–93).

Kipling had introduced a kindred type the decade before, and London was quick to acknowledge his debt to the master of the "plain tale" (*Letters*, 216).[7]

But the Klondike argonauts were not merely copies of those leathery cockneys and Irishmen in the Queen's Army whose individualism was subverted to the uses of British Imperialism and whose sporting ethic was at times gratuitously cruel. London's Northland heroes were, by contrast, a ruggedly independent yet a remarkably compassionate breed who paid allegiance only to the inexorable laws of nature and to the authority of conscience, and who possessed a capacity for selflessness and comradeship very much like the agape of primitive Christianity. Theirs was a situational ethic, predicated on integrity, charity, and pragmatism. They had invaded a hostile land where the ruling law was "survival of the fittest" and where the key to survival was adaptability, but this did not simply mean physical fitness or brute strength: "The man who turns his back upon the comforts of an elder civilization, to face the savage youth, the primordial simplicity of the North, may estimate success at an inverse ratio to the quantity and quality of his hopelessly fixed habits," explains the narrator in his prologue to the story "In a Far Country":

> The exchange of such things as a dainty menu for rough fare, of the stiff leather shoe for the soft, shapeless moccasin, of the feather bed for a couch in the snow, is after all a very easy matter. But his pinch will come in learning properly to shape his mind's attitude toward all things, and especially toward his fellow man. For the courtesies of ordinary life, he must substitute unselfishness, forbearance, and tolerance. Thus, and thus only, can he gain that pearl of great price,—true comradeship. He must not say "Thank you"; he must mean it without opening his mouth, and prove it by responding in kind. In short, he must substitute the deed for the word, the spirit for the letter. (*Wolf*, 70)

This is not merely a statement about individual survival but also about community, about "true comradeship." The emphasis on such "spirit" in these tales led Fred Lewis Pattee to remark that his gallery of supermen and superwomen has about it the myth atmosphere of the older world. . . . It is a new Northern mythology, and the stories . . . have the quality of sagas. Contrary to his own belief, [London] was not a realist at all. His tales were not written on the spot, but after they had mellowed for years in his imagination. Everywhere [are] exaggerations, poetizations, utter marvels described as commonplaces. . . .[8]

The code of the Northland, with the mystique of comradeship at its heart, is dramatized in "To the Man on Trail," the first of London's Klondike stories that had so excited the editors of the *Overland Monthly*. A Yuletide story, it is trimmed with the rich assortment of symbols, pagan as well as Christian, appropriate to the occasion. The setting is Christmas eve in the cabin of the Malemute Kid, who dominates *The Son of the Wolf* collection as high priest of the code. Gathered are representatives from a dozen different lands, swapping yarns, reminiscing about home, and sharing the heady Christmas punch concocted by the Kid. At midnight the convivialities are suddenly interrupted by the jingling of bells, "the familiar music of the dogwhip, the whining howl of the Malemutes and the crunch of a sled"; then comes "the expected knock, sharp and confident" and the entrance of "the stranger": ". . . a striking personage, and a most picturesque one, in his Arctic dress of wool and fur. Standing six foot two or three, with proportionate breadth of shoulders and depth of chest, . . . his long lashes and eyebrows white with ice, . . . he seemed, of a verity, the Frost King, just stepped in out of the night. . . . An awkward silence had fallen, but his hearty 'What cheer, my lads?' put them quickly at ease, and the next instant Malemute Kid and he had gripped hands. Though they had never met, each had heard of the other, and the recognition was mutual" (*Wolf*, 105–7).

The apparition suggests Saint Nicholas himself—but in a peculiar Klondike guise. He has been on the frozen trail for 12 hours running, and he is burdened, not with the traditional sack of gifts, but, instead, with "two large Colt's revolvers and a hunting knife . . . the inevitable dogwhip, a smokeless rifle of the largest bore and latest pattern" (*Wolf*, 106). Jack Westondale, the stranger, explains that he is pursuing a gang of dog thieves. While the guest is eating the Christmas snack hospitably prepared for him, the Kid studies his face and finds it worthy: "Nor was he long in deciding that it was fair, honest, and open, and that he liked it. Still youthful, the lines had been firmly traced by toil and hardship. Though genial in conversation, and mild when at rest, the blue eyes gave promise of the hard steel-glitter which comes when called into action, especially against odds. The heavy jaw and square-cut chin demonstrated rugged pertinacity and indomitability. Nor, though the attributes of the lion were there, was there wanting the certain softness, the hint of womanliness, which bespoke the emotional nature" (*Wolf*, 108).

Westondale apparently embodies all the vital traits of the code hero: "The trouble with him is clean grit and stubbornness" (*Wolf*, 111). After a short three hours of sleep the Kid sends him on his way with fresh provisions and wise counsel. Fifteen minutes later the festivities are stopped a second time—by a nearly exhausted stranger who wears the red coat, not of St. Nick, but of the Royal Canadian Mounted Police. He demands fresh dogs and information about Westondale, who is running—he discloses—not for, but *from,* the law after having robbed a Dawson gambling casino of $40,000!

Though the revelers have kept silent according to the Kid's example, they furiously demand an explanation after the Mountie has gone: Why has the Kid given sanctuary and aid to a man who has doubly violated the code by robbery and by deception? "It's a cold night, boys—a bitter cold night," the Kid begins. "You've all traveled trail, and know what that stands for. Don't jump a dog when he's down. You've heard only one side." As the Kid explains, Westondale was betrayed by his partner who robbed him of $40,000 by gambling it away and then getting himself killed. "You'll notice he took exactly what his partner lost,—forty thousand," the Kid explains. "Well, he's gone out; and what are you going to do about it?" The Kid glances around the circle of his judges, noted the softening of their faces, then raised his mug aloft. "So a health to the man on trail this night; may his grub hold out; may his dogs keep their legs; may his matches never miss fire. God prosper him; good luck go with him; and—Confusion to the Mounted Police!' cried Bettles, to the crash of the empty cups" (*Wolf,* 117–18). Without belaboring his symbolism, London has provided a fitting epiphany to the conclusion of his Christmas carol; moreover, the situational ethic that informs the story was sure to appeal to a reading public less than one generation removed from frontier justice.

The mystique of comradeship is obversely dramatized in the fourth story in *The Son of the Wolf* collection, "In a Far Country," which had first appeared in the June 1899 issue of the *Overland Monthly.* In this tale about "two Incapables" named Carter Weatherbee and Percy Cuthfert, who elect to spend the long Arctic winter snugly marooned in a deserted cabin rather than suffer the hardships of breaking trail with their comrades for the remaining 1,000 miles to Dawson, London reiterates the idea that survival is not primarily a matter of physical fitness.

Both Incapables are healthy, husky men, whereas Merritt Sloper, the wiry little argonaut who functions as moral norm in this and in several other Klondike episodes, weighs less than 100 pounds and is still yellow and weak from the fever he picked up in South America: "The fresh young muscles of either Weatherbee or Cuthfert were equal to ten times the endeavor of his; yet he could walk them into the earth in a day's journey . . . , [for he] held the flesh in the bondage of the spirit" (*Wolf,* 77–78). Sloper predicts the Incapables' fate as he and the remaining members of the party pull out from the cabin: "[Ever] hear of the Kilkenny cats?" he asks Jacques Baptiste, the party's half-breed guide. "Well, my friend and good comrade, the Kilkenny cats fought till neither hide, nor hair, nor yowl, was left. . . . Now, these two men don't like work. They won't work. We know that. They'll be all alone in that cabin all winter,—a mighty long, dark winter" (*Wolf,* 80).

At first, Sloper's prophecy appears to be wrong, for the Incapables are determined to prove their compatibility; in addition, they are plentifully stocked with food and fuel. But, representatives of a degenerate society, they are fatally undersupplied in the moral staples needed for subsistence in the Northland. Weatherbee, formerly a clerk, is an unimaginative, materialistic fool who has joined the gold rush to make his fortune; Cuthfert, opposite as well as apposite, is an overripe cultural dilettante afflicted with "an abnormal development of sentimentality [that he mistakes] for the true spirit of romance and adventure" (*Wolf,* 72). Moreover, the two men lack that "protean faculty of adaptability"—the capacity to slough off the callous of "self" along with the specious comforts of civilization—which is the most vital insurance against the dangers of the wilderness.

After an overeager show of industrious cooperation, they abandon the austere discipline of the code. Their spiritual degeneration, as they succumb to each of the Seven Deadly Sins, is initially dramatized in their social relationship. First, pride is manifest in a foolish arrogance that precludes the mutual trust requisite to survival in the wilderness: "The one was a lower-class man who considered himself a gentleman, and the other was a gentleman who knew himself to be such. From this it may be remarked that a man can be a gentleman without possessing the first instinct of true comradeship" (*Wolf,* 82–83).

Next appears lust, as they consume with sensual promiscuity their supply of sugar, mixing it with hot water and then dissipating "the rich, white syrup" over their flapjacks and breadcrusts. This is followed by sloth, as they sink into a lethargy that makes them "rebel at the performance of the smallest chore," including washing and personal cleanliness— "and for that matter, common decency" (*Wolf,* 84–85). Accelerated by gluttony, their moral deterioration now begins to externalize itself in their physical appearance: "Afraid they were not getting their proper shares, and in order that they might not be robbed, they fell to gorging themselves. . . . In the absence of fresh vegetables and exercise, the blood became impoverished, and a loathsome, purplish rash crept over their bodies. . . . Next, their muscles and joints began to swell, the flesh turning black, while their mouths, gums, and lips took on the color or rich cream. Instead of being drawn together by their misery, each gloated over the other's symptoms as the scurvy took its course" (*Wolf,* 85). Covetousness and envy appear when they divide their sugar supply and hide their shares from each other, obsessed with the fear of losing the precious stuff.

The last of the cardinal sins, anger, is delayed awhile by another trouble: "the Fear of the North . . . the joint child of the Great Cold and the Great Silence" (*Wolf,* 86), which preoccupies each man according to his nature. For the dilettantish Cuthfert, the Fear manifests itself quietly and inwardly: "He dwelt upon the unseen and unknown till the burden of eternity appeared to be crushing him. Everything in the Northland had that crushing effect—the absence of life and motion; the darkness; the infinite peace of the brooding land; the ghastly silence, which made the echo of each heartbeat a sacrilege; the solemn forest which seemed to guard an awful, inexpressible something, which neither word nor thought could compass" (*Wolf,* 88). The coarser sensibilities of the clerk are more sensationally aroused in necrophilic nightmares: "Weatherbee fell prey to the grosser superstitions, and did his best to resurrect the spirits which slept in the forgotten graves. . . . He shrank from their clammy contact as they drew closer and twined their frozen limbs about him, and when they whispered in his ear of things to come, the cabin rang with his frightened shrieks" (*Wolf,* 86–87).

The symbolism grows richer as the drama moves toward its ghastly climax. Although London had not yet read the works of Sigmund Freud, his metaphors reveal an instinctive grasp of dream symbolism, particularly of the unconscious associations of sexual impotency and death. Cuthfert is obsessed with the absolute stillness of the phallic, arrow-shaped weathervane atop the cabin: "Standing beneath the wind-vane, his eyes fixed on the polar skies, he could not bring himself to realize that the Southland really existed, that at that very moment it was a-roar with life and action. There was no Southland, no men being born of women, no giving and taking in marriage. . . . He lived with Death among the dead, emasculated by the sense of his own insignificance . . ." (*Wolf,* 88–89). The metaphors of potency/life versus emasculation/death coalesce in the story's vivid climax, as anger completes the allegoric procession of the deadly sins. Thinking that his companion has pilfered his last tiny cache of symbol-laden sugar, Weatherbee attacks Cuthfert in the cold fury of insanity and severs his spine with an axe, thereby fulfilling the premonition of symbolic emasculation; and then falls heavily upon him as the bullet from his victim's Smith & Wesson explodes in his face.

The closing tableau—a grotesque inversion of the primal scene—dramatically reveals London's pre-Freudian intuitions: ". . . they drew very close to each other in that last clinch" (*Wolf,* 98). Passages such as this one apparently substantiate Maxwell Geismar's observation that London seemed to be more at home in the "world of dream and fantasy and desolate, abnormal emotion . . . than the world of people and society" and that "his best work was often a transcript of solitary nightmares."[9] But such an assessment, notwithstanding the brilliance of Geismar's Freudian interpretation of London's life and work, is too limited. Although a considerable amount of his fiction does fit into this category, London's best is something more than "a transcript of solitary nightmares": it is the artistic modulation of universal dreams—that is, of myths and archetype.

The Primordial Vision

"A great work of art is like a dream," explains C. G. Jung in *Modern Man in Search of a Soul;* "for all its apparent obviousness it does not explain itself and is never unequivocal. A dream never says: 'You ought,' or 'This is the truth.' It presents an image in much the same way as nature allows a plant to grow, and we must draw our own conclusions."[10] In his essay "Psychology and Literature" Jung draws a sharp line between the fundamental approaches of the artist: the "psychological mode" and the "visionary mode." The former, rational and objective, always takes its materials from the vast realm of conscious human experience: "Even the basic experiences themselves, though non-rational . . . are that which has been known from the beginnings of time—passion and its fated outcome, man's subjection to the turns of destiny, eternal nature with its beauty and its horror" (Jung 1933, 156). But the visionary mode "is a strange something that derives its existence from the hinterland of man's mind— that suggests the abyss of time separating us from pre-human ages, or evokes a super-human world of contrasting light and darkness. It is a primordial experience which surpasses man's understanding. . . . We are reminded of nothing of everyday, human life, but rather of dreams, night-time fears and the dark recesses of the mind that we sometimes sense with misgiving" (Jung 1933, 156–58). In other words, the visionary mode derives its materials from what Jung calls the "collective unconscious": the deep psychological reservoir of "racial memories" that transcend both personal consciousness and the individual unconsciousness—or, as he explains, "a certain psychic disposition shaped by the forces of heredity [from which] consciousness has developed."

Because the language of normal discourse is inadequate to express such visions, the artist must resort to the metaphorical language of symbol and myth to express the unfathomable primordial experience, the source of creativeness. The work of the visionary artist is informed by what Jung calls *archetypes:* symbols of such transcendent and universal force that they would seem to be instinctual predispositions toward certain forms of psychic response rather than simple conditioned or learned responses.[11]

One of the many ironies of Jack London's career is that he thought himself as a thoroughly professional craftsman working quite consciously in what Jung would have termed the *psychological mode;* but while most of his works can be superficially thus categorized, those with the most enduring force derive their potency from his instinctive mythopoeic vision. Readily apparent in the great fiction such as "To Build a Fire" and *The Call of the Wild,* evidence of the visionary and mythic may be traced throughout the Northland Saga. In an obscure tale such as "In the Forests of the North," for example, the hero is described as undergoing a "weary journey beyond the last scrub timber and straggling copses, into the heart of the Barrens . . . the bad lands of the Arctic, the deserts of the Circle, the bleak and bitter home of the musk ox and lean plains wolf . . . treeless and cheerless" and beyond this across "the white blank spaces on the map" into a weird hyperborean region where he finds "undreamed-of rich spruce forests and unrecorded Eskimo tribes."[12] Long journeys far beyond the last outposts of civilization that penetrate into the great blank places—mysterious quests deep into the *Urwelt,* the elder world of human memories beyond space and time—form the recurrent pattern of the Northland Saga.

"In the saga," Mircea Eliade explains, "the hero is placed in a world governed by the gods and fate."[13] In this same world London has placed his sourdoughs, Native Americans, and *chechaquos* (newcomers to the Northland); and the ruling gods are not flatly indifferent ones like the typical deities of Naturalistic literature, but are actively hostile and sometimes vengeful. In dramatizing these forces London's vision is essentially primordial rather than logical or "psychological," and the mode of his fiction is often symbolic rather than discursive. In this sense his work could be described as *anti*naturalistic Naturalism, for as much as it dwells on material reality, it ultimately rejects materialism in favor of something more. At his best, he reaches the level of other great American symbolists such as Poe, Hawthorne, and Melville.

The White Silence

When Jack London writes in *The God of His Fathers,* "It was very natural, Death came by many ways, yet was it all one after all,—a manifestation of the all-powerful and inscrutable,"[14] he seems to echo Melville's lines in *Moby-Dick:* "Is it by its indefiniteness it shadows forth the heartless voids and immensities of the universe, and thus stabs us from behind with the thought of annihilation, when beholding the white depths of the milky way? Or is it, that as in essence whiteness is not so much a color as the visible absence of color, and at the same time the concrete of all colors; is it for these reasons that there is such a dumb blankness, full of meaning, in a wide landscape of snows—a colorless, all-color of atheism from which we shrink?"[15]

In his pioneering study of the symbolic mode in primitivism, James Baird identifies the "authentic primitivist" as an extreme individualist, as "the egoist-romanticist, as Santayana has described him . . . who 'disowns all authority save that mysteriously exercised over him by his deep faith in himself,' the man who would be 'heir to all civilization, and, nevertheless . . . take life arrogantly and egoistically, as if it were an absolute personal experiment,'" a man who will "entertain the idea of God in every form" and who will demonstrate "the custom of making symbols for the meaning of his own existence before a God whose nature he sees as inscrutable." Sensing that the traditional symbols of his spiritually impoverished civilization have lost their potency, the primitivist will attempt to replace these with symbols derived from his own personal experience and from "the richest and least exhaustible alien cultures," particularly those of Polynesia and the Orient: "The symbolist's awareness of cultural failure becomes atavism, reversion, thoroughly dependent upon feeling, to the past in search for a prototypic culture. This atavism . . . permits the use of archetypal concepts in the making of new and 'personal' religious symbols."[16]

This definition applies to Jack London as well as to Herman Melville. For all London's insistence on Realism, he was a blatant Romantic and an arrogant, inner-directed egoist with a profound faith in his own resources, who lived life as if it were "an absolute personal experiment." Born into an age when the larger religious structures of Western civilization were tottering, and reared in a home without any formal religious orientation, London gravitated logically toward the secular doctrines of Karl Marx and Herbert Spencer, and he described himself as a revolutionary Socialist and as a materialistic monist. In theory, he generally managed to remain true to these faiths; in practice, however, he demonstrated time and again that he was not only an individualist but also a dualist; an instinctive mysticism, not a logical positivism, dominates his Northland fiction. An example is the following passage from "The White Silence," the first story in *The Son of the Wolf:*

> The afternoon wore on, and with the awe, born of the White Silence, the voiceless travelers bent to their work. Nature has many tricks wherewith she convinces man of his finity,—the ceaseless flow of the tides, the fury of the storm, the shock of the earthquake, the long roll of heaven's artillery,—but the most tremendous, the most stupefying of all, is the passive phase of the White Silence. All movement ceases, the sky clears, the heavens are as brass; the slightest whisper seems sacrilege, and man becomes timid, affrighted at the sound of his own voice. Sole speck of life journeying across the ghostly wastes of a dead world, he trembles at his audacity, realizes that his is a maggot's life, nothing more. Strange thoughts arise unsummoned, and the mystery of all things strives for utterance. And the fear of death, of God, of the universe, comes over him,—the hope of the Resurrection and the Life, the yearning for immortality, the vain striving of the imprisoned essence,—it is then, if ever, man walks alone with God. (*Wolf,* 6–7)

London's Northland Deity, like the "inscrutable tides of God" in Melville's *Moby-Dick,* is the polar opposite of the philanthropic God-in-Nature celebrated by such sentimental "exoticists" as Jean-Jacques Rousseau and François René de Chateaubriand.[17] But where Melville had combined whiteness with the fish, an archetype of creation and the life-force, London fused it with images of space, silence, and cold—and he thereby created an autotype more subtly terrifying than the warm-blooded whale. Yet like the whale, the suggestion of an unnerving sentience is what most appalls in the White Silence. Cuthfert in "In a Far Country" is reduced to craven depression by "the ghastly silence [of] the solemn forest which seemed to guard an awful inexpressible something, which neither word nor thought could compass" (*Wolf,* 88). Still more explicit is the opening section of *White Fang:* "A vast silence reigned over the land. The land itself was a desolation, lifeless, without movement, so lone and cold that the spirit of it was not even that of sadness. There was a hint of laughter, but of a laughter more terrible than any sadness—a laughter that was mirthless as the smile of the Sphinx, a laughter cold as the frost and partaking of the grimness of infallibility. It was the masterful and incommunicable wisdom of eternity laughing at the futility of life and the effort of life."[18] Thus conceived, London's White Silence is not merely a convenient setting for adventurous plots; it emerges as a dramatic antagonist charged with the special potency of universal dream symbolism—that is, of myth.

This potency is displayed nowhere to better advantage than in "To Build a Fire," a masterpiece of short fiction that has become one of the most widely anthologized works ever produced by an American author. The central motif is simple enough, as London himself suggested: "Man after man in the Klondike has died alone after getting his feet wet, through failure to build a fire" (*Letters,* 777).[19] Plot and characterization are spare: a nameless *chechaquo,* accompanied by a large husky, is taking a day's hike across the frozen wilderness to join his partners at their mining claim. Although he has been warned by the old-timers against traveling alone in the White Silence, he, a strong, practical man, is confident of his ability to cope with the forces of nature. Yet we sense from the outset that he is doomed, as the narrator begins to weave his dark spell: "Day had broken cold and gray, exceedingly cold and gray, when the man turned aside from the main Yukon trail and climbed the high earth-bank, where a dim and little-traveled trail led eastward through the fat spruce timberland."[20]

The key to the story's impact is not plot, but—as in much of London's best work—mood and atmosphere, which is conveyed through repetitive imagery of cold and gloom and whiteness:

> There was no sun nor hint of sun, though there was not a cloud in the sky. It was a clear day, and yet there seemed an intangible pall over the face of things, a subtle gloom that made the day dark, and that was due to the absence of sun. . . . The man flung a look back along the way he had come. The Yukon lay a mile wide and hidden under three feet of snow. It was all pure white. . . . North and south, as far as his eye could see, it was unbroken white, save for a dark hair-line [trail]. (*Lost,* 63–64)[21]

London's story manifests in its stark eloquence many of those same elements that Aristotle indicated in his *Poetics* as requisite to tragedy. It is a representation of an action that is serious, whole, complete, and of a certain magnitude. The action is rigorously unified, taking place between daybreak and nightfall. The protagonist, neither an especially good man nor an especially bad man, falls into misfortune because of a tragic flaw, notably hubris, an overweening confidence in the efficacy of his own rational faculties and a corresponding blindness to the dark, nonrational powers of nature, chance, and fate: "He was quick and alert in the things of life, but only in the things, and not in the significances. Fifty degrees below zero meant eighty-odd degrees of frost. Such fact impressed him as being cold and uncomfortable, and that was all. It did not lead him to meditate upon his frailty as a creature of temperature, and upon man's frailty in general, able only to live within certain narrow limits of heat and cold; and from there on it did not lead him to the conjectural field of immortality and man's place in the universe" (*Lost,* 64–65). The narrator tells us that "The cold of space smote the unprotected tip of the planet, and he, being on that unprotected tip, received the full force of the blow. The blood of his body recoiled before it. The blood was alive, like the dog, and like the dog it wanted to hide away and cover itself up from the fearful cold" (*Lost,* 80). Here, as throughout the story, the narrator functions as the chorus, who mediates between the action and the reader and who provides moral commentary upon the action. The setting, a mask of the scornful gods ("the cold of space"), functions as antagonist. Aside from these, the only other character is the reluctant dog, who acts as foil or "reflector" by displaying the humility and natural wisdom the man fatally lacks; for "its instinct told it a truer tale than was told to the man by the man's judgment" (Lost, 76).

Also in keeping with the tragic mode is the sense of inevitability in the catastrophe that must befall the hero. Even when he builds his first fire for lunch, we know that the reprieve is temporary: "For the moment the cold of space was outwitted." There is no doubt in our suspense, only a dreadful waiting for the disaster. "And then it happened" (*Lost,* 78): the curt announcement is almost a relief. Still, knowing the cruel irony of the gods, we sense that although the man must surely die, he will first be mocked in his delusion of security. The man himself does not know this, of course, but he does know the gravity of the situation. Having broken through the snow crust over a hidden spring and having wet his legs halfway to the knees, he realizes he must immediately build a fire: "He knew there must be no failure. When it is seventy-five below zero, a man must not fail in his first attempt to build a fire—that is, if his feet are wet. If his feet are dry, and he fails, he can run along the trail for half a mile and restore his circulation. But the circulation of wet and freezing feet cannot be restored by running when it is seventy-five below. No matter how fast he runs, the feet will freeze the harder" (*Lost,* 79–80). The man is fully cognizant of these facts, for they have been told him by the sour-doughs, yet he remains obtuse to their significance. Working rationally and carefully, he manages to build his fire and believes himself safe: "He remembered the advice of the old-timer on Sulphur Creek and smiled. The old-timer had been very serious in laying down the law that no man must travel alone in the Klondike after fifty-below. Well, here he was; he had had the accident; he was alone; and he had saved himself. Those old-timers were rather womanish, some of them, he thought. All a man had to do was to keep his head, and he was all right" (*Lost,* 81). The irony is dramatic as well as tragic.

Being human and therefore fallible, London's protagonist makes a simple, human mistake: he builds his fire under a large, snow-laden spruce tree, and the heat precipitates a small avalanche that blots out the fresh blaze. Reversal and discovery are virtually simultaneous: "The man was shocked. It was as though he had just heard his own sentence of death. For a moment he sat and stared at the spot where the fire had been. Then he grew very calm. Perhaps the old-timer on Sulphur Creek was right. If he had only had a trail-mate he would have been in no dan-ger now. The trail-mate could have built the fire" (*Lost,* 83–84).

From this dramatic climax, the story moves through a brilliant dénouement toward its inescapable conclusion. Fighting off panic, the man tries vainly to build another fire, but his fingers are already dead from the cold. Next, he tries ineffectually to kill the dog, thinking he can warm his hands in its body. Then, panic-stricken, he tries running on his frozen feet until he falls exhausted in the snow. Finally, he grows calm and decides to meet his death with dignity: "His idea of it was that he had been making a fool of himself, running around like a chicken with its head cut off. . . . Well, he was bound to freeze anyway, and he might as well take it decently. . . . There were lots worse ways to die" (*Lost,* 96). In thus resigning himself to his fate, the man achieves a certain heroic stature; and his tragic action inspires both pity and fear in leading his audience toward the cathartic relief prescribed by Aristotle:

> "You were right, old hoss; you were right," the man mumbled to the old-timer of Sulphur Creek.
>   Then the man drowsed off into what seemed to him the most com-fortable and satisfying sleep he had ever known. The dog sat facing him and waiting. The brief day drew to a close in a long, slow twilight. There were no signs of a fire to be made, and, besides, never in the dog's experi-ence had it known a man to sit like that in the snow and make no fire. . . . A little longer it delayed, howling under the stars that leaped

and danced and shone brightly in the cold sky. Then it turned and trot-
ted up the trail in the direction of the camp it knew, where were the
other food-providers and fire-providers. (*Lost,* 97–98)

With this concluding image the tone of the action has been transmuted from dramatic irony into cosmic irony. Gazing at the cold mockery of the heavens, we sense that we are not on the side of the gods and
that the man's frailty is also ours. Such is the effect of London's artistry
that few of us finish "To Build a Fire" without a subtle shiver of relief to
be—at least for the moment—among the "food-providers and fire-
providers." "To Build a Fire" has established itself as a world classic, and
while it is instructive to see how much of Aristotle's formula is reflected
in this work, we should realize that the story's greatness does not depend
on this formal coincidence and that London himself was probably
unaware of these nice parallels with Greek tragedy. The story is great
because it derives its informing power from the communal mystery that
animates the plays of Sophocles and Aeschylus—and of all great tragedi-
ans—and because it has articulated this mystery with such force that we
become mutual participants in the celebration of what Joseph Conrad
called "the unavoidable solidarity" of our human destiny.[22] In that sense
we indeed "never travel alone."

Longer Fictions

In the late summer of 1900 Jack wrote to his friend Johns, "Have or
rather am winding up the first chapter of novel. Since it is my first
attempt, I have chosen a simple subject and shall simply endeavor to
make it true, artistic, and interesting" (*Letters,* 203). Five months later, he
wrote, "Well, I am on the home stretch of the novel, and it is a failure"
(*Letters,* 240). The novel, *A Daughter of the Snows,* published in October
1902 by J. B. Lippincott, was indeed a failure: it is neither true, nor artistic, nor very interesting. C. C. Walcutt has said that the novel is "lavishly
prodigal of ideas,"[23] and this lavishness is largely the reason for its failure.
"Lord, Lord," London sighed, looking back on it; "how I squandered into
it enough stuff for a dozen novels!" (*Book,* I, 384). This work is a pot-
pourri of his pet ideas on social Darwinism, Anglo-Saxon supremacy,
environmentalism, and joy-through-fitness. So preoccupied is the author
with ideology that he confuses fiction with essay. Consequently, ideas
assume precedence over characterization. "The great defect of the novel of
ideas," says Aldous Huxley's Philip Quarles in *Point Counter Point,* "is that

it's a made-up affair. Necessarily; for people who can reel off neatly formulated notions aren't quite real; they're slightly monstrous. Living with
monsters becomes rather tiresome in the long run."[24]

Old Jacob Welse, the Klondike robber baron with his Spencer-
Carnegie rationalizations; Vance Corliss, the Yale "sissy" who gets the
girl after reverting atavistically to the he-manhood of his forbears;
Gregory St. Vincent, the smooth-talking ladies' man who turns graceless
under pressure; and, above all, the astonishing Frona Welse, who, we are
supposed to believe, captivates every male in the Yukon Territory with
her feminine charm, even while flexing her biceps, spouting the doctrines of racist imperialism, and bragging that she can do 20 pull-ups:
such characters do, indeed, "become rather tiresome in the long run." It
must be noted, however, that one important contribution of *A Daughter
of the Snows* that becomes central to London's later work is his use of a
feminist heroine. Clumsy though she is here, Frona is a precursor of more
successful characters such as Lucy of "The Night-Born" or Saxon Brown
Roberts of *The Valley of the Moon.*

London claimed afterward that he had learned a great deal about
writing novels from the mistakes he had made in *A Daughter of the Snows,*
but the simple truth is that he was a born sprinter who never acquired
the artistic stamina of the long-distance runner. The basic technical
weaknesses revealed in his first novel were chronic: his longer plots tend
to be episodic and disjointed; his dialogue is strained; and his characters
often degenerate into caricatures because they are stretched flat on ideological frames. London asserted, "I will sacrifice form *every time,* when it
boils down to a final question of choice between form and matter. The
thought is the thing." But he did not realize that the literary artist has
no such option. It was extremely difficult for him to articulate the larger
structures of the novel without doctrinal meddling such as we find in
Martin Eden, The Iron Heel, The Mutiny of the Elsinore; and, ironically, his
last attempt at writing a novel—*Hearts of Three*—ended in worse failure
than his first.[25]

Neither of London's two most successful works of long fiction is a
conventional novel: *The Call of the Wild* is a mythic romance; *White Fang,*
a sociological fable. Both works are beast fables in that they provoke our
interest—unconsciously if not consciously—in the human situation, not
in the plight of the lower animals.[26] By using canine rather than human
protagonists, London was able to say more about this situation than he
might have been otherwise permitted by the editors of magazines such
as the *Saturday Evening Post* and *Cosmopolitan,* who were extremely careful

not to offend the general sensibilities of their Victorian readership. Just as two generations earlier Poe had muffled sexual aberrations under the dark mantle of Gothicism, so London hid sex under a heavy cloak of fur as in the vivid scene of "love-making in the Wild, the sex-tragedy of the natural world" in the early pages of *White Fang* when old One Eye and the ambitious young wolf fight to the death while "the she-wolf, the cause of it all," sits and watches with pleasure. And we also have the example of Buck's ethical retrogression in *The Call of the Wild:* his learning to steal and rob without scruple and to kill without pity does not morally offend us because he is just a dog, not a human.[27]

Full appreciation of *The Call of the Wild* and *White Fang* begins with "Bâtard," London's first dog story, published in the June 1902 issue of *Cosmopolitan* under the euphemistic title "Diable—A Dog." Although its thematic relationship to the two later works is inverse, this fine tale shares with both of them the characteristics of fable and, especially with *White Fang,* the theme of hereditary and environmental determinism. "Bâtard" is an anatomy of hatred, and its canine protagonist— "Hell's Spawn," as he is called by some—is the antithesis of everything that man's best friend is supposed to be. It is clear that such devils are not merely born; they are also made:

> Bâtard did not know his father—hence his name—but, as John Hamlin [the storekeeper of the Sixty Mile Post] knew, his father was a great gray timber wolf. But the mother of Bâtard, as he dimly remembered her, was a snarling, bickering, obscene husky, full-fronted and heavy-chested, with a malign eye, a cat-like grip on life, and a genius for trickery and evil. . . . Much of evil and much of strength were there in these, Bâtard's progenitors, and, bone and flesh of their bone and flesh, he had inherited it all. And then came Black Leclère, to lay his heavy hand on the bit of pulsating puppy life, to press and prod and mould till it became a big bristling beast, acute in knavery, overspilling with hate, sinister, malignant, diabolical. With a proper master Bâtard might have been an ordinary, fairly efficient sled-dog. He never got the chance: Leclère but confirmed him in his congenital iniquity.[28]

His sadistic treatment at the hand of his human antagonist, the dissolute voyageur, finally transforms Bâtard into the incarnation of evil. Half-starved, tortured, beaten, and cursed, the dog grows progressively more vicious and cunning—yet he refuses to leave his master because he bides with uncanny patience his time for revenge. Nor can Black

Leclère resist his compulsion to cultivate this hatred. Even after Bâtard has attacked him in his sleep and has slit his throat, he refuses to accept the advice of old-timers who urge him to let them shoot the dog. But Leclère is no match for the preternatural malevolence he has unleashed. Near the end of the story, unjustly convicted of murdering a gold miner, he is forced to mount a large box, hands tied and noose around his neck. He gets a last-minute reprieve, but the miners leave him alone, standing precariously on the box, to meditate upon his sinful ways while they go downriver to apprehend the real murderer. When the miners have gone, the dog, grinning "with a fiendish levity in his bearing that Leclère [cannot] mistake," casually retreats a few yards—then hurls himself against the box on which his helpless master is standing. "Fifteen minutes later, Slackwater Charley and Webster Shaw, returning, caught a glimpse of a ghostly pendulum swinging back and forth in the dim light. As they hurriedly drew in closer, they made out the man's inert body, and a live thing that clung to it, and shook and worried, and gave to it the swaying motion" (*Faith,* 231).

London said he wrote *The Call of the Wild* to redeem the species. "I started it as a companion to my other dog story 'Bâtard,' which you may remember; but it got away from me, and instead of 4,000 words it ran 32,000 before I could call a halt" (*Book,* I, 388). Joan London tells us that as far as her father was concerned, this masterpiece was "a purely fortuitous piece of work, a lucky shot in the dark that had unexpectedly found its mark," and that, when reviewers enthusiastically interpreted *The Call of the Wild* as a brilliant human allegory, he was astonished: "'I plead guilty,' he admitted, 'but I was unconscious of it at the time. I did not mean to do it'"(*Times,* 252).[29] However, he was not entirely oblivious to the story's unusual merit.

London's story was utterly different from the humanized beasts in Kipling's "Mowgli" stories and from the sentimental projections of Margaret Marshall Saunders's *Beautiful Joe* and Ernest Seton's *Biography of a Grizzly,* which were enormously popular in London's day and are still found in the children's sections of libraries. Charles G. D. Roberts, writing about the appeal of such literature at the turn of the century, explained that "the animal story, as we now have it, is a potent emancipator. It frees us for a little while from the world of shop-worn utilities, and from the mean tenement of self of which we do well to grow weary. . . . It has ever the more significance, it has ever the richer gift of refreshment and renewal, the more humane the heart and spiritual the understanding which we bring to the intimacy of it."[30] This explanation holds true for *The Call of the Wild* as well as for the other wild animal stories: London's work offers the "gift of refreshment and renewal," as well as a certain escapism. The difference is its radical departure from the conventional animal story in style and substance—the manner in which it is, to use the psychoanalytic term, *overdetermined* in its multilayered meaning.[31]

Maxwell Geismar gives a clue to the deeper layer of meaning when he classifies the work as "a beautiful prose poem, or *nouvelle*, of gold and death on the instinctual level" and as a "handsome parable of the buried impulses."[32] We need only interpolate that these "buried impulses" are essentially human, not canine, and that readers identify more closely than they may realize with this protagonist. The plot is animated by one of the most basic of archetypal motifs: the Myth of the Hero. The call to adventure, departure, initiation, the perilous journey to the mysterious life-center, transformation, and apotheosis: these are the phases of the Myth; and all are present in Buck's progress from the civilized world through the natural and beyond to the supernatural world.[33] His journey carries him not only through space but also through time and, ultimately, into the still center of a world that is timeless.

Richard Chase points out that in the type of long fiction most properly designated as the *romance,* character becomes "somewhat abstract and ideal," and plot is "highly colored": "Astonishing events may occur, and these are likely to have a symbolic or ideological, rather than a realistic, plausibility. Being less committed to the immediate rendition of reality than the novel, the romance will more freely veer toward mythic, allegorical, and symbolistic forms."[34] All of these remarks are directly applicable to *The Call of the Wild,* in which the richly symbolistic form ultimately becomes the content of the fiction. The seven chapters of the work fall into four major parts or movements. Each of these movements is distinguished by its own theme, rhythm, and tone; each is climaxed by an event of dramatic intensity; and each marks a stage in the hero's transformation from a phenomenal into an ideal figure.

Part 1, consisting of three chapters, is, with its emphasis on physical violence and amoral survival, the most Naturalistic—and the most literal—of the book. Its rhythms are quick, fierce, muscular. Images of intense struggle, pain, and blood predominate. Chapter 1, "Into the Primitive," describes the great dog's kidnapping from Judge Miller's pastoral ranch and his subsequent endurance of the first rites of his initiation—the beginning of the transformation that ultimately carries him deep into Nature's heart of darkness: "For two days and nights he nei-

ther ate nor drank, and during those two days and nights of torment, he
accumulated a fund of wrath that boded ill for whoever first fell foul of
him. His eyes turned blood-shot, and he was metamorphosed into a rag-
ing fiend. So changed was he that the Judge himself would not have recognized him; and the express messengers breathed with relief when they
bundled him off the train at Seattle."[35]

The high priest of Buck's first initiatory rites is the symbolic figure in
the red sweater, the man with the club who relentlessly pounds the hero
into a disciplined submission to the code of violence and toil. "Well,
Buck, my boy," the man calmly observes after the merciless beating,
"we've had our little ruction, and the best thing we can do is to let it go
at that. You've learned your place, and I know mine" (*Call,* 32). Like all
of London's heroes who survive the rigors of the White Silence, Buck has
passed the first test: that of adaptability.

Chapter 2, "The Law of Club and Fang," takes the hero to the
Northland. On Dyea Beach he encounters the dogs and men who are to
become his traveling companions in the long, hard months ahead. He
also continues to absorb the lessons of survival. Curly, the most amiable
of the newly arrived pack, is knocked down by a veteran husky, then
ripped apart by the hordes of canine spectators. The scene remains vivid-
ly etched in Buck's memory: "So that was the way. No fair play. Once
down, that was the end of you" (*Call,* 45). Later, as he is broken into his
traces for the trail, he awakens to the great driving motivation of the
veteran sled dogs: the extraordinary love of toil. But more significant is
the metamorphosis of his moral values. He learns, for example, that
stealing, an unthinkable misdeed in his former state, can be the difference between survival and death: "It was all well enough in the
Southland, under the law of love and fellowship, to respect private prop-
erty and personal feelings; but in the Northland, under the law of club
and fang, whoso took such things into account was a fool, and in so far
as he observed them he would fail to prosper" (*Call,* 59–60).

Chapter 3, "The Dominant Primordial Beast," marks the conclusion
of the first major phase of Buck's initiation, for it reveals that he is not
merely qualified as a member of the pack but that he is worthy of leadership. This chapter has a pronounced modulation of style to signal the
glimmerings of Buck's mythic destiny; instead of sharply detailed physical description, we begin to encounter passages of tone poetry:

With the aurora borealis flaming coldly overhead, or the stars leaping in
the frost dance, and the land numb and frozen under its pall of snow, this

song of the huskies might have been the defiance of life, only it was pitched in minor key, with long-drawn wailings and half-sobs, and was more the pleading of life, the articulate travail of existence. When he moaned and sobbed, it was with the pain of living that was of old the pain of his wild fathers, and the fear and mystery of the cold and dark that was to them fear and mystery. (*Call*, 84–87)

London's style becomes increasingly lyrical as the narrative rises from literal to symbolic level, and it reaches such intensity near the end of chapter 3 that we now realize Buck's is no common animal story:

There is an ecstasy that marks the summit of life, and beyond which life cannot rise. And such is the paradox of living, this ecstasy comes when one is most alive, and it comes as a complete forgetfulness that one is alive. This ecstasy, this forgetfulness of living, comes to the artist, caught up and out of himself in a sheet of flame; it comes to the soldier, war-mad on a stricken field and refusing quarter; and it came to Buck, leading the pack, sounding the old wolf-cry, straining after the food that was alive and that fled swiftly before him through the moonlight. He was sounding the deeps of his nature, and of the parts of his nature that were deeper than he, going back into the womb of Time. He was mastered by the sheer surging of life, the tidal wave of being, the perfect joy of each separate muscle, joint, and sinew in that it was everything that was not death, that it was aglow and rampant, expressing itself in movement, flying exultantly under the stars and over the face of dead matter that did not move. (*Call*, 91)

This paragraph is a thematic epitome of the whole work, and it functions as a prologue to the weird moonlit scene in which Buck challenges Spitz for leadership of the team, a scene noted by Geismar as "a perfect instance of the 'son-horde' theory which Frazer traced in *The Golden Bough,* and of that primitive ritual to which Freud himself attributed both a sense of original sin and the fundamental ceremony of religious exorcism" (Geismar, 150–51).

Even though Buck has now "Won to Mastership" (chapter 4), he is not ready for apotheosis. He is a leader and a hero—but he is not yet a god. His divinity must be confirmed, as prescribed by ritual, through death and rebirth. After the climactic pulsations of chapter 3, a slowing of beat occurs in the second movement. Death occurs symbolically, almost literally, in chapter 5 ("The Toil of Trace and Trail"). Clustering darkly, the dominant images are those of pain and fatigue as Buck and his teammates suffer under the ownership of the three *chechaquos:*

Charles, his wife Mercedes, and her brother Hal— "a nice family party."
Like the two Incapables of "In a Far Country," they display all the fatal
symptoms of incompetence and unfitness: "Buck felt vaguely that there
was no depending upon these two men and the woman. They did not
know how to do anything, and as days went by it became apparent that
they could not learn. They were slack in all things, without order or discipline" (*Call,* 138). Without a sense of economy or the will to work and
endure hardship themselves, they overwork, starve, and beat their
dogs—then they turn on one another:

> Their irritability arose out of their misery, increased with it, doubled
> upon it, outdistanced it. The wonderful patience of the trail which comes
> to all men who toil hard and suffer sore, and remain sweet of speech and
> kindly, did not come to these two men and the woman. They had no
> inkling of such a patience. They were stiff and in pain; their muscles
> ached, their bones ached, their very hearts ached; and because of this they
> became sharp of speech, and hard words were first on their lips in the
> morning and last at night. (*Call,* 141)

This ordeal is the second long and difficult phase of Buck's initiation.
The "long journey" is described in increasingly morbid imagery as the
"perambulating skeletons" and "wayfarers of death" approach closer to
their fatal end in the thawing ice of Yukon River; the journey ends with
Buck's symbolic crucifixion as he is beaten nearly to death by Hal shortly before the ghostly caravan moves on without him and disappears into
the icy maw of the river.

Buck's rebirth comes in chapter 6, "For the Love of Man," which also
functions as the third and transitional movement of the narrative.
Having been rescued by John Thornton, the benign helper who traditionally appears in the Myth to lead the hero toward his goal, Buck is
now being readied for the final phase of his odyssey. Appropriately, the
season is spring; and the mood is idyllic as he wins back his strength,
"lying by the river bank through the long spring days, watching the
running water, listening lazily to the songs of the birds and the hum of
nature . . ." (*Call,* 161). And, during this same convalescent period, the
hints of his destiny grow more insistent: "He was older than the days he
had seen and the breaths he had drawn. He linked the past with the
present, and the eternity behind him throbbed through him in a mighty
rhythm to which he swayed as the tides and seasons swayed. . . . Deep in
the forest a call was sounding. . . . But as often as he gained the soft
unbroken earth and the green shade, the love for John Thornton drew

him back . . ." (*Call*, 168–71). The passionate devotion of Thornton climaxes in the final scene of chapter 6 when Buck wins a $1,000 wager for his master by moving a half-ton sled 100 yards; this legendary feat, which concludes the third movement of the narrative, foreshadows the hero's supernatural appointment in the fourth and final movement.

Chapter 7, "The Sounding of the Call," consummates Buck's transformation. In keeping with this change, London shifts both the setting and the tone. Thornton, taking the money earned by Buck in the wager, begins his last quest "into the East after a fabled lost mine, the history of which was as old as the history of the country . . . steeped in tragedy and shrouded in mystery." As the small party moves into the wilderness, the scene assumes a mythic atmosphere and the caravan is enveloped in a strange aura of timelessness:

> The months came and went, and back and forth they twisted through the uncharted vastness, where no men were and yet where men had been if the Lost Cabin were true. They went across divides in summer blizzards, shivered under the midnight sun on naked mountains between the timber line and the eternal snows, dropped into summer valleys amid swarming gnats and flies, and in the shadows of glaciers picked strawberries and flowers as ripe and fair as any the Southland could boast. In the fall of the year they penetrated a weird lake country, sad and silent, where wild-fowl had been, but where then there was no life nor sign of life—only the blowing chill winds, the forming of ice in sheltered places, and the melancholy rippling of waves on lonely beaches. (*Call*, 195–96)

The weirdness of the atmosphere is part of the "call to adventure" described by Joseph Campbell in *The Hero with a Thousand Faces*, which "signifies that destiny has summoned the hero and transferred his spiritual center of gravity from within the pale of society to a zone unknown. This fateful region of both treasure and danger may be variously represented: as a distant land, a forest, . . . or profound dream state; but it is always a place of strangely fluid and polymorphous beings, unimaginable torments, superhuman deeds and impossible delight" (58). This "fateful region of both treasure and danger" is a far cry from Judge Miller's pastoral ranch and from the raw frontier of the Klondike gold rush: it is the landscape of myth. The party finally arrives at its destination, a mysterious and incredibly rich placer valley where "Like giants they toiled, days flashing on the heels of days like dreams as they heaped the treasure up" (*Call,* 197).

His role fulfilled as guide into the unknown zone, Thornton and his party are killed by the savage Yeehats, and Buck is released from the bond of love to fulfill the last phase of his apotheosis as he is transformed into the immortal Ghost Dog of Northland legend. He incarnates the eternal mystery of creation and life: "[And when] the long winter nights come on and the wolves follow their meat into the lower valleys . . . a great, gloriously coated wolf, like, and yet unlike, all other wolves . . . may be seen running at the head of the pack through the pale moonlight or glimmering borealis, leaping gigantic above his fellows, his great throat abellow as he sings a song of the younger world, which is the song of the pack" (*Call,* 228–31).

Although *The Call of the Wild* was perhaps no luckier than any other great artistic achievement, it was "a shot in the dark" in an unintended sense—into the dark wilderness of the unconscious. And as with other great literary works, its ultimate meaning eludes us. But at least a significant part of that meaning relates to the area of human experience that cannot be translated into discursive terms and that must therefore be approached tentatively and obliquely. After granting this much, we may infer that the animating force of London's wild romance is the vital energy Jung called *libido* and that London's hero is a projection of the reader's own *self* eternally striving for psychic integration in the process called *individuation.* Such an inference accounts for the appropriateness of London's division of his narrative into seven chapters that fall naturally into four movements, quaternity symbolizing, in Jung's words, "the ideal of completeness" and "the totality of the personality," and seven, the archetypal number of perfect order and the consummation of a cycle.[36] But, of course, we do not need such a technical explanation to know that the call to which we respond as the great Ghost Dog flashes through the glimmering borealis singing his song of the younger world is the faint but clear echo of a music deep within ourselves.

In 1904, following the immediate success of *The Call of the Wild,* London wrote to Macmillan's president, George P. Brett, that he had decided to compose a "complete antithesis [and] companion-book": "I'm going to reverse the process. Instead of devolution or decivilization of a dog, I'm going to give the evolution, the civilization of a dog—development of domesticity, faithfulness, love, morality, & all the amenities & virtues" (*Letters,* 454). Two years later this "companion-book" was published under the title of *White Fang.* Instead of being a true companion piece, however, *White Fang* is a completely different kind of book from *The Call of the Wild,* clearly illustrating the basic distinctions between

Jung's "visionary mode" and "psychological mode." Structured upon ideas rather than upon myth, *White Fang* is a sociological fable intended to illustrate London's theories of environmentalism.

More Naturalistic than *The Call of the Wild,* the opening description of the frozen-hearted Northland is as powerful as anything London ever wrote in this vein. Here he depicts nature as a vast intransigent force utterly hostile to puny, inconsequential men who are "pitting themselves against the might of a world as remote and alien and pulseless as the abyss of space" (*White,* 5). Unlike the animated Wild to which Buck reverts, this is the Wild of the White Silence, predicated upon the death principle: "Life is an offense to it, for life is movement; and the Wild aims always to destroy movement. It freezes the water to prevent it running to the sea; it drives the sap out of the trees till they are frozen to their mighty hearts; and most ferociously and terribly of all does the Wild harry and crush into submission man—man, who is the most restless of life, ever in revolt against the dictum that all movement must in the end come to the cessation of movement" (*White,* 4–5). Into this forbidding world the young wolf cub is born, and he learns early that life is an eat-or-be-eaten affair and that the forces of life move inexorably toward death in one violent form or another.

Set against this principle and providing the central tension of the work is a cluster of contrasting values: life, love, civilization, the Southland. Toward these the protagonist moves during his rites of passage. In *White Fang,* a proper initiation story, the hero follows the conventional pattern of separation, ordeal, transformation, return, and full integration as a full-fledged, responsible member of society. At the conclusion, White Fang has been transformed by love from a savage beast into a thoroughly domesticated pet: "Not alone was he in the geographical Southland, for he was in the Southland of life. Human kindness was like a sun shining upon him, and he flourished like a flower planted in good soil" (*White,* 305). From this perspective, *White Fang* may be regarded as a companion piece and antithesis, not to the *Call of the Wild,* but to "Bâtard," in which a misbegotten brute is shaped by maltreatment into a fiend. To make sure the reader perceives the message, the author inserts into the closing pages of *White Fang* the episode of the escaped convict Jim Hall, who is a human version of Bâtard. Hall has been "ill-made in the making," we are told; and the harsh treatment he has received from society, "from the time he was a little pulpy boy in a San Francisco slum—soft clay in the hands of society and ready to be formed into something," has turned him into "so terrible a beast that he can best be characterized as carnivorous" (*White*, 315–16).

The dramatic confrontation between these two contrasting products of environmental determinism—the brutalized man and the civilized beast—occurs when the escaped convict breaks into Judge Scott's home to "wreak vengeance" on the man who he thinks "railroaded" him to prison. Jim Hall is a mad dog who must be destroyed for the safety of respectable citizens, but London makes it clear, as he had done in "Bâtard," that the responsibility for such creatures rests squarely on the society that has molded them. As he said to George Wharton James,

> "I know men and women as they are—millions of them yet in the slime stage. But I am an evolutionist, therefore a broad optimist, hence my love for the human (in the slime though he be) comes from my knowing him as he is and seeing the divine possibilities ahead of him. That's the whole motive of my 'White Fang.' Every atom of organic life is plastic. The finest specimens now in existence were once all pulpy infants capable of being moulded this way or that. Let the pressure be one way and we have atavism—the reversion to the wild; the other the domestication, civilization. I have always been impressed with the awful plasticity of life and I feel that I can never lay enough stress upon the marvelous power and influence of environment."[37]

White Fang is an effective dramatization of this theme and continues to be widely read, but from the artistic viewpoint it is less impressive than *The Call of the Wild* because it is written in what Eliseo Vivas has called the "transitive" mode: its function is to point toward the cognitive and the moral. *The Call of the Wild* is, on the other hand, purely aesthetic and intransitive: it engages the reader in a rapt attention for no other purpose than the unique experience of art.[38] Rather than pointing outward to society, *The Call of the Wild* points inward to something marvelous within humanity—the everlasting mystery of life itself.

The artistic significance of *The Call of the Wild* was recognized at once in one of those rare instances when critical taste and popular appetite agree, and Jack London was acclaimed by the world as a major writer. During the years afterward, he had other moments of "primordial" inspiration, but none surpassed the sustained vision of this extraordinary "parable of the buried impulses."

Chapter Three

Success

Jack London made no bones about his reasons for writing. "If cash come with fame, come fame," he wrote to Clondesley Johns; "if cash comes without fame, come cash" (*Letters,* 129). But it was not the money itself or the making of the money that he really wanted; he wanted what the money would buy: "I shall always hate the task of getting money," he confessed in 1900; "every time I sit down to write it is with great disgust. I'd sooner be out in the open wandering around most any old place. So the habit of money spending, ah God! I shall always be its victim" (*Letters,* 164–65). There is some truth in Granville Hicks's remark that "in his attitude towards money London was indistinguishable from any middle-class man on the make,"[1] but it is the kind of partial truth often conveyed through condescension: by ignoring the larger implications, it risks missing the point entirely.

The point is that London was forever playing the role of the American Adam. As in the case of Fitzgerald's Jay Gatsby—and London's own Martin Eden—the obsession to get money was materialistic and vulgar only in the most superficial way; fundamentally, the conception was ideal. In this ideal sense, money—though essential—was the means to an end, never an end in itself. The concept was part of the old American Dream again, older than Ben Franklin, who popularized this myth derived from the Puritan ethic: Material gain was a sign of spiritual grace; through His special providence, the Almighty smiled visibly upon His saints by rewarding their labors with profit in the affairs of this world. Older than the Puritans, material gain was inextricable from the age-old dream for the better life. Money was in truth the coin of the New Realm, for would it not buy happiness, esteem, the richer life? "More money means more life to me," said London, and this statement was a key to his meteoric career, just as it is a key to the larger Dream.

Portrait of the Artist as a Professional

Jack London's open confession—or boast—that his motives were commercial has provided modern critics with a handy excuse for consigning

both him and his work to the literary dustbin. However, as the British
critic Winifred Blatchford has written, "Jack London is known as a 'popular' writer, and certainly he is more greatly read by all classes of readers
than are most writers. But his popularity was not gained by cheapness,
as is usually the case. He had a great public not because he wrote down
to the public, but because what he wrote was always intensely alive and
understandable."[2]

A fair assessment of London's artistic integrity must begin with the
recognition that his attitude toward writing was thoroughly professional—that is, he deliberately chose writing as the sole means of making his
livelihood; he underwent rigorous training to acquire the special exper-
tise of his chosen field; he wrote with the full expectation of being paid
well for his investment; he maintained the discipline of steady application of his time and energies to his vocation, and once having become
secure in his accomplished skill, he regarded it with a confidence border-
ing on contempt. At the same time, his work was generally governed by
a clear-cut professional code comprising an ethic, a mystique, and a practical aesthetic.

The ethic was sincerity. In 1907, reacting to the suggestion by Brett
that publication of his disreputable tramping experiences might damage
the sales of his other works, London asserted: "In *The Road,* and in all my
work, in all that I have said and written and done, I have been true. This
is the character I have built up; it constitutes, I believe my big asset. . . .
I have always insisted that the cardinal literary virtue is sincerity, and I
have striven to live up to this belief" (*Letters,* 675). Earlier, he prescribed
for aspiring young writers: "The three great things are: GOOD
HEALTH; WORK; and a PHILOSOPHY OF LIFE. I may add, nay,
must add, a fourth—SINCERITY. Without this, the other three are
without avail; with it you may cleave to greatness and sit among
giants."[3] To be candid was to tell the truth as he saw it in relationship to
his philosophy of life; it was to be true to his artistic self as that self had
been shaped by experience; and it meant that he must in his fiction
articulate the basic, cosmic realities.

The mystique was imaginative Realism or, as London phrased it in
Martin Eden, "an impassioned realism, shot through with human aspira-
tion and faith . . . life as it [is], with all its spirit-groping and soul-reach-
ing left in," a truthful compromise between "the school of god" and "the
school of clod," charged with vitality and with "humanness." The impassioned Realist "must seize upon and press into enduring art-forms the
vital facts of our existence." And, while he will always endeavor to fuse

his Realism with imaginative beauty and with the spirit of romance and adventure, he must never shun the terrible and the tragic in favor of the illusion of life's "sweet commonplaces." The sincere writer will be as forceful as he is honest—for "what more is the function of art than to excite states of consciousness complementary to the thing portrayed? The color of tragedy must be red." In sum, the supreme fiction will be truer than phenomenal reality because the writer's imagination will have seized upon the cosmic essence, thereby making it "LIVE, and spout blood and spirit and beauty and fire and glamor."[4]

London's aesthetic, informed by the same vital honesty, manifested itself in functionalism: "Art, to be truly effective, should be part and parcel of life and pervade it in all its interstices."[5] Only so much beauty does an object possess as it has utility: "What finer beauty than strength—whether it be airy steel, or massive masonry, or a woman's hand? . . . A thing must be true, or it is not beautiful, any more than a painted wanton is beautiful, any more than a sky-scraper is beautiful that is intrinsically and structurally light and that has a false massiveness of pillars plastered on outside." Praising Spencer's "Philosophy of Style," London wrote:

> It taught me to transmute thought, beauty, sensation and emotion into black symbols on white paper; which symbols, through the reader's eye, were taken into his brain, and by his brain transmuted into thoughts, beauty, sensations and emotions that fairly correspond with mine. Among other things, this taught me to know the brain of my reader, in order to select the symbols that would compel his brain to realize my thought, or vision, or emotion. Also, I learned that the right symbols were the ones that would require the expenditure of the minimum of my reader's brain energy, leaving the maximum of his brain energy to realize and enjoy the content of my mind, as conveyed to his mind. (*Book,* II, 50)

Simplistic as such comments seem by late twentieth-century critical standards, London was fully representative of his own age when he remarked that "it tolerates Mr. James, but it prefers Mr. Kipling";[6] and he was well in advance of that age when he asserted that "there is no utility that need not be beautiful" and that "construction and decoration must be one."[7]

Because London discovered early in his career that writing fiction paid better than writing literary criticism, he published relatively few essays on the art of fiction; but the many letters of advice he so generously wrote, along with the handful of his critical essays, reveal his mastery of his craft.[8] Dissimilar though the two writers appear to be in so many ways, London would have agreed with Henry James that the absolute requirement for a work of fiction is that it be interesting and that the quality of the work of art is directly proportional to the quality of the mind of the producer: "You must have your hand on the inner pulse of things," London admonished the young writer; "the very form of the thinking is the expression . . . if your expression is poor, it is because your thought is poor, if narrow, because you are narrow."[9] He would have agreed, moreover, with James's concept of experience as a state of mind, though for James artistic sensibility was an exquisite silken web while for London it was a trawling net. Yet in both cases the supreme virtue was the illusion of life conveyed through the artistic transaction. Long before T. S. Eliot circulated his "objective correlative," London advised Johns, "Don't you tell the reader. [INSTEAD,] HAVE YOUR CHARACTERS TELL IT BY THEIR DEEDS, ACTIONS, TALK, ETC. Then, and not until then, are you writing fiction and not a sociological paper. . . . Atmosphere stands always for the elimination of the artist, that is to say, the atmosphere is the artist . . ." (*Letters,* 191–92).

The most thorough exposition of London's attitude toward the artist as a professional craftsman is found in his early article "First Aid to Rising Authors," first published in the December 1900 issue of *Junior Munsey Magazine* and posthumously reprinted as "The Material Side" in *The Occident.* In this seminal essay London divides writers into two major categories. The first group consists of three types for whom writing is a part-time, secondary activity: (1) the specialist—the doctor, the lawyer, the professor, the scientist—who writes in order to disseminate knowledge of a profession; (2) the social gadfly who writes merely to get his name into print; and (3) the literary dabbler or dilettante who writes for the same reason one hunts, travels, or attends the opera—for diversion and pleasure. By contrast, the second group are the serious authors for whom writing is a way of life, and these also comprise three major types: (1) the true poet "who sings for the song's sake" and "because he cannot help singing"; (2) the didactic "heavenly, fire-flashing, fire-bringing" soul who has—or thinks he has— "a message the world needs or would be glad to hear" and whose "ambition is to teach, to help, to uplift"; and (3) the ambitious, practical writer who is driven by "belly need" and by an obsession to achieve the good life. Without compunction London places himself in this last group:

We are joy-loving, pleasure-seeking and we are ever hungry for the things which we deem the compensation of living: . . . good food . . . nice houses with sanitary plumbing and tight roofs . . . books, pictures, pianos . . . saddle horses, bicycles, and automobiles; cameras, shot guns, and jointed rods; canoes, catboats, and yawls . . . railroad tickets, tents, and camping outfits. . . . When India starves, or the town needs a library, or the poor man in the neighborhood loses his one horse and falls sick, we want to put our hands in our pockets and help. And to do all this, we want cash!

Because we want these things, . . . we are going to rush into print to get them. . . . We have chosen print because we were better adapted for it; and, further, because we preferred it to pulling teeth, mending broken bones, adding up figures, or working with pick and shovel.[10]

If one chooses to write for cash, one should write the kind of stuff that will pay best, and fiction pays best. Even so, London urges, one should avoid "the inanely vapid sort which amuses the commonplace public, and the melodramatic messes which tickle the palates of the sensation mongers. . . . Of course it pays; but . . ."—and here is the key to the paradox of London's view of his work—

. . . because we happen to be mercenarily inclined, there is no reason why we should lose our self-respect. A man material enough of soul to work for his living is not, in consequence, so utterly bad as to be incapable of exercising choice. . . . Though the dreamers and idealists scorn us because of our close contact with the earth, no disgrace need attach to the contact. The flesh may sit heavily upon us, yet may we stand erect and look one another in the eyes.

And in this connection we may well take a lesson from those same dreamers and idealists. Let us be fire-bringers in a humble way. Let us have an eye to the ills of the world and its needs; and if we find messages, let us deliver them. Ah, pardon me, purely for materialistic reasons. We will weave them about with our fictions, and make them beautiful, and sell them for goodly sums.

Of course there is a danger in this. It is liable to be catching. We may become possessed by our ideas, and be whisked away into the clouds. But we won't inoculate. Honor bright, we won't inoculate. ("Material," 145)

The complexity of London's theory of his craft is revealed in these playful ironies. By his own admission he was a commercial artist who wrote from "belly need" and for the material accoutrements of the Great Society—but he was also a self-respecting professional. More than this, he was also on occasion a true poet, a dreamer, and an idealist. Finally, he was an ideological "fire-bringer" who wrote a good many messages with a sharper eye to indoctrination than to profit.

Ideological Inoculations

Porter Garnett, in an early assessment of London's work, wrongly predicted that London would "take his place in the encyclopedias as a philosopher and a propagandist rather than as a literary artist."[11] His was an understandable error. The amount of London's work written primarily to indoctrinate rather than to sell should easily disprove the accusations that he was a hack. Although he was fully aware of the unpopularity and, therefore, of the economic risks of his Socialist preachings, he authored a half-dozen overtly propagandistic titles. Less obvious but no less important is the quantity of his profit-motivated work that is also didactic. Few major fictionists have committed themselves more openly to ideology in so much of their writing, and no American author has been more transparent or, for that matter, less secretive. In his writing London told everything he knew—and unwittingly revealed more than he knew.

If we glance back a few years before his successes with *The Call of the Wild* and *White Fang,* his literary collaboration with Anna Strunsky on *The Kempton-Wace Letters* is a case in point. When they met in the fall of 1899 at a lecture by Socialist Austin Lewis, London was immediately attracted to the brilliant young liberal: "I shall be over Saturday night," he announced in a letter to her a few days afterward. "If you draw back upon yourself, what have I left? Take me this way: a stray guest, a bird of passage, splashing with salt-rimed wings through a brief moment in your life—a rude and blundering bird, used to large airs and great spaces, unaccustomed to the amenities of confined existence" (*Letters,* 136). Reminiscing years later, Strunsky wrote: "He was youth, adventure, romance. He was a poet and a social revolutionist. He had a genius for friendship. He loved and was greatly beloved."[12]

Yet, despite his great affection for Anna, he married Bessie Maddern the following spring, not because of romantic love but because of ideology: he wanted "seven sturdy Saxon sons and seven beautiful daughters."[13] A few months later he rationalized his decision in an epistolary dialogue with Strunsky published pseudonymously by Macmillan in

1903 as *The Kempton-Wace Letters*. As he wrote to Johns in October 1900, "Didn't I explain my volume of letters? Well, it's this way: A young Russian Jewess of 'Frisco and myself have often quarreled over our conceptions of love. She happens to be a genius. She is also a materialist by philosophy, and an idealist by innate preference, and is constantly being forced to twist all the facts of the universe in order to reconcile herself with her self. So, finally, we decided that the only way to argue the question out would be by letter" (*Letters*, 214). The question was argued out, to be sure, but not in the way London had intended. The ultimate effect of the debate was to purge him of his rational-scientific attitude toward love.

"Love is something that begins in sensation and ends in sentiment," he writes behind the persona of a young economics professor named Herbert Wace who is attacking the romantic views of his older friend Dane Kempton (Strunsky); it is *"a disorder of the mind and body and is produced by passion under the stimulus of imagination."* The entire tradition of romantic love is nothing but "pre-nuptial madness," "an artifice, blunderingly and unwittingly introduced by man into the natural order."[14] The deluded romantic lover, unable to reconcile his carnal passions with his idealized sentiment, agonizes in his "sense of sin and shame and personal degradation," for he fails to realize that "the need for perpetuation is the cause of passion; and that human passion, working through imagination and worked upon by imagination, becomes love" (*Kempton*, 89). This emotion is simply *"a means for the perpetuation and development of the human type"* and may be improved through the application of human reason. A sensible marriage "is based upon reason and service and healthy sacrifice. . . . In a word, and in the fullest sense of the word, it is sex comradeship" (*Kempton*, 67, 69).

Ironically, London soon abandoned the tough reasonableness of his own attitude. As Strunsky later remarked, "He held that love is only a trap set by nature for the individual. One must not marry for love but for certain qualities discerned by the mind. This he argued in 'The Kempton-Wace Letters' brilliantly and passionately; so passionately as to again make one suspect that he was not as certain of his position as he claimed to be" (*Book*, I, 360). Between the inception and publication of the *Letters*, something happened to change radically London's views about love. At the end of the book, Herbert Wace, smugly rational, is rejected by his fiancée, thereby signifying a victory for Dane Kempton's romantic argument. Apparently the course of London's own marriage, which had been predicated on the same thesis argued in the book, had altered his belief that one could successfully marry without passion. Writing to Johns in the late summer of 1903, a few weeks after his separation from Bessie, he drily commented: ". . . it's all right for a man sometimes to marry philosophically, but remember, it's damned hard on the woman" (*Letters*, 381). Two years later, as soon as the divorce was final, he married Charmian Kittredge for romantic love.

On 21 July 1902, a few weeks after London had finished his collaboration with Strunsky and his proofing of *A Daughter of the Snows*, he received a wire from the American Press Association asking him to go to South Africa to report the aftermath of the Boer War. He left the next day, stopping over in New York to meet with Brett and to discuss publication of *The Kempton-Wace Letters*. During the discussion he also made an agreement to publish a study of conditions in the London slums, which he planned to research during his layover in England. It was a fortunate agreement, for his South African series was canceled before he left for England. Despite dire predictions that he would never be seen alive again by his friends, he spent 10 shillings at a secondhand clothing shop in Petticoat Lane for a change of wardrobe and, disguised as a stranded and broke American seaman, disappeared into the black heart of the East End. On 9 August he stood in Trafalgar Square indistinguishable from the thousands of derelicts who threw their dirty caps into the air amid shouts of "God save the King!" as Edward VII rode by in his Coronation Day parade.

London had endured considerable hardship and had lived close to poverty most of his life, but nothing in his past experiences compared with what he saw in that "City of Degradation." "Am settled down & hard at work," he wrote to Strunsky on 16 August. "The whole thing, all the conditions of life, the intensity of it, everything is overwhelming. I never conceived such a mass of misery in the world before" (*Letters,* 305). The next week he wrote again that his book was one-fifth done: "Am rushing, for I am made sick by this human hell-hole called London Town. I find it almost impossible to believe that some of the horrible things I have seen are really so" (*Letters,* 306). When he emerged a month later from the jungle, he had the vivid record—manuscript and photographs—ready for the press.

The salient feature of this record is its Blakean compassion. "Of all my books on the long shelf," Jack said near the end of his life, "I love most 'The People of the Abyss.' No other book of mine took so much of my young heart and tears as that study of the economic degradation of the poor" (*Book,* I, 381). What affected him most deeply was the hopeless plight of the very old and the inevitable doom of the very young. For example, there are "the Carter" and "the Carpenter," decent, respectable tradesmen who are now too old to compete with vigorous younger men in a ruthless industrial system; their children are dead, and, with no one to care for them, they have been set loose without shelter or money to scavenge for bits of garbage along filthy sidewalks and to drift aimlessly and painfully toward death. At the other end of the Abyss are the children. From every 100 of these, 75 will die before age five, and perhaps they are the luckier ones—

> There is one beautiful sight in the East End, and only one, and it is the children dancing in the street when the organ-grinder goes his round. It is fascinating to watch them, the new-born, the next generation, swaying and stepping, with pretty little mimicries and graceful inventions all their own, with muscles that move swiftly and easily, and bodies that leap airily, weaving rhythms never taught in dancing school. . . . They delight in music, and motion, and color, and very often they betray a startling beauty of face and form under their filth and rags.
>
> But there is a Pied Piper of London Town who steals them away. They disappear. One never sees them again, or anything that suggests them. You may look for them in vain amongst the generation of grown-ups. Here you will find stunted forms, ugly faces, and blunt and stolid minds. Grace, beauty, imagination, all the resiliency of mind and muscle, are gone.[15]

Only the beasts in the jungle remain.

> It is rather hard to tell a tithe of what I saw. Much of it is untellable. But in a general way I may say that I saw a nightmare, a fearful slime that quickened the pavement with life, a mess of unmentionable obscenity that put into eclipse the "nightly horror" of Piccadilly and the Strand. . . . They reminded me of gorillas. Their bodies were small, ill-shaped, and squat. There were no swelling muscles, no abundant thews and wide-spreading shoulders. . . . But there was strength in those meagre bodies, the ferocious, primordial strength to clutch and gripe and tear and rend. . . .
>
> The unfit and the unneeded! . . . The miserable and despised and forgotten, dying in the social shambles. The progeny of men and women and children, of flesh and blood, and sparkle and spirit; in brief, the prostitution of labor. If this is the best that civilization can do for the human, then give us howling and naked savagery. Far better to be a people of the

wilderness and desert, of the cave and the squatting-place, than to be a people of the machine and the Abyss. (*People,* 284–288)

Even with such appalling descriptions of human degradation, *The People of the Abyss* is not merely a sensational diatribe; in light of the conditions it depicts, the style and tone are remarkably restrained. London's compassion was so profound that it overwhelmed his compulsion to preach. He might easily have made the book into a profitable venture in "muckraking," or just as easily, he could have made it a useful vehicle for economic propaganda. He deliberately chose to do neither, and he resented the labeling of the work as a "Socialistic treatise": "I merely state the disease as I saw it," he said, "I have not, within the pages of *that* book, stated the cure as I see it" (*Book,* I, 381).

London's next venture proved to be one of his most profitable works: a novel closely rivaling *The Call of the Wild* and *White Fang* in reprints and total sales, and outranking them in motion picture productions.[16] *The Sea-Wolf* seems to have all the necessary ingredients for greatness. It pulses with the vitality of its creator; it is structured upon the universal, timeless motif of initiation; its setting is likewise archetypal, with the ship as microcosm and the eternal sea as the most fitting matrix, symbolic as well as literal, for death and rebirth. It also has an excellent cast: convincingly delineated, "round" characters who can stand both as individuals and as representative types—headed by Wolf Larsen, one of the most unforgettable figures in American literature. As Ambrose Bierce wrote in a letter to George Sterling in 1905, "The great thing—and it is among the greatest of things—is that tremendous creation Wolf Larsen. If that is not a permanent addition to literature, it is at least a permanent figure in the memory of the reader. You 'can't lose' Wolf Larsen. He will be with you to the end."[17]

Assuredly it is not easy to "lose" a character who, on the one hand, can quote from memory long passages of Robert Browning's poetry and the Bible and who, on the other, can squeeze a raw potato or a man's arm to a pulp. Praised by Robert Spiller as "London's most fully conceived character" and by Gordon Mills as "London's most enduring example of the intense life,"[18] Larsen is a fascinating composite of Shakespeare's Hamlet, Milton's Satan, Browning's Caliban, and Nietzsche's *Übermensch.* But more than this composite, he is the Captain Ahab of literary Naturalism, and he bridges the gap between the Byronic hero and the modern antihero. Like the earlier Romantic hero, Larsen is sensitive, intelligent, domineering, arrogant, uninhibited,

actively rebellious against conventional social mores, and—above all—
alone. He rules alone; he suffers alone. But, like the twentieth-century
man, he lacks purpose and direction. Although he possesses the personal
force of Melville's Ahab and to some extent shares the desire for revenge
in his search for his brother, Death, he has no real quest—not even a
mad quest—into which to channel this force; and the result is disorien-
tation, frustration, senseless violence, and finally self-destruction. The
thwarting of Larsen's tremendous vitality manifests itself physically in
his brutal treatment of his crew and intellectually in his materialistic
nihilism:

> "Do you know, I am filled with a strange uplift; I feel as if all time were
> echoing through me, as though all powers were mine. . . . But,"—and his
> voice changed and the light went out of his face,— "what is this condi-
> tion in which I find myself? . . . It is what comes when there is nothing
> wrong with one's digestion, when his stomach is in trim and his appetite
> has an edge, and all goes well. And I shall know that I must die, at sea
> most likely, cease crawling of myself to be all acrawl with the corruption
> of the sea; to be fed upon, to be carrion, to yield up all the strength and
> movement of my muscles that it may become strength and movement in
> fin and scale and the guts of fishes."[19]

Physically and morally, Larsen is a prototype of Eugene O'Neill's "Yank"
Smith and of T. S. Eliot's ape-neck Sweeney; psychologically, he has
more in common with Prufrock and Gerontion: he is cursed with a
hyperrational sensibility.[20] In Larsen's gradual deterioration—first
headaches, then blindness and paralysis, and finally death from a brain
tumor—he is symbolic of a modern type: the psychopathic overreacher
who is alienated both from nature and from his fellow man by the lep-
rous disease of self. London told his wife Charmian that the underlying
motif of *The Sea-Wolf* was that "the superman is anti-social in his tendencies, and in these days of our complex society and sociology he cannot be
successful in his hostile aloofness" (*Book,* II, 57). Even with his amazing
physical strength and his great force of personality, Larsen cannot survive. "It is true that [London] admired, even worshipped, strength,"
observes Conway Zirkle, "but he had learned that strength was increased
by cooperation, by union. The atavistic individual, the lone wolf, was
truly a hero, but a tragic hero who was doomed to extinction. The well-
integrated group was stronger than any individual could ever be. . . .
Those who co-operated won because they were fit. The social virtues,
altruism, co-operation—even self-sacrifice—were justified biologically

for they made gregarious living possible and the strength of the strong was the strength of the group."[21]

The character best equipped for survival in *The Sea-Wolf* is clearly not Larsen; nor is it the courageous young sailor Johnson, whose survival index is lowered by his readiness to die for the principle of manhood; nor is it the greasy cook, Thomas Mugridge, whose cowardice and meanness fit him for survival only as something less than a man. The character endowed with a potential for survival is, curiously enough, a thorough-going "sissy" at the beginning of the novel. But the latent adaptability of Humphrey Van Weyden, enhanced by his intelligence, his vital optimism, and his capacity to love, marks him for survival while Larsen is drawn inexorably toward Death, his spiritual as well as his literal brother. Van Weyden's rise to self-sustaining maturity and Larsen's decline into paralytic oblivion provide an "X" structure for the novel: Van Weyden starts at the bottom—poles apart from Larsen—and, as he gains in strength and toughness, he moves steadily upward and nearer his demoniacal antagonist. The two lines converge at the moment "Hump" finds the courage to defend Maud Brewster against Larsen's wolfish advances. From this point onward, Larsen's power wanes rapidly. Van Weyden and Brewster escape from the *Ghost* during one of their captor's disabling headache attacks, and the two lines of the "X" begin to diverge. By the time Van Weyden encounters Larsen again, the two are once again, and finally, at opposite extremes: Larsen has lost his crew and is blind and partially paralyzed; Van Weyden has gained a mate and has reached his full maturity.

Van Weyden is the central, if not the most memorable, character in *The Sea-Wolf;* for his growth from effete snobbery into dynamic manhood constitutes the main plot. The sinking of the ferryboat *Martinez,* at the beginning of the novel, Van Weyden's immersion, and his dramatic delivery from near drowning by Larsen signify the protagonist's rebirth into a raw, unfamiliar world—one of harsh reality where his culture, wealth, and social position are worthless. The first step in his initiation is an awakening to the reality of death as he stares in horror at the alcoholic convulsions of the *Ghost*'s first mate, whose death elicits a volley of oaths from Larsen. "To me," confesses Van Weyden, "death had always been invested with solemnity and dignity. It had been peaceful in its occurrence, sacred in its ceremonial. But death in its more sordid and terrible aspects was a thing with which I had been unacquainted till now" (*Sea-Wolf,* 21).

The next step for Van Weyden is learning the value of hard physical work: "You stand on dead men's legs," Larsen tells him. "You've never had any of your own. You couldn't walk alone between two sunrises and hustle the meat for your belly for three meals. Let me see your hand. . . . Dead men's hands have kept it soft. Good for little else than dish-washing and scullion work" (*Sea-Wolf*, 26). Scorning Van Weyden's demands to be put ashore, Larsen impresses him into the ship's service as a lowly cabin boy—no longer "Mr. Van Weyden" but just plain "Hump"— under the sadistic domination of the Cockney cook, and the ordeal begins during which Van Weyden gradually hardens into manhood. He discovers quickly that the conventions of society, the rules that protect the weak and strong alike, are irrelevant in this new environment: he must survive by countering tooth with claw. He clears his first hurdle in the dramatic knife-sharpening episode with "Cooky." Only after he has met the cook's abuse by whetting his own dirk does Hump gain the crew's respect. He is subsequently promoted to first mate and is never again without his knife, the crude metonymy of his manhood.

However, the brutal masculine world of the *Ghost* is no truer than the anemic, conventionally feminine world that Van Weyden has left behind. Larsen's bleak materialism is ultimately no better than Van Weyden's blind idealism: a truer philosophy may be found somewhere between these two extremes in a pragmatic optimism that comprehends the equally real meanness and magnificence of human potentiality. To keep a man's vision on the stars instead of the slime, he needs the Feminine: "It strikes me as unnatural and unhealthful that men should be totally separated from women," remarks Van Weyden. "Coarseness and savagery are the inevitable results. These men about me should have wives, and sisters, and daughters; then would they be capable of softness, and tenderness, and sympathy. . . . There is no balance in their lives. Their masculinity, which in itself is of the brute, has been overdeveloped. The other and spiritual side of their natures has been dwarfed—atrophied, in fact" (*Sea-Wolf*, 128–29). Neither the emasculating world of social culture nor the brutalized world of club and fist can produce the truly balanced human being. There must be a sensible equipoise of the two worlds. Until taken aboard the *Ghost,* Van Weyden is only a half-man lacking in virility because he has been reared in a woman's world. Not until he has viewed woman from a man's world is his perspective complete, for only then may he assume his role in society as a full-fledged male—as mate and father. Sam Baskett has defined the subject of *The Sea-Wolf* itself as the need for psychic androgyny; this view certainly sheds light on the role of Maud Brewster, a role often slighted by critics.[22]

On the surface London's motive for introducing Maud Brewster into the plot of *The Sea-Wolf* was apparently to dramatize Van Weyden's newly won manhood and fitness for survival. From that perspective the gambit might have been thematically justifiable, but technically, it was risky. From the moment of the incredible coincidence in the middle of the Pacific Ocean when Humphrey Van Weyden, the Dean of American Letters, meets Maud Brewster, the First Lady of American Poetry, *The Sea-Wolf* begins to deteriorate in the minds of some readers along with Captain Larsen of the *Ghost*. By the time the two lovers have escaped and have become chaste castaways on Endeavor Island, the novel might seem a sentimental shambles.

"The 'love' element, with its absurd suppressions and impossible proprieties, is awful," wrote Ambrose Bierce. "I confess to an overwhelming contempt for both sexless lovers."[23] One finds it difficult to demur, even when one realizes that a proper Victorian lady and gentleman might, in fact, have behaved just so.[24] Certainly London needed another bestseller; if pandering to sentimental popular taste would better his odds, he was willing to gamble. In his prospectus of the novel he wrote, "My idea is to take a cultured, refined, super-civilized man and woman (whom the subtleties of artificial, civilized life have blinded to the real facts of life), and throw them into a primitive sea-environment where all is stress and struggle and life expresses itself, simply, in terms of food and shelter; and make this man and woman rise to the situation and come out of it with flying colors." London's intention from the outset was clearly to have a ripping good sea-story with "adventure, storm, struggle, tragedy, and love," but he also insisted that "the love-element will run throughout, as the man and woman will occupy the center of the stage pretty much all of the time. Also, it will end happily" (*Letters*, 337).

The androgynous balance is the key, for only when they are able to transcend traditional gender roles are Humphrey and Maud able to prevail over the circumstances of their sea journey and return to civilization freed of its stifling conventions. They are transformed, Baskett notes, even as London transforms the metaphysical quest motif of the story by uniting it with the social implications of the theme of androgyny. Using evidence from London's letters as to his notion of the ideal androgynous mate and following Humphrey and Maud's escape from both the effeminacy of their culture and Wolf's brutish, one-dimensional masculinity,

Baskett convincingly demonstrates that London achieved "a significant highly original thematic and textual contribution to the American literary canon" (Baskett, 21).

The profitable success of *The Sea-Wolf,* which remains one of his most reprinted and most readable novels, enabled London to concern himself with the intensification of his Socialist activities. In the spring of 1905 he ran again as the Socialist candidate for the mayoralty of Oakland, receiving almost 1,000 votes in defeat (as the Socialist Labor Party candidate in 1901 he had received 245 votes). That fall, as the first president of the Intercollegiate Socialist Society, he launched a widely publicized lecture tour that shocked the Establishment and delighted the young radicals. "A great ovation was given Jack London at the Harvard Union," reported Hearst's *Boston American* on 22 December 1905: "Every available inch of space was occupied; even the gallery was jammed, and the doorways were filled by rows and rows of students. Never before has the student body of Harvard University turned out in such numbers to hear a speaker." London obviously told the young people what they wanted to hear. "I went to the University . . . but I did not find the University alive," he said a few nights later at Yale. "If [collegians] cannot fight for us, we want them to fight against us—of course, sincerely fight against us, believing that the right conduct lies in combating socialism because socialism is a great growing force. But what we do not want is that which obtains today and has obtained in the past of the university, a mere deadness and unconcern and ignorance so far as socialism is concerned. Fight for us or fight against us! Raise your voices one way or the other; be alive!" The student body gave him a standing ovation. "You have mismanaged the world, and it shall be taken from you!" he announced the next week to a meeting of wealthy New Yorkers: "Look at us! We are strong! Consider our hands! They are strong hands, and even now they are reaching forth for all you have, and they will take it, take it by the power of their strong hands; take if from your feeble grasp."[25] This audience did not applaud.

The following spring London started to work on his fiercest literary inoculation, the "first apocalyptic novel of the century," according to Joseph Blotner.[26] "You have failed in your management of society, and your management is to be taken away from you," announces Ernest Everhard, hero of *The Iron Heel,* in his sensational speech to the wealthy Philomaths. He warns them, "We are going to take your governments, your palaces and all your purpled ease away from you, and in that day you shall work for your bread even as the peasant in the field or the starved and runty clerk in your metropolises. Here are our hands. They are strong hands!"[27]

The Iron Heel purports to be a copy of the "Everhard Manuscript," a fragment written and hidden away by Avis Everhard, widow of the leader of the "Second [unsuccessful] Revolt," and edited seven centuries later by the historian Anthony Meredith in the year 419 B.O.M. (Brotherhood of Man). Mrs. Everhard's document covers the 20-year period from 1912 to 1932 when the capitalist oligarchy, called "the Iron Heel" by her husband Ernest, rises to complete power, grinding underfoot all opposing political systems. In the early stages of the conflict, Ernest works against this oppression by use of democratic methods, finally winning election to Congress, where he is joined by 50 Socialist representatives.

Realizing the threat to its power, the plutocracy consolidates its ranks and moves forcefully to suppress all opposition. Union leaders are bought off, secret police and mercenaries are employed as terrorists, and political antagonists are arrested and murdered. Everhard's group is now forced to move underground and to counter violence with violence. The narrative rises to a bloody climax when an oppressed subhuman mob erupts from the great Chicago ghetto and is methodically slaughtered by the mercenaries of the Iron Heel. Although Ernest survives the holocaust and works to reorganize the forces of the revolution, the manuscript ends abruptly, and we are told in Professor Meredith's concluding footnote that Everhard has been mysteriously executed. Meredith also reminds us that the oligarchy held its power for another three centuries and throughout numerous revolts before Herbert Spencer's prophecy of Socialist evolution was at last fulfilled.

Politically speaking, *The Iron Heel* was Jack London's bravest novel. "It was a labor of love, and a dead failure as a book," he later wrote. "The book-buying public would have nothing to do with it, and I got nothing but knocks from the socialists."[28] Although he had not anticipated the hostile Socialist reaction, he did know that the book would be unpopular and that its sales would be limited; nevertheless, he was compelled to write it. The work was motivated by a variety of influences: his experiences in the London slums in 1902 (the climactic chapter of the novel is titled "People of the Abyss"); the abortive Russian Revolution of 1905; the dramatic events of his own lecture tour that winter; the San Francisco earthquake the following spring, which provided background material for the novel's cataclysmic last chapters; and the reading of W. J. Ghent's *Our Benevolent Feudalism* (1902), which predicted a twentieth-century feudal state dominated by capitalist overlords.[29] London's motivation may also have been sharpened by his unconscious guilt feelings: in 1905, he had used his profits from *The Sea-Wolf* to begin buying land in the Sonoma Valley, and by the spring of 1906 he was well on his way to creating his own agrarian fief.

Psychologically speaking, *The Iron Heel* is one of London's most revealing books; it is the fictional articulation of his private dreams of revolutionary glory. The novel's hero, earnest and "ever-hard," is a fantasy figure of Jack London purged of his obsession to win the good life of the American Dream. A "natural aristocrat" and a "blond beast" with blacksmith's biceps and prizefighter's neck, Ernest is London's exact physical replica. With his Spencerian weltanschauung and his Marxist rhetoric, he is also London's metaphysical replica, for, as Joan London remarks, "His best knowledge of the class struggle and the socialist movement, his best speeches and essays he gave to Everhard. . . ." Even the love affair between Ernest and Avis Cunningham Everhard is a replica of that between Jack and Charmian Kittredge London. "Few of Jack London's books, even those which were consciously autobiographical, are so intensely personal," says his daughter (*Times,* 307). And this personal involvement accounts for the failure of the book as a novel. There is some merit in Irving Stone's judgment of the book as London's "greatest contribution to the economic revolution," but his claim that it is "one of the most . . . beautiful books ever written"[30] denotes an astonishing lapse of aesthetic sensibility. Viewed strictly from the artistic standpoint, *The Iron Heel* is—except for the vivid description of mob violence near the end—a lifeless novel. The hero, haranguing his various audiences with his pretentious ideological pieties, is a relentless boor. The other characters are merely cardboard foils to the much-bruited force of Ernest's magnetic personality and to his irrefutable logic, neither of which is authenticated within the narrative. Time and again we are told of his splendid virtues; seldom are these virtues dramatically discovered through his actions.

And clearly, a major flaw lies in the telling—in London's unfortunate choice of narrator. Even Professor Meredith's dry, pseudoscholarly footnotes cannot relieve the cloying sentimentality of Avis Everhard's prose: "When I do not think of what is to come, I think of what has been and is not more—my Eagle, beating with tireless wings the void, soaring toward what was ever his sun, the flaming ideal of human freedom" (*Iron,* 2). Ernest "was a humanist and a lover. And he, with his incarnate spirit of battle, his gladiator body and his eagle spirit—he was as gentle and tender to me as a poet. He was a poet. A singer in deeds. And all his life he sang the song of man. And he did it out of sheer love of man, and for man he gave his life and was crucified." "We loved love, and our love was never smirched by anything less than the best. And this out of all remains: I did not fail. I gave him rest—he who worked so hard for others, my dear, tired-eyed moralist" (*Iron,* 182, 187). It is *1984* as it might have been penned by a Harlequin romance writer.

But, if it is less than an artistic success, *The Iron Heel* must nevertheless be regarded as an important book. It was enthusiastically commended by Eugene V. Debs, Leon Trotsky, and Anatole France. Robert E. Spiller has called it "a terrifying forecast of Fascism and its evils"; Philip Foner ventures that it is "probably the most amazingly prophetic work of the twentieth century"; Maxwell Geismar suggests that it is "a key work—perhaps a classic work—of American radicalism"; Walter B. Rideout classifies it as "a minor revolutionary classic"; and Max Lerner concludes that "the real point about *The Iron Heel* is not what Jack London failed to foresee, but how remarkably much he did foresee."[31] What he failed mainly to foresee was that the middle class would not only survive but actually grow stronger through the capitalistic system. But what he did foresee was humankind's inexhaustible capacity for oppression and violence even in the midst of economic prosperity. And his apocalyptic vision of urban holocaust still has a disquieting immediacy.

The Iron Heel is also significant for another reason. It represents one of London's major fictional modes: fantasy. Much of his writing in this genre is "transitive," that is, it is intended to serve some purpose more important in the author's mind than mere art or entertainment. Such is the obvious case with *The Iron Heel,* which is little more than an ideological treatise cast in narrative form, as are shorter fictions such as "The Dream of the Debs," a vision of the triumph of organized labor by means of a great general strike; "The Strength of the Strong," a parable that dramatizes the superiority of collective strength over individual power; "The Minions of Midas," an early potboiler about a group of homicidal blackmailers who label themselves as the inevitable "culmination of industrial and social wrong[,] the successful failures of the age, the scourges of a degraded civilization"; and "Goliah," the juvenile tale of a mild-mannered little scientist who invents a machine to stop all wars and who is subsequently loved by all mankind "for his simplicity and comradeship and warm humanness, and for his fondness for salted pecans and his aversion to cats." However, London's appetence for fantasy may be traced to something subtler and deeper than his desire to propagandize.

Fearful Fantasies

Startling as it may be to think of Jack London and Edgar Allan Poe as similar, their careers, minds, and personalities were comparable in several ways. Both were masters of the art of the short story. Both were also moody, often lonely, individuals who yearned for the securities of home, companionship, and love—and whose basic insecurities were concealed under the cloak of reckless egotism only to be manifest in a weakness for alcohol and in genius for oneiric fiction. Thanks to Princess Marie Bonaparte, Gaston Bachelard, and other French analysts, Poe's dark secrets have long since become part of the public domain. London's critical psychoanalysis, on the other hand, has barely begun, although Maxwell Geismar made a start in *Rebels and Ancestors* when he observed that it is the "world of dream and fantasy and desolate, abnormal emotion that [London] inhabits far more completely than the world of people and society—for all his stress on that."[32]

London's fantasies may not constitute his best work, but they are both readable and revealing. As with Poe, they disclose more about the author than he probably realized, and they are often not an escape from reality so much as a symbolic path into the deeper, inchoate reality of the unconscious mind. Seldom overt, the telltale clues to the heart of this dark world are the images and metaphors that set the story's mood. Almost without exception London's fantasies are woven within a framework of violence and death; they are textured by metaphors of darkness, chaos, pain, and terror; seldom do they end happily. Their characteristic attitude is one of fear and trembling. In one novel only (*The Star Rover*) do we find a concluding affirmation, and it is for the next world, not this one. Apocalyptic gloom overshadows the rest. "Putting the horror-story outside the pale, can any story be really great, the theme of which is anything but tragic and terrible?" London asked rhetorically. "It would not seem so. The great stories in the world's literary treasure-house seem all to depend upon the tragic and terrible for their strength and greatness" (*Reports,* 334).

London was fascinated by the atavistic, primal force at work in the human psyche:

What is it that lures boys to haunted houses after dark, compelling them to fling rocks and run away with their hearts going so thunderously pit-a-pat as to drown the clatter of their flying feet? What is it that grips a child, forcing it to listen to ghost stories which drive it into ecstasies of fear, and yet forces it to beg for more and more? . . . Is it a stirring of the savage in them?—of the savage who has slept, but never died, since the time of the river-folk crouched over the fires of their squatting-places, or the tree-folk bunched together and chattered in the dark? (*Reports*, 331–32)

This same phenomenon is central to London's most popular "dream vision," the psychological and mythic saga *Before Adam*, written in 40 days, completed on 7 June 1906, and published that fall in *Everybody's Magazine* (*Letters*, 961). "Pictures! Pictures! Pictures!" begins the narrative. "Often, before I learned, did I wonder whence came the multitudes of pictures that thronged my dreams; for they were pictures the like of which I had never seen in real wake-a-day life. They tormented my childhood, making of my dreams a procession of nightmares and a little later convincing me that I was different from my kind, a creature unnatural and accursed."[33] It seems that the narrator of *Before Adam* has a recurrent dream that takes him back to a previous existence as one of man's remote ancestors in the mid-Pleistocene Age. He dreams his life as Big-Tooth, who is one of the Folk caught between monkey-like Tree People and the advanced Fire People (homo sapiens), and who is threatened not only by these but also by the terrifying presence of "Red-Eye, the atavism," within the Folk tribe: "Ogres and bugaboos and I had been happy bed-fellows, compared with these terrors that made their bed with me throughout my childhood, and still bed with me, now, as I write this, full of years" (*Before*, 11).

Yet, filled as Big-Tooth's life is with misery and danger, it is not devoid of happiness. There is "the peace of the cool caves in the cliffs, the circus of the drinking-places at the end of the day . . . the bite of the morning wind in the tree-tops [and] the taste of young bark sweet in your mouth" (*Before*, 2–3). There is also the companionship of his bosom friend Lop-Ear, steadfast, affectionate, protective—who possesses, in short, the traits normally associated with a good parent. For instance, Lop-Ear risks his own life to save Big-Tooth from the arrows of the deadly Fire Men. And, above all, Big-Tooth has the precarious happiness of freedom—freedom from the restrictions of social conformity, freedom for adventure and exploration.

In an episode rich with Freudian implications, Big-Tooth defies the brutal authority of Red-Eye and has to run away for safety along with Lop-Ear. Forced out of the security of their small cave by Red-Eye, set to flight by this avenging father figure, deprived of the protection of a natural as well as symbolic mother, the two youths begin their long journey into the vast unknown: "a desolate land of rocks and foaming streams and clattering cataracts . . . mighty canyons and gorges . . . [and] in all directions, range upon range, the unceasing mountains. . . . And then, at last, one hot midday, dizzy with hunger, we gained the divide. From this high backbone of earth, to the north, across the diminishing down-falling ranges, we caught a glimpse of a far lake. The sun shone upon it, and about it were open, level grasslands, while to the eastward we saw the dark line of a wide-stretching forest" (*Before*, 155–56).

From the lofty reaches of the world spine, the young hero and his companion descend to the world center, a region of incredible abundance where the streams are "packed thick with salmon that had come up from the sea to spawn" and are surrounded by rich grasslands. Moving eastward from this matrix of fecundity, "we came out upon the river, but we did not know it for our river. We had been lost so long that we had come to accept the condition of being lost as habitual. As I look back I see clearly how our lives and destinies are shaped by the merest chance. We did not know it was our river—there was no way of telling; and if we had never crossed it we would most probably have never returned to the horde; and I, the modern, the thousand centuries yet to be born, would never have been born" (*Before*, 157).

Because of "merest chance," however, Big-Tooth achieves his rebirth, finally returns to his tribe, mates with Swift One, and becomes the father of many children, thus maintaining the long line of descent between his primal world and the civilized one of the narrator. In mythological terms, Big-Tooth's story is a re-creation of the "rites of passage" archetype; it is moreover, a fictive manifestation of what Mircea Eliade has called "the myth of the eternal return"—our universal compulsion to return to the beginning of things and to the innocence and simplicity of the childhood of the race. But London does not conclude the novel on this happy note; instead, the countenance of the terrible Red-Eye leaves a last, haunting impression on the narrator's memory: "I can see him now, as I write this, scowling, his eyes inflamed, at his peers about him at the circle of the Tree People. And he crooks one monstrous leg and with his gnarly toes scratches himself in the stomach. He is Red-

Eye, the atavism." So the vision, originated in fear, ends on the characteristic note of ominous terror.

The same vision, along with its atavistic theme, reappears in *The
Scarlet Plague,* published in 1912. In this work London demonstrates that
Red-Eye, the archetypal monster of the id, has never been eradicated
from the racial unconscious; he has only been slumbering within us,
awaiting the right moment to leap forward in all his terrifying brutality.
In *The Scarlet Plague,* London provides that moment in the form of a cataclysmic epidemic that sweeps over the world, wiping out most of its
inhabitants. The germ of this story may be discovered in Poe's "The
Masque of the Red Death," wherein the symptoms are described as
"sharp pains, and sudden dizziness, and then dissolution[,] the whole
seizure, progress, and termination [being] the incidents of half an hour."
The symptoms of the scarlet plague are similar: "Many died within ten
or fifteen minutes of the appearance of the first signs. . . . Usually, they
had convulsions at the time of the appearance of the [scarlet] rash. . . .
And another strange thing was the rapidity of decomposition. No sooner was a person dead that the body seemed . . . to melt away even as you
looked at it. That was one of the reasons the plague spread so rapidly. All
the billions of germs in a corpse were so immediately released."[34]

In addition to the disease, London also borrowed the theme of Poe's
story: the idea that no one can escape the terrible realities of disease and
death—or that everyone ultimately shares the brotherhood and sister-
hood of mortality. Just as Poe's Prince Prospero and his followers try to
shut out the contagious sufferings of their fellow men, so London's hero
and his colleagues at the University of California blockade themselves in
the massive chemistry building. And just as surely as the Red Death follows Prospero's vainglorious court through the sealed portals of the
castellated abbey, so the scarlet plague filters through the barricaded
walls of Science's ivory tower. Only James Howard Smith—not a scientist, but a professor of English—escapes to witness civilization disinte-
grating in chaos and red terror.

From the point of his hero's escape, London departs from the inspiration of Poe's tale. The long-journey motif manifests itself as Smith wanders through the desolated land in search of some remnant of humanity.
For three years, almost crazy from loneliness, he searches for some fellow
human being who has survived the devastation of the plague. Finally, in
the region of Lake Temescal, California, he finds the signs of humanity—
but, instead of an intelligent, sensitive, refined creature of his own kind,
he stumbles across the thing that his race is to become: the atavism, "a

large, dark hairy man, heavy-jawed, slant-browed, fierce-eyed." In this book he is called the Chauffeur, but his brutish characteristics are the same as those of Red-Eye in *Before Adam,* and the force symbolized in him has survived the plague to carry humankind back to the primeval wilderness.

The narrator observes a vicious irony in the survival of this "iniquitous moral monster" while millions of better people died—but he also notes a grim poetic justice. By the time of the plague, 2013 A.D., the United States had developed into a totalitarian plutocracy, the mass of its population in bondage to the wealthy, physically degenerate upper classes. Without realizing it, Americans of intellectual and aesthetic refinement had sown the seeds of destruction within the very lap of their society: "In the midst of our civilization, down in our slums and labor-ghettos, we had bred a race of barbarians, of savages; and now, in the time of our calamity, they turned upon us like the wild beasts they were and destroyed us" (*Scarlet,* 105–6).

After the plague, the Chauffeur had discovered another survivor, Vesta Van Warden, beautiful young widow of one of the world's richest men ("Warden" of wealth and keeper of the keys for an oppressive economic system). Although she fled in terror, she was finally caught, beaten, subdued, and mated to this coarse epitome of lower-class brutality, who gloats over his new social position: "'We've got to start all over and replenish the earth and multiply. You're handicapped, Professor. You ain't got no wife, and we're up against a regular Garden-of-Eden proposition. But I ain't proud. I'll tell you what, Professor.' He pointed at their little infant, barely a year old. 'There's your wife, though you'll have to wait till she grows up. It's rich, ain't it. We're all equals here, and I'm the biggest toad in the splash'" (*Scarlet,* 158–59).

But the Chauffeur is not Ernest Everhard in loin cloth, and *The Scarlet Plague* is not a primitivistic rerun of *The Iron Heel.* Allowing mood to overshadow message, London creates a much more telling indictment of twentieth-century civilization than in his idea-ridden earlier novel. As occasionally happens in his fantasies, the compulsion to preach is forgotten in the heat of the poetic moment. The English Professor who watched his world vanish in a "sheet of flame and a breath of death" is now an old man known as "Granser" who, standing at the end of time, is trying bravely to shore up the ruins of a once-mighty civilization:

> "'The fleeting systems lapse like foam,'" he mumbled what was evidently a quotation. "That's it—foam and fleeting. All man's toil upon the plan-

et was just so much foam. He domesticated the serviceable animals, destroyed the hostile ones, and cleared the land of its wild vegetation. And then he passed, and the flood of primordial life rolled back again, sweeping his handiwork away—the weeds and the forest inundated the fields, the beasts of prey swept over his flocks, and now there are wolves on the Cliff House beach." He was appalled by the thought. "Where four million people disported themselves, the wild wolves roam to-day, and the savage progeny of our loins, with prehistoric weapons, defend themselves against the fanged despoilers." (*Scarlet,* 33–34)

Apocalyptic pessimism notwithstanding, the conclusion of *The Scarlet Plague* has a wild, lyrical beauty reminiscent of the final note of mythic rapture in *The Call of the Wild.* Often in London's work, when his outlook for civilized humanity is bleakest, his vision of nature's eternal fecundity—his mystical faith in the strength of the life force itself—presents itself most powerfully. The ebbing of his faith in social reform seems to have been accompanied by a tendency to turn more and more for solace toward the seemingly inexhaustible vitality of nature. The dramatic power of his conclusion to *The Scarlet Plague* derives from the tension between these two forces: a civilization tottering on its last leg (symbolized in the figure of the old man who has narrated the story) and the animation of nature in her wilder forms (signified in the concluding tableau of the horses, mountain lions, sea lions, and skin-clad boy):

Edwin was looking at a small herd of wild horses which had come down on the hard sand. There were at least twenty of them, young colts and yearlings and mares, led by a beautiful stallion which stood in the foam at the edge of the surf, with arched neck and bright wild eyes, sniffing the salt air from off the sea.

"What is it?" Granser queried.

"Horses," was the answer. "First time I ever seen 'em on the beach. It's the mountain lions getting thicker and thicker and driving 'em down."

The low sun shot red shafts of light, fan-shaped, up from a cloud-tumbled horizon. And close at hand, in the white waste of shore-lashed waters, the sea-lions, bellowing their old primeval chant, hauled up out of the sea on the black rocks and fought and loved.

"Come on, Granser," Edwin prompted.

And the old man and boy, skin-clad and barbaric, turned and went along the right of way into the forest in the wake of the goats. (*Scarlet,* 180–81)

This final vivid montage is as fine as anything London ever created. For a moment, sea and wilderness are fused in the image of the stallion that stands triumphantly at the water's edge. The foam image, used earlier to symbolize the fleeting systems of humanity, now assumes an additional dimension—that of the eternal fecundity of the sea, that mighty womb from which life emerges and to which life returns in a never-ending cycle. Against a backdrop of crimson sky, white waters, and black rocks, the timeless pageant of fighting and loving—of life itself—is enacted by the sea lions. And, lurking always in the background, is the grim specter of Darwinistic survival, nature red in tooth and claw, suggested in the image of the mountain lions. Juxtaposed against these primal natural forces is the bent, pathetic figure of the old man, the last remnant of a dying culture.

More complex both thematically and structurally than either *Before Adam* or *The Scarlet Plague* is *The Star Rover,* published the year before London's death. This strange novel, ignored by most of London's critics, is perhaps the most difficult of all his works to assess fairly. Maxwell Geismar dismisses it as "incredibly bad" (Geismar, 210). Irving Stone calls it "a magnificent literary accomplishment" (Stone, 311). Joan London has made the most cogent assessment: "Into this extraordinary and little-known book he flung with a prodigal hand riches which he had hoarded for years, and compressed into brilliant episodes notes originally intended for full-length books" (*Times,* 362). Even in praising the novel Joan London indicates the source of its principal weakness, which is structural: where London should have concentrated on one narrative, he tried to handle a half-dozen, thus vitiating the effect of his central theme.

The main plot of the novel is based on the experiences of an actual California former convict named Ed. Morrell, who appears as one of the characters. Morrell's own story, published as *The Twenty-Fifth Man* in 1924, is as fantastic as London's fictional account in *The Star Rover.* One of a band of rancher-outlaws who fought the railroad monopoly, the "octopus" indicted in Frank Norris's famous novel, Morrell was convicted and sentenced to a life term in the California prisons. During his several years of imprisonment he endured incredible tortures. One of the most diabolical devices for punishing intractable inmates was "the jacket," a heavy canvas square into which the prisoner was tightly laced for several days until his spirit was broken. After almost dying in the jacket, Morrell mastered a form of self-hypnosis or "astral projection," which, he claimed, enabled him to leave his physical body and travel at will through both time and space. After receiving a pardon by the acting governor of California in 1909 (an event Morrell had predicted four years earlier), he devoted his life to penal reform. He met Jack London in 1912, and he gives the following brief account of their relationship: "Jack London and I were very dear friends, and we had often talked about my experience in the dungeon, particularly those phases pertaining to the 'little death' in the strait-jacket . . . 'God, Ed., do you know what this means to me?' he often said. 'It has often been the ambition of my life to put across a staggering punch against the whole damnable, rotten American Jail System. I want it to be my masterpiece.'"[35]

If *The Star Rover* is not "the staggering punch" that London wanted, it is not a dull book. Taking Morrell's story as the basis for his main narrative, London added a series of soul-flight adventures, any one of which would have made a solid short story: Darrell Standing, the narrator, through astral projection relives parts of former lives as (1) the French Count Guillaume Sainte-Marie, who loves and fences during the late Renaissance in the best Dumas style; (2) the youth Jesse Fancher, who, traveling with a wagon train from Arkansas, is killed by the Mormons and Indians in the notorious Mountain Meadow Massacre; (3) a fourth-century Christian ascetic who inhabits a tiny cave in the Egyptian desert; (4) Adam Strang, a superman who fights nobly in the sixteenth-century Orient; (5) the herculean Dane, Ragnar Lodbrog, who is captured in a battle with the Roman Army and subsequently becomes a legionary officer under Pilate during the time of the Crucifixion; and (6) Daniel Foss, a castaway who lives for eight years on a desert island during the early nineteenth century. In addition to these major projections, other fragmentary reincarnations take Darrell Standing back to prehistoric existences.

But *The Star Rover* is considerably more than a loose-knit sequence of adventure stories. A cogent exposé of a corrupt, brutalizing penal system, it "truly states prison conditions," as London wrote to Roland Phillips, editor of *Cosmopolitan:* "It is the law to-day [in prison] that a man can be hanged by the neck until dead, for punching another man in the nose. . . . It is also legal in California to sentence a man to life-imprisonment in solitary. . . . I have really understated the severity of the use of the jacket" (*Letters,* 1314–15). However, more than an exposé, it is a dramatic tribute to humankind's historic capacity for suffering, comparable to such novels as Arthur Koestler's *Darkness at Noon* and Bernard Malamud's *The Fixer.*

But most intriguing of all is London's philosophical ground shifting. Gone are his hard-nosed materialism and scientific rationalism; instead, we encounter a curious mixture of idealism, mysticism, and metempsychosis. "The key-note of the book is: THE SPIRIT TRIUMPHANT," wrote London (*Letters,* 1315). He contended that he was deliberately playing tricks with philosophy in order to appeal to the widest possible audience, but more probably—and more characteristically—he was playing tricks on himself in refusing to acknowledge the nonrational element that was a vital part of his creative genius, a natural gift perhaps in part inherited from his spiritualist mother. Certainly London progressively turned toward the spiritual side of things as his career progressed; one finds it even in his "purest" Naturalism. "We know life only phenomenally, as a savage may know a dynamo," Darrell Standing muses; "but we know nothing of life noumenally, nothing of the nature of the intrinsic stuff of life. . . . I say, and as you, my reader, realize, I speak with authority—I say that matter is the only illusion."[36] Wolf Larsen had asserted with equal authority that "life is a mess . . . a thing that moves and may move for a minute, an hour, or a hundred years, but that in the end will cease to move"; but this Naturalistic view was small comfort to a writer whose own once-splendid physique had begun to deteriorate from too many years of too little exercise and too many cigarettes, too much work and too little rest. "I have lived millions of years. I have possessed many bodies, . . ." exclaims Darrel Standing; "I am life. I am the unquenched spark ever flashing and astonishing the face of time, ever working my will and wreaking my passions on the cloddy aggregates of matter, called bodies, which I have transiently inhabited" (*Star,* 123). Perhaps death and dissolution were not the words final, after all— "For look you. This finger of mine, so quick with sensation, so subtle to feel, so delicate in its multifarious dexterities, so firm and strong to crook and bend or stiffen by means of cunning leverages—this finger is not I. Cut it off. I live. The body is mutilated. I am not mutilated. The spirit that is I, is whole" (*Star,* 123).

Soul flight! This might indeed be an escape from the old biological trap, a release of the triumphant spirit from its decaying prison house. Unfortunately, escape from the old American trap—Success—was another matter.

Another American Tragedy

The following comment was written not by a college student, nor by a literary critic, but by a well-trained, successful young businessman. It is cited because it so accurately reflects a common response to what is considered London's most intensely personal novel: "I have for the past two evenings been absorbed completely (and I do mean *completely*) in *Martin Eden*. I am profoundly moved. Nothing else I have ever read has had this effect upon me and I am not capable of analyzing it just yet."[37]

Although its artistic merits may be open to question, *Martin Eden* is a profoundly moving book for many readers, and any serious attempt to assess Jack London's work must involve this novel. Critics have variously considered it to be his best book or his worst book. Franklin Walker is probably closest to the mark in saying it is one of London's most puzzling books, for although it is "uneven in structure, sometimes clumsy in expression, at times mawkish in tone[,] it possesses great lasting power, having more vitality today than it did the day it issued from the press."[38] *Martin Eden* has maintained its power for several reasons: it belongs to a fictional genre that never seems to lose its appeal for sensitive, youthful readers; it is archetypal both in theme and in structure; it articulates an especially potent cultural myth; and it is tremendously charged with London's personal vitality.

Martin Eden is part of a literary tradition that includes such classics as Goethe's *Wilhelm Meister's Apprenticeship,* Melville's *Pierre,* Somerset Maugham's *Of Human Bondage,* D. H. Lawrence's *Sons and Lovers,* and Thomas Wolfe's *Look Homeward, Angel.* A bildungsroman or "education novel," its basic pattern involves the hero's painful transition from a state of innocence into one of "knowing"; and, because *Martin Eden* is drawn largely from London's own formative ordeal as a writer, it is necessarily an agonized—and agonizing—novel.

In the plot, which is relatively straightforward and uncomplicated, a husky sailor rescues a young gentleman from the attack of a gang of waterfront toughs and is rewarded by an invitation to the luxurious home of the stranger, Arthur Morse. The sailor is, significantly, 21 years old when he is introduced into this dazzling new world of upper-middle-class refinement. Lacking in manners and formal education, he is nevertheless sensitive and intelligent. He meets and immediately falls in love with Arthur's pale, ethereally beautiful sister, Ruth, who—university-educated, exquisitely poised, articulate—is wholly unlike any girl he has ever met. Inspired to become worthy of this genteel goddess, Martin

Eden becomes ambitious: he quits drinking, smoking, and swearing; starts bathing and brushing his teeth regularly; presses his trousers; and initiates a rigorous program of self-education through the local library. Although Ruth does not at first share his powerful infatuation, she is amused by his immense vitality; she volunteers to become his cultural tutor, and they begin to see each other regularly.

Martin learns with amazing rapidity and within a few months has become conversant not only with the best-known writers but also with philosophers such as Adam Smith, Karl Marx, Henry George, and, above all, Herbert Spencer; but, the more he learns, the more clearly he sees the hollowness and hypocrisy of the Morse world. Ruth's parents become alarmed about Martin's alleged radicalism and about the possibility that their daughter is becoming attached to this wild young man. When Ruth finds herself falling in love with him and urges him to find a steady, respectable occupation, Martin decides to embark upon a career in writing. He rents a typewriter, sets himself to work in a frenzy of creativity, allows himself no more than five hours of sleep a night, and grinds out stories, articles, poems, and jokes by the dozen. Then after pawning his bicycle, his only decent suit, and his overcoat to buy stamps, he waits for word from the magazine editors: that word is *No* as manuscript after manuscript comes back.

Broke and desperate, Martin takes a job in the laundry at a large resort hotel where he becomes a 14-hour-day work beast. After several weeks of this drudgery, he quits and returns again to the frustrating cycle of rejected manuscripts. Only Russ Brissenden, a brilliant but cynical poet, assures him that his work shows genuine talent—too genuine for the cheap commercialized literary marketplace. All the others—friends, relatives, Ruth—keep nagging him to get a steady job. Confused, Martin oscillates between the society of Brissenden and his radical leftist intellectual friends and the Morse parlor, unable as well to find a home amongst his own plodding lower class. When he is falsely publicized in the local newspapers as a notorious revolutionary, Ruth rejects him. Shortly afterwards, he learns that his closest companion, Brissenden, has committed suicide. Exhausted by his ordeal and profoundly depressed by these personal tragedies, Martin lapses into a neurasthenic daze. Almost simultaneously he starts to receive acceptances for the many manuscripts he has sent out; his success snowballs; he is lionized by the cultural elite; the magazines and publishers clamor for his work; and Ruth comes back, begging his forgiveness and declaring her love. But she is too late. Disenchanted and passive, he books passage on a ship to the South Seas. Halfway across the Pacific Ocean, he squeezes through a porthole, drops into the ocean, and at last finds peace.

Discernible even in this rough summary is the larger structural pattern of the novel: the hero emerges from the sea at the outset and returns to the sea at the end. The ocean metaphor, usually set forth in nautical imagery, recurs throughout and serves to unify the novel. When Martin first enters the Morse home, he feels as if he were on the unsteady deck of a ship in rough seas; and one of the first sights his eyes focus on is an oil painting of a pilot schooner surging through a heavy sea against a stormy sunset sky; later in the evening, he likens himself to "a sailor, in a strange ship, on a dark night, groping about in the unfamiliar running rigging" (*Martin,* 10). These images are prophetic as well as descriptive: during his nervous breakdown, he thinks of himself as "chartless and rudderless" with no port to make, as drifting nowhere (*Martin,* 349).

Set against the sea and providing the basic tension of the novel is the metaphor of the trap. Martin feels he is being led into a cage like some wild animal on display when he enters the Morse house, which, though spacious by society's standards, is a dark, cramped cell by natural standards—by perspectives of the ocean that have hitherto set the reaches of Martin's vision: "The wide rooms seemed too narrow for his rolling gait, and to himself he was in terror lest his broad shoulders should collide with the doorways or sweep the bric-a-brac from the low mantel" (*Martin,* 1). And, though his intellectual horizons are widened, the image of the trap recurs with increasing force as the novel progresses. From the sea, Martin's Garden of Eden, he has moved first into the stuffy hothouse of Victorian gentility represented by the Morses; from that, into the stifling hell of the steam laundry, where he suffers through a midsummer's nightmare of killing toil; and then to the living tomb at Maria Silva's house, where he sleeps, studies, writes, and keeps house in a cubicle so small that two-thirds of the total space is used up by his bed. In brief, his quest for knowledge, imaged at first in the cold, white light of the stars, has led him down a progressively narrowing blind tunnel to the tiny cabin aboard the steamship *Mariposa* (Spanish for "night taper").[39]

Like all education novels, *Martin Eden* is a book about *seeing.* Early in the story we are told that our young hero "saw with wide eyes, and he could tell what he saw. . . . He communicated his power of vision, till they saw with his eyes what he had seen" (*Martin,* 20). But, though this power of vision is the key to his artistic genius, Martin is blinded by his false romantic idol. He does not see Ruth at all when he enters the Morse home; he sees a lovely, golden-haloed princess: "No, she was a spirit, a divinity, a goddess; such sublimated beauty was not of the earth. Or perhaps the books were right, and there were many such as she in the upper walks of life. She might well be sung by that chap Swinburne" (*Martin*, 4–5). Ruth, whose very name is a mockery, is a lifeless spirit; and she might truly have been celebrated by Algernon Swinburne, the notorious versifier of fin-de-siècle Victorianism; therefore, it is fitting that Martin finds himself again thinking of Swinburne in his cabin aboard the *Mariposa*. It is also fitting that his state of apathy that precedes this last voyage is represented by a corresponding vagueness in the images of his reveries: "Once in his rooms, he dropped into a Morris chair and sat staring straight before him. . . . Then his mind went blank again, and the pictures began to form and vanish under his eyelids. There was nothing distinctive about the pictures. They were always masses of leaves and shrub-like branches shot through with hot sunshine. . . . It was not restful, that green foliage. The sunlight was too raw and glaring. It hurt him to look at it, and yet he looked, he knew not why" (*Martin*, 388, 396). Martin has lost his sense of focus, and his sight is without insight.

Martin Eden is a story about the Dark Fall—about the price paid for the unhappy gift of knowledge. Martin was happy, innocent, unselfconscious, naturally graceful: Adam before the Fall. Ruth, his Eve, acts as his guide to the deadly fruit of knowledge, though she is not the agent of his destruction. As he emerges from the Edenic sea and enters her world, the modern capitalist world, he becomes for the first time in his life *self*-conscious, shamed by his social and intellectual nakedness: "All his life, up to then, he had been unaware of being either graceful or awkward. Such thoughts of self had never entered his mind. . . . He felt lost, alone there in the room with that pale spirit of a woman" (*Martin*, 6). It is a premonition of his ultimate disaster, his lostness and aloneness.

Viewed symbolically, Martin's "education" is a growth in consciousness: a breaking away from the primal rhythms of the unconscious—symbolized by the sea—into the fractured world of overreason—culture, intellect, civilization, money. As Lizzie Connolly tells him, his sickness is in his "think machine." Martin's is also the universal sickness of a modern man caught in the Naturalistic trap—the same "middle stage" Theodore Dreiser defined so poignantly at the beginning of chapter 17 in *Sister Carrie:* ". . . scarcely beast, in that [he] is no longer wholly guided by instinct; scarcely human, in that [he] is not yet wholly guided by reason. . . . As a beast, the forces of life aligned him with them; as a man, he has not yet wholly learned to align himself with the forces. In this intermediate stage he wavers—neither drawn in harmony with nature by his instincts nor yet wisely putting himself into harmony by his own free will."

Unable to regain his former state, intolerably miserable in his present state, Martin falls inevitably into the pattern of eternal return. C. G. Jung, echoing Herman Melville's Ishmael, has written that "the way of the soul in search of its lost father—like Sophia seeking Bythos—leads to the water, to the dark mirror that reposes at its bottom. . . . This water is no figure of speech, but a living symbol of the dark psyche." Or, as he observes elsewhere, "The sea is the favourite symbol for the unconscious, the mother of all that lives" (Jung, 1968, 17, 177–78). Jung's remarks provide the clue to the last lines of *Martin Eden:* "And somewhere at the bottom he fell into darkness. That much he knew. He had fallen into darkness. And at the instant he knew, he ceased to know" (*Martin,* 411). The resolution of the novel's underlying tension—the paradox of knowing and unknowing, sight and insight, light and darkness—is a fine ending. Although many critics have objected that the reader is not properly prepared for Martin's death, London's closure is artistically superb.[40]

Martin Eden, in addition to its universal appeal, has special impact upon the American reader because it involves one of the most potent myths in the American culture, the Dream of Rags-to-Riches, and because its hero so clearly represents the values of that culture even while ostensibly rejecting them. London had originally selected the title "Success" for his novel, with "Star-Dust" his second choice (*Letters,* 738). Either would have been appropriate, but neither would have been quite so fitting as the name of the hero himself,[41] for "Martin Eden" is a symbolic epitome of the archetypal American male: "Martin," the "man of war," incongruously gifted with the innocence of "Eden," deadly but incorruptible; the American Adam who, despite his pure white soul, is, as D. H. Lawrence tells us, "a man with a gun." Martin Eden belongs to that long, red line of Adamic warriors in American literature headed by Leatherstocking and followed by such characters as Henry Fleming, Frederick Henry, Francis Macomber, and Isaac McCaslin.

But Martin is also a member of another American literary fraternity comprising Horatio Alger, Frank Algernon Cowperwood, and Jay

Gatsby. Like Gatsby especially, Martin is destroyed by the delusions that an ideal goal may be attained through material means and that success is synonymous with happiness. He also shares with Gatsby the vague confusion of the American Dream with the decadent avatar of courtly love mythology—the notion that the true knight may achieve blessedness simply by winning the princess. Martin's inability to see that the girl of his dreams, like the world of which she is a representative product, is not golden but merely gilded is—in the same way as Gatsby's—symptomatic of his greater blindness in his quest. Gatsby's Daisy, we finally learn, is nothing but a voice full of money; Martin's Ruth, a silver laugh— "like tinkling silver bells" (*Martin,* 9). Both are cold, hollow vessels, and both have a false ring. But in their culture it is not the substance but the image that counts: Gatsby and Martin fail to realize that in America the value does not lie in substance but in the appearance of substance. *Work performed* is the phrase that haunts Martin's brain. "It is work performed! And now you feed me, when then you let me starve, forbade me your house, and damned me because I wouldn't get a job. And the work was already done, all done. And now, when I speak, you check the thought unuttered on your lips and hang on my lips and pay respectful attention to whatever I choose to say. . . . And why? Because I'm famous; because I've a lot of money. Not because I'm Martin Eden . . ." (*Martin,* 378). The joy was in becoming, not in being. And that is why, having arrived, Martin, like Gatsby, finds himself nowhere, and why, therefore, he has nothing left except to die.

Martin Eden cannot be taken for Jack London's spiritual autobiography—unlike Martin, London was fully aware of "the collective human need" and lived for much more than himself. London believed the book to be an indictment of individualism and a testament to the need for a socialist philosophy. As he put it,

> Martin Eden lived only for himself, fought only for himself, and, if you please, died for himself. He fought for entrance into the bourgeois circles where he expected to find refinement, culture, high-living and high-thinking. He won his way into those circles and was appalled by the colossal, unlovely mediocrity of the bourgeoisie. He fought for a woman he loved and had idealized. He found that love had tricked him and failed him, and that he had loved his idealization more than the woman herself. These were the things he had found life worth living in order to fight for. When they failed him, being a consistent Individualist, being unaware of the collective human need, there remained nothing for which to live and fight. And so he died. (*Letters,* 865)

Yet the novel still has a certain symbolic credibility and an element of prophecy. Youthful vitality is the key to Martin Eden's charismatic appeal, and the profligate expenditure of this tremendous energy is the key to his tragedy—just as it is the key to London's own personal tragedy. London was no suicide,[42] but he stubbornly refused to conserve his resources. Perhaps the supreme irony of his life was that, after striving so long and so hard to break out from the underworld of the work-beast, he succeeded in working himself to death.

Chapter Four

The Symbolic Wilderness

Not surprisingly, water symbolism is predominant in *Martin Eden;* for the novel was written at sea during the most highly publicized of all Jack London's many wanderings. "It was all due to Captain Joshua Slocum and his *Spray,* plus our own wayward tendencies," explained Charmian. "We read him aloud to the 1905 camp children at Wake Robin Lodge, in the Valley of the Moon, as we sat in the hot sun resting between water fights and games of tag in the deep swimming pool. *Sailing Alone Around the World* was the name of the book, and when Jack closed the cover on the last chapter, there was a new idea looking out of his eyes."[1] That new idea was taking shape before the next year was out. If Joshua Slocum could sail a 37-foot sloop around the world by himself, so could Jack and Charmian London together.[2]

No ingenuity nor expense would be spared in making Jack London's the finest sailing vessel of her size ever built. She would set sail from Oakland on 1 October 1906, and, though a sailboat, she would carry a rugged 10-horsepower gasoline engine for added safety and convenience; she would be constructed of the finest buttless planking that money could buy; with three watertight bulkheads, she would be not only unsinkable but virtually unleakable; she would be stocked with six months' provisions including dozens of crates of fresh fruits and vegetables; she would be 45-feet long (including an extra five feet for an indoor bathroom); her beautiful bow would defy the heaviest seas; and she would be called the *Snark* (from Lewis Carroll's famous mock epic).

The *Snark* was, however, something of a *Boojum,* to use Carroll's word. Unfortunately, London's careful planning had not taken into consideration the April 1906 San Francisco earthquake, the subtler disasters of modern industrial production standards, nor the vagaries of sheer chance. The *Snark,* costing more than five times the $7,000 originally calculated, did not sail until April 1907. Before she cleared the harbor, her engine broke loose from its bed plate and fell on its side; she was discovered to have multiple butts in her beautiful planking; her bottom, her sides, and her water-tight compartments leaked; leaking kerosene spoiled the provisions; she was two feet short; the bathroom plumbing failed on the first day at sea; and her beautiful bow could not be made to heave to. No boat had ever been more fatefully named.[3]

With more courage than discretion the Londons persisted in their travel scheme and somehow managed to get the *Snark* to Hawaii, where she underwent major repairs, and then across the Pacific to the Marquesas, the Fijis, the Solomons, and Australia. There, two years after embarking, bad health forced them to abandon their circumnavigation and head for home. But, abortive as the voyage was, the *Snark* did provide some "big moments of living" that the veteran writer could convert to ready cash and, occasionally, to the sounder currency of art. Perhaps most significant from the critic's viewpoint, the *Snark* experience served as a catalyst—much in the same way the Klondike had done 10 years before—for London's mythopoeic genius.

A critical commonplace today is that the American literary genius from Jonathan Edwards onward has tended to express itself in symbolism. All major American novelists, in this view, are Transcendental—not because they share Emerson's hearty optimism—but because they see the phenomenal world as essentially a projection of the spiritual or psychological world, because they posit an affinity between Nature and Soul, and because they are all, finally, moral idealists. In the case of Jack London this moral idealism—despite his protestation of materialistic monism—manifested itself principally in two ways: first, in his scientific and sociological progressivism; second, in this fictional projection of moral values onto Nature, especially onto natural settings. Both relate to the same universal pattern in that they reflect the human yearning to recapture the perfection of Eden.

This motif, the quest for Paradise, is recurrent throughout London's work, both fictional and autobiographical; his career might well be studied as a lifelong series of attempts to escape the corruptions of civilization and to recapture the simple, maternal security of Nature. The first major revelation of this archetype was the White Silence: the vast, still wilderness of the Northland Saga. There, Nature was cold, impassive, awesome; humans puny and insignificant. Even so, a cosmic orderliness existed in the harsh, immutable laws of the White Silence, and a moral certitude resulted from the country's effects upon the people who inhabited it. The unfit—the morally weak, the selfish, the foolhardy—perished. Those who survived were improved because of their adaptation to the Northland Code. The outer cold stimulated an inner warmth: humans were drawn closer together in the bond of cooperation and sympathy because these were the virtues necessary to survival, as were integrity, courage, forebearance, and—above all—imagination. This highest of human faculties enabled its possessor to understand the ways of the Northland so well that he or she could anticipate emergencies before they occurred, adapt to Nature's laws, and never attempt foolishly to impose the devious customs of civilization upon the inviolable wilderness. Still, the Northland was a far cry from Eden. Its spiritual wellsprings were pure—but they were frozen. Although an agent of moral reformation, the region provided neither warmth nor security. One could discover a certain serenity in the Arctic wastes, but it was the blank serenity of death. In short, it was a region to escape *from*—not *to*.

The South Seas held forth the promise of warmth, life, and new symbolic vistas.

Paradise Lost

"This is the twentieth century, and we stink of gasoline," mutters Prince Akuli, the Oxford-educated gentleman whose sole legacy from a past age rich in myth is the dry shin bone of a great Earth-Princess three centuries dead.[4] The statement might have been borrowed directly from T. S. Eliot but for the fact that the first volume of this great poet's work did not appear in print until the year after Jack London died. It may come as a surprise to many contemporary scholars that several years before Eliot immortalized Jessie L. Weston by poeticizing the cruelties of April, London had already discovered a similar key—perhaps the skeleton key—to the "lost-ness" of modern man in the primitive folklore of Polynesia and in the writings of C. G. Jung.

In the same symbolic tradition that included James Fenimore Cooper ahead of him and William Faulkner after him, London was acutely sensitive to the tragic consequences of the white man's exploitation of the wilderness and his pollution of the earth. When London first landed in Hawaii in 1904 en route to the Russo-Japanese War, he thought he had found Elysium, a paradise of flower-swept valleys peopled by bronzed youths and golden maidens. "When Hawaii was named the Paradise of the Pacific," he wrote afterwards, "it was inadequately named. The rest of the Seven Seas and the islands in the midst thereof should have been included with the Pacific. 'See Naples and die'—they spell it differently here: *See Hawaii and live*."[5] To live there would be to experience the climate of Eden both in weather and in human relations: "Hawaii and the Hawaiians are a land and a people loving and lovable. By their language may ye know them, and in what other land save this one is the commonest form of greeting, not 'Good day,' nor 'How d'ye do,' but 'Love'? That greeting is *Aloha*—love, I love you, my love to you." Hawaii and the other islands of Polynesia inspired outbursts of lyrical description:

> As I write these lines I lift my eyes and look seaward. I am on the beach of Waikiki on the island of Oahu. Far, in the azure sky, the trade-wind clouds drift low over the blue-green turquoise of the deep sea. Nearer, the sea is emerald and light olive-green. Then comes the reef, where the water is all slaty purple flecked with red. Still nearer are brighter greens and tans, lying in alternate stripes and showing where sandbeds lie between the living coral banks. Through and over and out of these wonderful colors tumbles and thunders a magnificent surf. As I say, I lift my eyes to all this, and through the white crest of a breaker suddenly appears a dark figure, erect, a man-fish or a sea-god, on the very forward face of the crest where the top falls over and down, driving in toward shore buried to his loins in smoking spray, caught up by the sea and flung landward, bodily, a quarter of a mile. It is a Kanaka on a surfboard. And I know that when I have finished these lines I shall be out in that riot of color and pounding surf, trying to bit those breakers even as he, and failing as he never failed, but living life as the best of us may live it. (*Cruise,* 58–59)

Though London returned again to Hawaii in his later years literally as well as fictionally, and though a handful of his Polynesian stories of volumes such as *The House of Pride* (1912) and *On the Makaloa Mat* (1919) rival the greatness of his best Northland tales, it was not then the Eden of his dreams: it was, instead, Paradise Lost, a land whose economy had been commercialized, whose politics had been usurped, whose ecology had been upset, and whose beautiful natives had been contaminated by the "civilized" *haoles.* What he wrote of Tahiti was also true in Hawaii: "And now all this strength and beauty has departed, and the Valley of Typee is the abode of some dozen wretched creatures, afflicted by leprosy, elephantiasis, and tuberculosis. . . . Life has rotted away in this wonderful garden spot, where the climate is as delightful and healthful as any to be found in the world. . . . When one considers the situation, one is almost driven to the conclusion that the white race flourishes on impurity and corruption" (*Cruise,* 170). As the central character of "Koolau the Leper" remarks, "They came like lambs, speaking softly. . . . They were of two kinds. The one kind asked our permission, our gracious permission, to preach to us the word of God. The other kind asked our permission, our gracious permission, to trade with us. That was the beginning. Today all the islands are theirs, all the land, all the cattle—everything is theirs." Also theirs is the "rotting sickness" of civilization, the leprosy that has metamorphosed people into hideous monsters with stumps for arms and gaping holes for faces: "The sickness is not ours. We have not sinned. The men who preached the word of God and the word of Rum brought the sickness with the coolie slaves who work the stolen land."[6]

"Koolau" is the story of a community, the inhabitants of the Kalalau Valley on the island of Kauai, condemned to ostracism upon Molokai because they have been stricken with leprosy. Rather than accept the injustice of this sentence, they decide to resist any efforts to force them from their beloved island. As one old native, a former judge in the Hawaiian court, reasons, "We love Kauai. Let us live here, or die here, but do not let us go to the prison of Molokai. . . . I have been a judge. I know the law and the justice, and I say to you it is unjust to steal a man's land, to make that man sick, with the Chinese sickness, and then to put that man in prison for life" (*House,* 57).

The little band fights bravely to defend its home on Kauai, but their cause is foredoomed. Women and children, along with the warriors, are slaughtered by the white soldiers who come to enforce the law. Ironically, the killing occurs amidst idyllic beauty: superimposed upon the golden backdrop of *hau* blossoms, morning glories, and papaya fruit are the black clouds of exploding shells and the crimson stains of broken bodies, dark metonymies of the deadly *haole.*

Demoralized by the shell fire, the surviving lepers surrender—all but the proud Koolau. The soldiers pursue him for six weeks over the mountains and through the jungles of his valley—but unsuccessfully. He either eludes them, or when cornered, outshoots them with his old Mauser rifle. Maimed and deformed physically, he is indomitable spiritually—a pitiable yet magnificent rebel against the inevitable white man and the iron laws of civilization:

> Two years later, and for the last time, Koolau crawled unto [*sic*] a thicket and lay down among the *ti*-leaves and wild ginger blossoms. Free he had lived, and free he was dying. A slight drizzle of rain began to fall, and he drew a ragged blanket about the distorted wreck of his limbs. His body was covered with an oilskin coat. Across his chest he laid his Mauser rifle, lingering affectionately for a moment to wipe the dampness from the barrel. The hand with which he wiped had no fingers left upon it with which to pull the trigger. (*House,* 89)

"Koolau" is representative of London's attitude toward the underdog—whether Polynesian, Klondike Indian, East End slum dweller, or
American hobo. London was unusually touched, however, by the tragic plight of the Hawaiian leper. Hawaiian officials raised their eyebrows
when London and his wife celebrated the Fourth of July with the lepers on Molokai in 1907; they were scandalized by his frank, sympathetic treatment of the leprosy taboo in his Hawaiian chapters in *The
Cruise of the Snark* and in his three stories "Koolau the Leper," "Goody-
by, Jack," and "The Sheriff of Kona."[7] But the horrors of leprosy were
pale in comparison to what London encountered in the dark heart of
Melanesia.

Inferno

If Polynesia was Paradise Lost, Melanesia was Hell. The conglomeration
of tropical ailments suffered by London and his crew in Melanesia finally
sent them packing back home in full rout, thereby cutting short the projected world tour of the *Snark*. London was drawing directly from personal experience when he wrote that in Melanesia "fever and dysentery
are perpetually on the walk about, . . . loathsome skin diseases abound,
. . . the air is saturated with a poison that bites into every pore, cut, or
abrasion and plants malignant ulcers, [and] many strong men who
escape dying there return as wrecks to their own countries."[8] Melanesia,
not the Klondike, inspired London's bitterest Naturalistic writing; and
in it the wilderness-as-Eden symbol is wholly inverted.

The deity who presides over this putrescent waste land is the Prince of
Blackness himself; and the cannibalistic Melanesians are his myrmi-
dons— "a wild lot, with a hearty appetite for human flesh and a fad for
collecting human heads," London remarks in "The Terrible Solomons":

> Their highest instinct of sportsmanship is to catch a man with his back
> turned and to smite him a cunning blow with a tomahawk that severs the
> spinal column at the base of the brain. It is equally true that on some
> islands, such as Malaita, the profit and loss account of social intercourse is
> calculated in homicides. Heads are a medium of exchange, and white
> heads are extremely valuable. Very often a dozen villagers make a jack-
> pot, which they fatten moon by moon, against the time when some brave
> warrior presents a white man's head, fresh and gory, and claims the pot.
> (*South*, 199–200)

The moral effect of this rotting green hell is the exact opposite of the Northland Code. Rather than bringing out the best in those who survive, the Melanesian jungles bring out the worst. In the midst of ruthless savagery, the white man in Melanesia is just as savage. Instead of escaping from corruption when he enters this wilderness, he finds himself infected by a malaise even more pernicious than that of civilization. The theme of dissolution—moral as well as physical—recurs time and again in London's Melanesian fiction. "Oh, I don't mind being caught in a dirty trick," confesses one of his degenerates in *A Son of the Sun* (1912); "I've been in the tropics too long. I'm a sick man, a damn sick man. And the whiskey, and the sun, and the fever have made me sick in morals, too. Nothing's too mean and low for me now, and I can understand why the niggers eat each other, and take heads, and such things. I could do it myself. . . . I'd as soon shoot you as smash a cockroach."[9] Life is without worth or meaning; human beings are reduced to things, whether "niggers" or "cockroaches"; brutality and killing have become a game. Thematically, much of this is reminiscent of Joseph Conrad's tropical fiction; but in tone and style it is a remarkable forecast of Ernest Hemingway:[10] "The niggers spread out and headed for the shore, swimming. The water was carpeted with bobbing heads, and I stood up, as in a dream, and watched it all—the bobbing heads and the heads that ceased to bob. Some of the long shots were magnificent. Only one man reached the beach, but as he stood up to wade ashore, Saxtorph got him. It was beautiful. And when a couple of niggers ran down to drag him out of the water, Saxtorph got them, too" (*South,* 250–51). This writing is Naturalism with a vengeance. Additional intimations of the "new prose" are evident in the casual underplaying of human suffering described in "The Jokers of New Gibbon":

> "It *is* a devil island, and old Koho is the big chief devil of them all. . . . I remember six years ago, when I landed there in the British cruiser. The niggers cleared out for the bush, of course, but we found several who couldn't get away. One was his latest wife. She had been hung up by one arm in the sun for two days and nights. We cut her down, but she died just the same. And staked out in the fresh running water, up to their necks, were three more women. All their bones were broken and their joints crushed. The process is supposed to make them tender for eating. They were still alive. Their vitality was remarkable. One woman, the oldest, lingered nearly ten days." (*Sun,* 137–39)

It is possible for the white man to survive in this tropical Inferno—only by becoming worse than the natives themselves; those same virtues essential to his survival in the Northland—brotherhood and imagination—become fatal liabilities in Melanesia:

> A man needs only to be careful—and lucky—to live a long time in the Solomons; but he must be of the right sort. He must have the hall-mark of the inevitable white man stamped upon his soul. . . . He must have a certain grand carelessness of odds, a certain colossal self-satisfaction, and a racial egotism that convinces him that one white man is better than a thousand niggers. For such are the things that have made the white man inevitable. Oh, and one other thing—the white man who wishes to be inevitable, must not merely despise the lesser breeds and think a lot of himself; he must also fail to be too long on imagination. He must not understand too well the instincts, customs, and mental processes of the blacks, the yellows, and the browns; for it is not in such fashion that the white race has tramped its royal road around the world. (*South*, 200–1)

Critics who have classified London as an unmitigated proponent of "the white man's burden" have missed the calculated irony in such passages as the foregoing.[11] It is true, of course, that London was a bundle of contradictions in such matters—and nothing illustrates these ambivalences better than his South Sea tales—but the fact remains that, in his better moods, he was anything but blind to the unconscionable enormities of the white race in its treatment of darker-skinned peoples. The sad historic fact is that many of the leading "scientific" thinkers of his age embraced various doctrines of white supremacy, and millions of decent Americans bought books that blatantly preached "racial egotism" and taught their readers to "despise the lesser breeds." London returned to problems of race again and again, and he addressed them in much more depth than most of his contemporaries. In his portraits of the cruelties of racial hatred one senses his search for spirit, something to transcend and outlast the ruthless struggle for survival in the world. For example, in one of his finest stories, "The Chinago," London's portrait of the title character's "sweet kindliness of spirit" as opposed to his white tormentors' "dominant, iron-clad, primeval brutishness," together with the way the narrator's irony exposes the whites' stupidity, endures and prevails in our imaginations long after such once-popular notions as white superiority have been discarded by history.

Occasionally, London's dark irony assumes the form of a grim poetic justice in his Melanesian tales, as in the story "Mauki." The protagonist is an inversion of the stereotyped Western hero: "He weighed one hundred and ten pounds. His hair was kinky and negroid, and he was black. He was peculiarly black. He was neither blue-black nor purple-black, but plum black. His name was Mauki, and he was the son of a chief" (*South*, 83). His appearance belies his sinister heroism: "There was no strength nor character in the jaws, forehead, and nose. In the eyes only could be caught any hint of the unknown quantities that were so large a part of his make-up and that other persons could not understand. These unknown quantities were pluck, pertinacity, fearlessness, imagination, and cunning, and when they found expression in some consistent and striking action, those about him were astounded" (*South*, 86–87).

Mauki's antagonist is Max Brunster, a hulking, psychopathic German whose principal delight is beating cripples, old men, and defenseless blacks. Bunster symbolizes the inevitable white man at his degenerate worst: "Semi-madness would be a charitable statement of his condition. He was a bully and a coward, and a thrice-bigger savage than any savage on the island. Being a coward, his brutality was of the cowardly order" (*South*, 103). "Mauki," a racial chiaroscuro, presents a dramatic tableau of a white man's sadistic cruelty juxtaposed against a black man's capacities for endurance and revenge. Theirs is an unwholesome "marriage" like that of Black Leclère and Batârd in London's early Klondike story: "For better or worse, Bunster and he were tied together. Bunster weighed two hundred pounds. Mauki weighed one hundred and ten. Bunster was a degenerate brute. But Mauki was a primitive savage. While both had wills and ways of their own" (*South*, 106). Bunster finds many ways to torment the black man—depriving him of his tobacco allowance, beating his head against the wall, knocking out his teeth, "vaccinating" him with the live end of a cigar, for example; but his most ingenious method of torture is "caressing" his servant with a mitten made of ray-fish skin: "The skin of a shark is like sandpaper, but the skin of a ray fish is like a rasp. In the South Seas the natives use it as a wood file in smoothing down canoes and paddles. . . . The first time he tried it on Mauki, with one sweep of the hand it fetched the skin off his back from neck to armpit. Bunster was delighted" (*South*, 111).

Mauki endures this treatment for week after week, but his chance for retribution finally comes when Bunster is stricken with a severe case of black-water fever. After the worst of the illness has passed, leaving the white man bedridden, Mauki carefully provisions a boat for his escape and then returns to bid farewell to his tormentor:

The house deserted, he entered the sleeping-room, where the trader lay in a doze. Mauki first removed the revolvers, then placed the ray fish mitten on his hand. Bunster's first warning was a stroke of the mitten that removed the skin the full length of his nose.

"Good fella, eh?" Mauki grinned, between two strokes, one of which swept the forehead bare and the other of which cleaned off one side of his face. "Laugh, damn you, laugh."

. . .

When Mauki was done, he carried the boat compass and all the rifles and ammunition down to the cutter, which he proceeded to ballast with cases of tobacco. It was while engaged in this that a hideous, skinless thing came out of the house and ran screaming down the beach till it fell in the sand and mowed and gibbered under the scorching sun. Mauki looked toward it and hesitated. Then he went over and removed the head, which he wrapped in a mat and stowed in the stern-locker of the cutter. (*South,* 115–16)

The irony is dark but clear: Bunster has paid for his moral callousness by having his thick hide removed entirely, and his sadistic head has become the trophy of its principal victim.

If Melanesia can be said to have had any salutary effect on Jack London, it was perhaps to convince him that the Eden he sought was not halfway round the globe but in his own backyard. "I also have a panacea," he confessed after suffering through the hellish ailments inflicted on him and his crew by the tropics. "It is California. I defy any man to get a Solomon Island sore in California" (*Cruise,* 276).

The Valley of the Moon

As early as 26 May 1905, London had written to Brett, "For a long time I have been keeping steadily the idea in mind of settling down somewhere in the country. I am in a beautiful part of California now, and I have my eyes on several properties, one of which I intend to buy, so I want to know how much money I possess in order to know to what extent I may buy" (*Letters,* 483). The letter was postmarked at Glen Ellen, a quiet hamlet nestled in the Sonoma Valley 55 miles north of San Francisco. Two weeks later he again wrote to Brett to tell him that he had bought the Hill Ranch a half mile from Glen Ellen:

There are 130 acres in the place, and they are 130 acres of the most beautiful, primitive land to be found in California. There are great redwoods on it, some of them thousands of years old—in fact, the redwoods are as fine and magnificent as any to be found anywhere outside the tourist groves. Also there are great firs, tan-bark oaks, maples, live-oaks, white-oaks, black-oaks, madrono and manzanita galore. There are canyons, several streams of water, many springs, etc., etc. In fact, it is impossible to really describe the place. All I can say is this—I have been over California off and on all my life, for the last two months I have been riding all over these hills, looking for just such a place, and I must say that I have never seen anything like it. (*Letters,* 489)

London spent the next 11 years developing his Beauty Ranch into one of the best model farms in the state. Moreover, it became the model for his next major version of the symbolic wilderness. The California wilderness figures as the setting in a score of London's stories and eight of his novels: *White Fang, The Iron Heel, Burning Daylight, The Abysmal Brute, The Valley of the Moon, The Little Lady of the Big House, Jerry of the Islands,* and *Michael Brother of Jerry.*

His problem, as London saw it, was how to place men and women in the wilderness, to enable them to live in nature and partake of its wholesome essence without contaminating the crystal springs from which they drank. This problem did not present itself in the other versions of wilderness: in the Northern wilderness, those springs were frozen; in the tropics, they were already polluted. In the American West, however, they were both accessible and pure, a prime requisite for his Eden: it must be tractable as well as virginal—it must be, above all, benevolent toward humanity. Yet, we must be spiritually purified *before* entering the wilderness; we must rid ourselves of all selfish materialistic motives. After undergoing a spiritual cleansing of the baser motives of civilization—in short, being reborn—we may impose social refinements and scientific methods upon nature—as long as these improve the wilderness without desecrating it. Finally, we must become self-appointed guardians of the wilderness, protecting it against all attempts to exploit and despoil. As a result of these considerations, London's fiction about the American wilderness assumes qualities of the pastoral romance necessarily alien to the White Silence and Melanesia.

London's attitude toward Nature was both paradigmatic and visionary. The following passage from Leo Marx's *The Machine in the Garden* provides a useful context for understanding London's own special vision:

If the city is corrupt, it is men who have made the journey of self-discovery who must be relied upon to restore justice, the political counterpart of

psychic balance. Thus the symbolic action, as in our American fables, has
three spatial stages. It begins in a corrupt city, passes through a raw
wilderness, and then, finally, leads back *toward* the city [emphasis
added]. . . . The model for political reform is . . . a symbolic middle landscape created by mediation between art and nature. . . . The landscape
thus becomes the symbolic repository of value of all kinds—economic,
political, aesthetic, religious.[12]

In presenting a chart of America's attitude toward Nature, we might
add one earlier stage to the three cited by Marx. The symbolic action
begins not in the corrupt city, but on the edge of the raw wilderness:
that is, on the frontier that precedes the city. We have only to dip into
the writings of the early settlers of the New World (for example, the
journals of William Bradford and John Winthrop) to realize that their
attitude toward Nature, like that of their ancestors, was at best ambiva-
lent and, more commonly, antagonistic. As Roderick Nash has percep-
tively written in *Wilderness and the American Mind,* the "main component
of that attitude is fear and hatred. Consequently, the appreciation of the
wilderness must be seen as recent, revolutionary, and incomplete."[13]
Only a nation that had conquered Nature—and thereby lost its frontier—could enjoy the luxuries of pastoralism and the sentimental yearnings for primitivism. Hence, for example, the extraordinary rush to the
Klondike in 1897 was motivated by something far deeper than the
desire for gold: it was the desire to recapture a lost frontier of the human
spirit.

It was essentially this spirit that informed London's attitude toward
Nature. But not at the outset—and not at the end. His attitude, like
that of his culture, was both dynamic and complex. It began with an
intense revulsion against farm life, for the accounts of his miserable boy-
hood on a series of California ranches given in his letters and *John
Barleycorn* are as bleak as those rendered in Hamlin Garland's stories
about the Middle Border. Moreover, any illusions he might have enter-
tained concerning the romantic beauty of Nature-in-the-raw were thoroughly dissipated during his nine months in the Klondike, an adventure
from which he was fortunate to emerge alive. The true wilderness (as
opposed to that of the Romantic poets and the academic primitivists)
was inimical to human beings—a hostile place to be escaped *from,* not
to—and London's early stories are filled with terror and dread of this
deadly landscape. It was several years later, only after the harshness of
that experience had been sublimated through the nostalgic alembic of
time—only after he had discovered through his traumatic six weeks in

the slums of London's East End that the city could be a more deadly wilderness than the Northland, and only when he was safe back home with family and friends in his snug bungalow in Piedmont—it was only then that he could afford to rhapsodize over *The Call of the Wild*. And it would be another two years, after his separation from Bessie and his daughters and after the Long Sickness described in *John Barleycorn*, before he would be ready to move permanently from the city to the country—not to the wilderness, but to the pastoral "middle landscape."

London's move from Oakland to the Valley of the Moon (Wake Robin Lodge in the hamlet of Glen Ellen) was initially motivated by what Marx calls "sentimental pastoralism": that is, "flight from the city" and "withdrawal from society into an idealized landscape" (Marx, 5–11). As London wrote to his socialist friend Frederick Irons Bamford at the Oakland Public Library on 28 May 1905, "The main thing is the country itself, and the fact that you are out of the high pressure of city life." Then, continuing in a remarkably Thoreauvian temper, he explains: "The thing is, to cease being intellectual altogether. To take delight in little things, the bugs and crawling things, the birds, the leaves, etc., etc. The thing is to get so keenly interested in decently cooking a pot of rice, that you will forget that there ever was a Socialist Revolution, or a library, or high school children getting books for collateral reading, or anything else under the sun except the one end—a decently cooked pot of rice. . . . I didn't come to Glen Ellen to see people, but to get away from people . . ." (*Letters,* 485). This same temper is reflected in a story London was writing at this time—his first fiction dealing with the pastoral scene, "All Gold Canyon"—obviously inspired by his own enthusiasm for the lovely setting of the Hill Ranch, which he purchased on 7 June 1905, the day before mailing his completed manuscript to *Century Magazine*.

"All Gold Canyon" is one of London's most crucially important stories. Not only does it embody some of his best lyrical description and dramatic narrative: it also demonstrates his newly awakened ecological conscience. There had been little evidence of such concern in his Alaskan stories; all his sympathies are with the brave souls who pit their heroic will against the awesome intractability of the wilderness. The gold itself is incidental, the moral fiber of the man himself being the important thing, but it is nonetheless a positive reward for those select few upon whom fate has endowed the rare combination of grit, determination, adaptability, good comradeship, and—most important—good luck. London's bonanza kings are almost invariably men of exceptional character who have also been blessed by Special Providence. Like their Puritan forebears, they see in wildness not the preservation of the world, but profit for the individual who has the strength of will to match force with force.

The main character of "All Gold Canyon," a pocket-miner simply named Bill, is such a frontier type, possessing the best qualities of the Northland heroes: courage, decency, industriousness, a sense of fair play, and humor. But his materialistic spirit is out of harmony with the spirit of the beneficent Southland wilderness, which London introduces in the characteristic imagery of the pastoral tradition:

> It was the green heart of the canyon, where the walls swerved back from the rigid plan and relieved their harshness of line by making a little shel-tered nook and filling it to the brim with sweetness and roundness and softness. Here all things rested. . . .
>
> There was no dust in the canyon. The leaves and flowers were clean and virginal. . . . Sunshine and butterflies drifted in and out among the trees. The hum of the bees and the whisper of the stream were a drifting sound. And the drifting sound and drifting color seemed to weave together in the making of a delicate and intangible fabric which was the spirit of the place.[14]

The quietness of this Western Sleepy Hollow is a far cry from the terri-fying silence of "the savage, frozen-hearted Northland Wild"[15] (*White*, 1), and its spirit is unmistakably Edenic (at one point the place is called "the canyon-garden").

This Edenic spirit is abruptly broken, however, by the pocket miner, who bursts noisily upon the scene in a cloud of dust, the metal of his hob-nailed boots clanging harshly against the rocks as he monotonously chants a hymn about "them sweet hills of grace." The man is immedi-ately struck by the loveliness of the place, but his motives are basically materialistic, not aesthetic, and he can only respond with cheap com-mercial clichés: "A pocket-hunter's delight an' a cayuse's paradise! Cool green for tired eyes! Pink pills for pale people ain't in it" (*Moon*, 154).

In London's pastoral wilderness the roles between Man and Nature are reversed from what they were in the Northland: It is Man who now becomes the savage destructive force, Nature the victim. Described in imagery that pits the eternal Feminine Earth against the destructiveness of Man, Bill proceeds methodically to desecrate the virginal canyon, dig-ging a series of scientifically calculated holes into the gently sloping hill in which he has located the secret gold pocket. But, while discovering his treasure, the man has also brought death into the garden: the deep hole he has dug almost becomes his own grave—and does, indeed, become the grave for the dark stranger who attempts to ambush him after he has mined his gold. Even so, "All Gold Canyon" ends on a hopeful note. After the miner has departed, "through the silence crept back the spirit of the place. . . . Only remained the hoof-marks in the meadow and the torn hillside to mark the boisterous trail of life that had broken the peace of the place and passed on" (*Moon,* 187).

Yet the lyrical pastoralism of "All Gold Canyon" represents only the first stage in London's dynamic attitude toward Nature and the land. His restless intelligence would not allow him to dwell long in this idyllic region without imposing his will upon the land. Shortly after purchasing the Hill Ranch, he contracted to build a magnificent barn from rock, reinforced concrete, and heavy redwood beams; and he began planting the orchard that would reach full maturity by the time he and Charmian returned from their projected seven years' cruise around the world. His own all-gold canyon was truly beautiful; he would preserve its beauty while also making it fruitful. Science, lovingly applied, could not merely preserve but enhance the best in Nature.

London's articulation of these two seemingly opposing forces— Science and Nature—is first effected in *White Fang,* which he started writing on 27 June 1905, the same day that ground was broken for the foundation of his new barn, the first structure he erected on his new ranch.[16] As indicated earlier (see chapter 2), the thematic crux of this novel is the encounter between the domesticated wolf and the bestialized man (the escaped convict Jim Hall, who, because he has been treated with neither kindness nor scientific understanding, has degenerated into a mad-dog psychopath). When White Fang is critically wounded saving his master's father, his extraordinary constitution coupled with the application of modern medicinal techniques saves his life, and he survives as the "Blessed Wolf." Building upon the imagery of "All Gold Canyon" and in keeping with the various ways he had portrayed the Feminine in works such as *The Sea-Wolf,* in the later Sonoma novels, as we shall see, the opposition between Science and Nature—sometimes resolved—is presented primarily through opposition of the Masculine and the Feminine.

Between 1909 and 1916 London increased the size of Beauty Ranch to 1,400 acres, one of the largest in the Sonoma Valley; and during those seven years he came to be regarded by the agricultural experts as "one of California's leading farmers," whose ranch was "one of the best in the country."[17] By combining modern agronomy with the wisdom of Oriental agriculture (terracing, drainage, tillage, etc.), he succeeded in growing bumper crops of prunes, grapes, and alfalfa on land that had been abandoned by previous owners. He built the first concrete-block silo in California and constructed a "pig palace" which was a model of sanitation and efficiency. His livestock regularly took high honors in the country and state fairs and brought top breeding prices. One of the finest tributes he ever received was that by the famous horticulturalist Luther Burbank in his autobiographical reminiscence *The Harvest of Years:* "Jack London was a big healthy boy with a taste for serious things, but never cynical, never bitter, always good-humored and humorous, as I saw him, and with fingers and heart equally sensitive when he was in my gardens."[18]

London was—like Thomas Jefferson—a rational humanist and a scientific progressivist; he was also—like Jefferson—strongly enamored of the pastoral dream, seeing in the return to the land the possibilities of spiritual as well as physical regeneration. This is the central theme of two of his three agrarian novels: *Burning Daylight* and *The Valley of the Moon.* What Howard Lachtman has called "the central tenet" of the latter applies just as well to both these works: "that self-reliant individuals who go back to the values of the land can create meaningful alternatives to the industrialized and urbanized blight of the twentieth century."[19] The two novels are remarkably complementary, as Peter J. Schmitt points out, the first depicting the evils of wealth, the second, the evils of poverty.[20] *Burning Daylight*—begun, according to Charmian London's diary, in Quito, Ecuador, on 5 June 1909—offers an interesting comparison with *White Fang:* both works begin in the Northland wilderness and end in the Southland idyll; the titular characters of both are domesticated through love and regenerated through contract with the beneficent spirit of the pastoral landscape. But *Burning Daylight* is the more complex because, after leaving the Northland, the hero has been initiated into the unnatural wilderness of the city and the corrupt savagery of big business; before he can achieve salvation he must be *de*-initiated through an act of renunciation; that is, it is only after he has relinquished his financial position that he can become wed to the spirit of the pastoral place, represented by the anima-figure of Dede Mason.

Apart from the significance of its theme, perhaps the most instructive observation concerning *Burning Daylight* is that in the central character are incarnated the three major types of the American hero. First, as Klondike bonanza king, he is a Northland Leatherstocking who combines extraordinary physical prowess with true grit to master the wilderness. As he boasts in typical frontier fashion during his showdown with the Robber Barons Dowsett, Letton, and Guggenhammer, "I'm Burning Daylight—savvee? Ain't afraid of God, devil, death, nor destruction. Them's my four aces, and they sure copper your bets."[21] (It is only fitting that, as archetypal Western hero, he backs his brag with a .44 Colt pistol.) Next, he becomes, as a Captain of Finance, the businessman as a hero. Finally, after renouncing his wealth, he becomes the yeoman farmer celebrated as the symbolic epitome of Jeffersonian democracy.

It is this last type that moves to the center of London's agrarian vision in his mature work. "In the solution of the great economic problems of the present age," he said, "I see a return to the soil. I go into farming because my philosophy and research have taught me to recognize the fact that a return to the soil is the basis of economics. . . . I see my farm in terms of the world, and I see the world in terms of my farm."[22] This vision is the main theme of *The Valley of the Moon,* generally regarded as the best of London's agrarian novels, but in it the Jeffersonian hero is supplanted by a Jeffersonian heroine.

London characterized the book as a traditional American call to move "back to the land," but he also emphasized that in place of a visionary hero "the woman gets the vision. She is the guiding force" (*Letters,* 1007–8). His androgynous heroine, Saxon Brown Roberts, is modeled on the figure of the New Woman of the era, but in addition Saxon's vitality and openness to development offer a refreshing contrast to the usual portraits of lower-class women in fiction of the day. As she and her husband Billy struggle for survival in a harsh capitalist world, they find that part of their success in creating a just economy for themselves involves dispensing with rigid sex roles, as do Maud Brewster and Humphrey van Weyden on Endeavor Island in *The Sea-Wolf.* But in a sense *The Valley of the Moon* is a tour de force—a "what if?" featuring a dramatic role reversal rather than merely a rejection of traditional roles. It is Saxon, not Billy, whose vision leads them to their pastoral home— her fortitude and sensitivity combine to make her London's most fully realized heroine. When Billy falters, she persists; when he gives up, she asks questions; when at the end he is full of grandiose plans to build housing developments in the beautiful valley, she is strangely silent.

London's innovation becomes more sharply defined when his sources are examined, including primarily some two dozen articles he tore out and annotated in 1910 and 1911 from publications including *The Saturday Evening Post, The Pacific Rural Press, Pacific Monthly,* and *Country*

Life in America. These articles, preserved in the Huntington Library's Jack London Collection, offer facts and figures about farming and land values, and nearly all of them are first-person accounts of entering the wilderness to begin a new life. They feature titles such as "How I Learned to Farm" or "Cutting Loose from the City." The most striking thing about them is that with one exception (across the top of which London wrote, "San Jose Woman"), they are all narrated by men and focused on masculine achievements. Often the new farmer's wife is barely mentioned. London's annotations, however, refer to Saxon in a different light than that in which these nearly forgotten women are presented in the articles. In addition to his general notes for the "farm novel," as he called it, London sketches possible dialogues between his two main characters that clearly place Saxon in charge of leading the dialogue and working through dialogue toward important decisions. For example, London noted in one margin: "Billy: 'Here's where we can do it.' Saxon: 'No, no, no redwoods here.'"

An early source, from the 12 November 1910 *Saturday Evening Post,* is the most telling of all: in an article entitled "The Man Who Came Back: Two Twentieth Century Pilgrims and Where They Landed," the author boasts of his achievements in leaving the corruption of Chicago and heading west to Colorado with his wife to become a farmer. He does mention that it was at her instigation that they left, and furthermore that she wants to find a special valley, which he calls "Mary's valley," where they can thrive. But though he says Mary is his inspiration to work hard, his favorite word seems to be "I." At the end of his piece, he tells us:

> I can make a living for myself and the family on a forty-acre farm, and raise the usual farm products too. I can make a fortune with twenty acres in fruit and nut trees, or in poultry. And the only thing I will have to give is just what I would have had to give if I had stuck to the trade back there in Chicago—work. The difference is now I work for myself. . . . I get the wages and the profits.[23]

Virtually no mention is made of what must have been a grueling life for Mary. London used several situations and events from this article in *The Valley of the Moon,* especially the notion of "Mary's valley." The change from male to female narrator and protagonist is a profound one. Saxon's valley and Mary's valley are two entirely different destinations.

Saxon and Billy Roberts abandon the strike-ridden city of Oakland after a series of domestic tragedies in an attempt to find a home somewhere in the country. Appropriately, they discover their sanctuary, just as London himself had done in 1905, in the Valley of the Moon. But theirs is no sentimental pastoral retreat. During their wandering they were observing, experiencing, and learning the ways of agrarian success. The basic lesson is that sincere motivation, good character, and hard work are not sufficient—the Anglo-Saxon pioneer farmers possessed these but failed nevertheless. Their major teacher is the "San Jose woman," Mrs. Mortimer, the widow of a university professor, herself a former librarian who managed to build a highly successful farming business because (like London himself) she read the right books on agronomy and subscribed to the best agricultural journals. As she explains to the young couple, "Remember, the soil is generous. But it must be treated generously, and that is something the old style American farmer can't get into his head. So it *is* head that counts" (*Valley,* 338). But it is not head *alone* that counts. And this, the ultimate key to London's agrarian vision, is also the central theme of his most misunderstood (and in some ways his most confused) novel, *The Little Lady of the Big House* to which we will presently turn.[24]

Saxon's importance in *The Valley of the Moon* is primarily realized through her ability to enter into dialogue both with Billy and with the people they meet as they look for their valley. London makes male-only dialogue seem quite limited, as when Billy and his friends grumble ineffectually about their union problems, or, even moreso, when they do not talk about painful personal subjects. But in marrying Saxon, whose mother, incidentally, was a poet, Billy manages—through language—to some extent to escape male stereotypes, and he moves toward androgyny and wholeness. Throughout the novel Saxon's voice leads them both to reason and reality; indeed, because she assists London in creating Billy as an integrated human being, she resembles an author herself, for she too relies on creating speech. The book has an extremely high preponderance of dialogue involving many characters, and dialogue promotes community between Billy and Saxon as well as between them and the world.

Yet why the compromised ending? Once they have attained their destination, Saxon falls silent before Billy's alarming plans to mine the mountain and to build a housing development in the valley. The reader is left to wonder whether Billy has been at all transformed by their experiences, whether Saxon's pregnancy will cast her in a more traditional role, whether their valley of the moon will indeed be a happy home, whether indeed it will revert to a "Mary's valley" after all. But London's twist at the ending seems supremely responsible, for it projects the need for future rejoinders in the dialogic structure the book establishes, the need for future transformations.[25]

Similarly and yet with a very different tone, *The Little Lady of the Big House* offers a woman as the moral and spiritual guide to the attainment of the pastoral dream. The gentle irony of *The Valley of the Moon*, however, is replaced by a dark, at times hopelessly dark, irony that lends the story its strangely decadent and apocalyptic feel.

In March 1913, a few days before the first installment of *The Valley of the Moon* appeared in *Cosmopolitan,* London wrote to Editor Roland Phillips that he had just gotten a "splendid motif" for a new novel in hand, featuring "Three characters only—a mighty trio in a mighty situation, in a magnificently beautiful environment enhanced by all the guts of sex, coupled with strength." His three main characters were not to be "puling weaklings and moralists," he continued. "They are cultured, modern, and at the same time profoundly primitive." Waxing more enthusiastic, London ventured that this book would be "what I have been working toward all my writing life. . . . Except for my old-time punch, which will be in it from start to finish, it will not be believed that I could write it—it is so utterly fresh, so absolutely unlike anything I have ever done. . . . It will be a cleancut gem, even in serial form—a jewel of artistry" (*Letters,* 374–75). But for many readers, so far did the author's reach seem to exceed his grasp that they would need an editorial footnote to recognize *The Little Lady of the Big House* from his prospectus. London had had bad luck with love trios, and in this new attempt he took some great risks that did not seem to pay off at all. *The Little Lady of the Big House* has been called the worst novel Jack London ever wrote.[26] However, this complex novel has been generally misunderstood because its irony and its radical treatment of gender have been overlooked. Most critics and many readers expect neither from Jack London.

An unmistakable personal element appears in the novel: its central characters, symbolically named Dick and Paula Forrest, are modeled after Jack and Charmian London; their efficient, scientific ranch resembles in many ways Beauty Ranch. Outwardly, the Forrests look like the all-American couple. Splendid physical specimens—dynamic, amiable, sensitive, fun loving, intelligent, and tremendously appreciative of each other's virtues—they live in a beautiful home and are apparently secure in the love of friends and the fruitfulness of nature. Yet, despite an idyllic aura, things are not quite right on the Forrest ranch: Paula is a chronic insomniac, Dick sleeps with a loaded .44 Colt pistol at his bedside, and—though he is a scientific breeder of prize stock—the marriage is barren.

Because the Forrests themselves have no children, the theme of natural fecundity that permeates the book assumes a pathological undertone. Dick reiterates this motif obsessively in his pagan chant, "The Song of Mountain Lad" (the Forrests' prize stallion): "Hear me! I am Eros. I stamp upon the hills. I fill the wide valleys. The mares hear me, and startle, in quiet pastures; for they know me. The grass grows rich and richer, the land is filled with fatness, and the sap is in the trees. It is the spring. The mares remember my voice. They know me aforetime through their mothers before them. Hear me! I am Eros. I stamp upon the hills, and the wide valleys are my heralds, echoing the sound of my approach."[27] Dick's oft-repeated song soon grates on the reader's nerves; its frequency is of a piece with Dick's overriding egoism.

Ostensibly the Forrests' marriage is broken up by Evan Graham, Dick's best friend, who falls in love with Paula; more subtly, the breach has already been made by Dick's failure to embrace Paula as a person in her own right—she is merely another entry in his ledger of possessions, and, despite his very vocal admiration of her, the values for which she stands are repudiated in his world. Dick contemplates suicide when he discovers his wife's attachment to Graham; but, before he can carry out his plan, Paula shoots herself with a rifle. Her dying words are, "I'm sorry there were no babies, Red Cloud" (*Little,* 391). The suppressed irony breaks through in harsh mockery at last: "After a long time, she sighed faintly, and began so easily to go that she was gone before they guessed. From without, the twittering of the canaries bathing in the fountain penetrated the silence of the room, and from afar came the trumpeting of Mountain Lad and the silver whinny of the Fotherington Princess" (*Little,* 392). Paula has outmanned her husband in the end, choosing the gun shot he would have chosen—the irony being that such "manliness" brings only death.

London's ambivalence about his hero is telling. Dick Forrest's name is an ironic travesty—just as his marriage has been. Dick, for all his horse play and erotic foot stampings, is the *un*natural man, an agronomical Ethan Brand, governed by head but lacking in heart; and just as Esther has been the victim of Brand's scientific egomania in Hawthorne's allegorical tale, so is poor Paula Forrest sacrificed to her husband's damnable efficiency. He is the *reductio ad horrendum* of the twentieth-century

mechanical man whose every working hour, sleeping hour—and playing hour—is governed by his watch. He is incapable of genuine love.
Somewhat peculiarly, he calls Paula his "boy girl, the child that never
grew up." Indeed she has never known what it is to be loved as a
mature woman; her only children are the cold marble cherubs in her
secret patio. Dick Forrest, though a success as a scientific farmer, is a
failure as a man. His alter ego, the artist-writer Evan Graham, possesses exactly those qualities lacking in Forrest, as the descriptive comparison of the two men reveals: "But the inch more in height and inch less
in chest-girth gave Evan Graham a grace of body and carriage that
Dick Forrest did not possess. . . . Graham was all light and delight,
with a hint—but the slightest of hints—of Prince Charming. Forrest's
seemed a more efficient and formidable organism, more dangerous to
other life . . ." (*Little*, 100). "Grace, light, delight": these are contrasted
against the deadly efficiency of Forrest, who is basically a sterile (but
deadly) clockwork figure. Yet in his selfish possession of her Evan is no
savior to Paula—and certainly he is no true friend to either Dick or
Paula. London's portrayal of both men seems to signal that it is pre-
cisely *Paula* who is missed.

As the last novel in which London dealt with the American wilderness
as Eden, *The Little Lady of the Big House* is disappointing because it has so
much unfulfilled potential. In a word, its ironies are too subtle. Also, if
London had hewed to the theme of agronomy, of successfully uniting
machine and garden through the loving application of scientific knowledge for purposes of redemption rather than exploitation—in other
words, if London had remained true by dramatizing in the novel the very
thing he himself was doing with Beauty Ranch—*The Little Lady of the
Big House* might have been a very significant book, not only for its treatment of women, but also in the light of modern ecology. It might have
also been a better book artistically.

The Little Lady of the Big House has often been said to show the failure
of the author's agrarian dream, a dream which, in the light of considerable evidence, seems to have lost none of its intensity during his last
years.[28] The biographical fallacy is a common critical trap, but London's
critics and biographers have been uncommonly prone to fall into it, and
not just when it comes to London's agrarianism. On the basis of Paula
Forrest's death, they have deduced that London was unconsciously trying to kill off Charmian. Yet there is overwhelming evidence that he
loved his wife deeply and loyally. Their marriage had recently survived
two near-affairs on Charmian's part—brought on by her husband's Dick

Forrest–like treatment of her—and as Charmian reports in her *Diary* she and Jack sat together and wept over the ending of *The Little Lady of the Big House*. It was a damning self-portrait of the author, but, like that in *Martin Eden,* it was one which London himself ultimately effaced. In short, it was a warning to himself—and to other men; it was a heart-felt testament to how a male-dominated and success-obsessed culture can fail to see, or, worse, destroy a woman like Paula. London wrote to one of his fans who was fearful that the pessimistic undertone in the novel was a reflection of the author's own philosophical outlook: "I assure you in reply to your question, that after having come through all the game of life, and of youth, at my present mature age of thirty-nine years I am firmly and solemnly convinced that the game is worth the candle. I have had a very fortunate life, I have been luckier than many hundreds of millions of men in my generation have been lucky, and while I have suffered much, I have lived much, seen much, and felt much that has been denied to the average man. Yes, indeed, the game is worth the candle . . ." (*Letters,* 461). *The Little Lady of the Big House* should be construed neither as London's own thinly veiled psychoauto-biography nor as the final rendition of his agrarian dream, but as a complex rendering of both these aspects subsumed by his constant per-sonal and artistic quest for the spirit that gives life.[29]

Within a fortnight after completing this novel London was hard at work on a new play for the Bohemian Grove; this would be published in February 1916 as *The Acorn-Planter—A California Forest Play—Planned to Be Sung by Efficient Singers Accompanied by a Capable Orchestra.*[30] It is this, if any single book may be so designated, which might be fairly called Jack London's "last will and testament to California possibilities."[31] The play is a mythopoeic fantasy beginning in "the morning of the world" and concluding in "the Epilogue, or Apotheosis" with "the celebration of the death of war and the triumph of the acorn-planters," incarnated in Red Cloud, the philosopher-agrar-ian. California is seen throughout as the place of Edenic possibilities, "A sunny land, a rich and fruitful land, / The warm and golden . . . land." Red Cloud, though killed by the Sun Men, is resurrected; and "In place of war's alarums, peaceful days; / Above the warrior's grave the golden grain / Turns deserts grim and stark to laughing lands" (*Acorn,* vi, 76, 77). The play ends on a strong note of affirmation as "The New Day dawns, / The day of brotherhood, / The day of man!" And in the protagonist's final paean to life may be discerned the author's own optimistic hopes:

The planters' ways are the one way.
Ever they plant for life.
For life more abundant.
For beauty of head and hand,
And the laughter of maids in the twilight
And the lover's song in the gloom.

                                                              (*Acorn*, 84)

Although he celebrated the way of the acorn planters, London was not reverting to a simplistic pastoralism in this fourth version of his symbolic wilderness. He saw with prophetic vision that the roots of humankind's social ills and conflicts are basically economic and that wars will end only when all people have enough to eat. What he envisioned here was a universal conversion of swords into plowshares—or, perhaps more accurately, of military tanks into tractors—for as a modern man he knew his agrarian dream could be realized only through modern technology, properly administered: that is, only if the machine were used sensibly in the garden.[32]

Chapter Five

Beyond the Literary Marketplace: The Quest for Self

Having explored the symbolic wilderness of the White Silence, Paradise Lost, the Inferno, and the Valley of the Moon, Jack London was increasingly attracted to yet another terra incognita during the last years of his life: that unexplored region of the human psyche that was in process of being charted by Sigmund Freud and C. G. Jung. As early as 1912 London had evidently read Freud, and four years later he incorporated a reference to psychoanalytic theory into one of his stories.[1] However, his major psychological epiphany came in the early summer of 1916, when he began reading Beatrice Hinkle's new edition of Jung's *Psychology of the Unconscious*.[2] It was at this point he exclaimed to Charmian that he was "standing on the edge of a world so new, so terrible, so wonderful" that he was "almost afraid to look over into it" (Book, II, 323).[3] That volume of Jung was to become the most heavily annotated book in his vast personal library.[4]

London's discovery of the Hinkle edition was clearly an instance of what Jung would have called *synchronicity*, for he had been readying himself for such a psychological and philosophical breakthrough for some time. His artistic "signature" (to use Leslie Fiedler's term)[5] had always been informed by myth and archetype, as witnessed in the best of his Northland tales—most brilliantly, of course, in *The Call of the Wild*. What his reading of Jung did, however, was enable him to comprehend and to articulate those powerful psychic forces that had unconsciously animated his creative genius earlier—unconscious promptings he had previously chosen willfully to ignore or to deny along with all the spiritualistic claptrap with which, thanks to his mother, his childhood memories had been cluttered. There is considerable irony in the fact that while consciously rejecting these maternal irrationalisms and supernaturalisms, London's psyche was being inspired by the "dark mother" of his unconscious to create his most potent and poetic fictions.

Neither London's mythic vision nor his creative energies declined during the post-*Snark* years, as witnessed by *The Valley of the Moon*, *The*

Scarlet Plague, and *The Star Rover.* Moreover, the short stories he wrote during this period, though fewer, contain passages of lyrical and narrative brilliance equal to the best of his Northland work. Most importantly, they not only body forth a cluster of archetypal motifs that demonstrate the dynamic vitality of his primordial vision, but they also show him experimenting with totally new subject matter, much of which was so alien to the current demands of the literary marketplace that even the famous name of Jack London was not enough to guarantee acceptance by the magazines. For example, London's reexamination of cultural "otherness" is brilliantly pursued in two stories on Anglo perceptions of Latino culture, "The Madness of John Harned" (1909) and "The Mexican" (1911). In both cases London condemns the whites' failures to address the racial "other" rather than reject or exploit him. And one of the most important continuing emphases in these tales is on the physical and spiritual strengths of women. James McClintock's pronouncement that most of the stories of this period "do not warrant individual attention" and that, collectively, "they reveal London's philosophical pessimism turning into artistic cynicism" could hardly be further off the mark.[6] London's originality, openness to new ideas, and his following his own inner search for value have unquestionably hurt him among those readers and critics determined to limit him to a particular "Jack London" canon.

Even in 1909, as the Londons were returning home via the tramp steamer *Tymeric* across the Pacific to Ecuador, across Panama to the Gulf of to Mexico and up to New Orleans, then west by rail with a stopover to see the Grand Canyon before finally arriving at Glen Ellen in late July, London was managing to produce a novel of middling quality along with a handful of first-rate stories, at least one of which was radically different from anything then in the magazines.[7] According to Charmian London, London got his idea for this tale—"Samuel"—from Robert McIlwaine, the captain of the *Tymeric,* and he worked very hard to transcribe the proper dialect of his Scotch-Irish protagonist (*Book,* II, 176). This protagonist is one of several memorable versions of the Great Mother archetype London portrayed in his fiction,[8] and she is more impressive than Synge's Maurya in *Riders in the Sea,* which "Samuel" resembles in both setting and theme if not in tone. London's ancient sea wife is named Margaret Henan. Past 70 and having borne 12 children, she represents the earth's timeless fecundity itself. When we first see her (through the eyes of London's anonymous first-person American narrator, a visitor to the Island Magill off the coast of Northern Ireland), she is—appropriate to her symbolic function—hauling hundred-weight sacks of grain:

> Six times she went between the cart and the stable, each time with a full sack on her back, and beyond passing the time of day with me she took no notice of my presence. Then, the cart empty, she fumbled for matches and lighted a short clay pipe, pressing down the burning surface of tobacco with a calloused and apparently nerveless thumb. The hands were noteworthy. They were large-knuckled, sinewy and malformed by labor, rimed with callouses, the nails blunt and broken, and with here and there cuts and bruises, healed and healing, such as are common to the hands of hard-working men. On the back were huge, upstanding veins, eloquent of age and toil. Looking at them, it was hard to believe that they were the hands of the woman who had once been the belle of Island McGill. This last, of course, I learned later. At the time I knew neither her history nor her identity. (*Strength*, 216)

Aside from her work-hewn appearance and extraordinary strength, her most noteworthy features are her forehead and her eyes. "Neither drifted hair nor serried wrinkles could hide the splendid dome of a forehead, high and broad without verging the slightest on the abnormal. . . . The sunken cheeks and pinched nose told little of the quality of the life that flickered behind those clear blue eyes of hers. Despite the minutiae of wrinkle work that somehow failed to wizen them, her eyes were as clear as a girl's—clear, out-looking and far-seeing, and with an open and unblinking steadfastness of gaze that was disconcerting" (*Strength*, 217).

Margaret Henan's story is an extraordinary one, indeed, and London's recounting of it is such that he considered "Samuel" one of his half-dozen best stories.[9] As the narrator learns in a multileveled dialogic narrative generated by the women villagers, after her youngest—and favorite—brother dies tragically, Margaret names her firstborn "Samuel" in his honor. The child dies, and the villagers insist that the name bears a curse. Defying their superstitious admonitions, she bestows the same name upon another and still another, both of whom also meet untimely ends. The third Samuel, a splendid young man who has given up a career as schoolteacher to follow the family sailing tradition, dies a heroic death trying to save his ship during a terrible storm at sea—long after his mother's childbearing days would seem to be over. Again, the villagers' ominous predictions appear to have been warranted. Then, incredibly, at age 47, Margaret Henan manages to conceive and give birth to a big, healthy baby boy—again to bear that fateful name. The rest of the islanders have long since ostracized her, branding her as lunatic and heretic. Yet the boy thrives: at age two he is as large as a normal child of five, and at three he is the size of a 10-year-old. But he is an idiot; instead of walking and talking, he can only creep on all fours, stare blinkingly at the sun, and bray like an ass. He is finally clubbed to death by his crazed, guilt-ridden father, who then hangs himself from a rafter in the stable.

On one level Margaret Henan is a fictional "grotesque," similar to Mrs. Grimes in Sherwood Anderson's "Death in the Woods": but, also like Anderson's portrayal of the Earth Mother, London's tale is a little masterpiece of tonal craftsmanship that reverberates with deeper chords of myth. By deftly modulating his descriptive images and dialogue, London sublimates the underlying morbidity of his plot, creating a fine texture of pathos, awe, and even a subtle strain of ironic humor. The mythic implications are reinforced through the narrator's description of the aura of certitude that radiates from the old woman:

> She looked at me with that strange, unblinking gaze, and she thought and spoke with a slow deliberateness that characterized everything about her, as if well aware of an eternity that was hers and in which there was no need for haste. Again I was impressed by the enormous certitude of her. In this eternity that seemed so indubitably hers, there was time to spare for safe-footing and stable equilibrium—for certitude, in short. . . . The feeling produced in me was uncanny. Here was a human soul that, save for the most glimmering of contacts, was beyond the humanness of me. (*Strength,* 218–19)

So taken is the narrator with Margaret Henan's strange destiny that he feels compelled to search out the motive for her awful persistence, wondering if she is "a martyr to Truth," the adherent to "some vaster, profounder superstition, a fetish-worship of which the Alpha and Omega was the cryptic Samuel," or merely a stolid, self-willed lunatic. The answer, as he discovers in his last meeting with her, is none of these exactly, but something at once as simple and as complex as life itself: for she is, in truth, the avatar of that mysterious force through which all living creatures are brought forth inexorably to bloom and die in the great cycle of nature. How fitting that her favorite sons are named after the personification of that wonderful force: "*Samuel* = his name is *God.*"[10] As the story concludes, Margaret (appropriately named after the patron saint of women in childbirth)[11] affirms that her motives transcend the merely logical and rational; she simply *likes* the name:

"Never yet hov I heard the answer tull the *why* o' like. God alone hoz thot answer. You an' me be mortal an' we canna know. Enough for us tull know what we like an' what we duslike. I *like*—thot uz the first word an' the last. An' behind thot *like* no mon can go an' find the *why* o' ut. I *like* Samuel, an' I like ut wull. Ut uz a sweet name, an' there be a rollun' wonder un the sound o' ut thot passes onderstandun. . . ."

"Have you any regrets, Margaret Henan?" I asked, suddenly and without forethought.

She studied me a moment.

"Ay, thot I no ha' borne another son."

"And you would . . . ?" I faltered.

"Ay, thot I would," she answered. "Ut would ha' been hus name."

I went down the dark road between the hawthorne hedges puzzling over the why of like, repeating *Samuel* to myself and aloud and listening to the rolling wonder in its sound that had charmed her soul and led her life in tragic places. *Samuel!* There was a rolling wonder in the sound. Ay, there was! (*Strength*, 256–57)

Another equally impressive version of the archetypal female may be found in one of London's least-known stories: "The Night-Born," composed in May 1910, one of the happiest periods in London's life when he was fully engaged in building Beauty Ranch and eagerly looking forward to the birth of his and Charmian's first child. Like "Samuel," it demonstrates London's engagement with the Feminine. The principal narrator of the story, a wealthy but debauched 47-year-old former Klondike argonaut named Trefethan, has, in Jungian terms, failed to embrace his anima-figure and is consequently drinking himself into an early grave. Both structurally and thematically, this is one of London's most complex narratives. Clell Peterson mentions the influence of Conrad's Marlow stories in the framing of London's narrative,[12] but "The Night-Born" goes a step further than even "Heart of Darkness" in this respect. It opens with the voice of an anonymous narrator describing a postdinner gathering of wealthy businessmen in an exclusive San Francisco men's club, and the symbolic implications are evident in the first paragraph:

It was the old Alta-Inyo Club—a warm night for San Francisco—and through the open windows, hushed and far, came the brawl of the streets. The talk had led on from the Graft Prosecution and the latest signs that the town was to be run wide open, down through all the grotesque sordidness and rottenness of man-hate and man-meanness until the name of O'Brien was mentioned—O'Brien, the promising young pugilist who had been killed in the prize-ring the night before. At

once the air had seemed to freshen. O'Brien had been a clean-living
young man with ideals. He neither drank, smoked, nor swore, and his
had been the body of a beautiful young god. He had even carried his
prayer-book to the ringside. They found it in his coat pocket in the
dressing-room . . . afterward.[13]

"Man-hate and man-meanness": these are the first symbolic keys to the
story's theme. Hatred, meanness, corruption, cynicism, and moral and
physical decadence are all associated with the corrupted masculine principle. "Here was Youth," continues the narrator, still musing over the
death of the young fighter, "clean and wholesome, unsullied—the thing
of glory and wonder for men to conjure with . . . after it has been lost to
them and they have turned middle-aged" (*Night,* 3). Clustered in opposition to the negative man-mean values of the city are Youth, Romance,
and Nature: "And so well did we conjure, that Romance came and for an
hour led us far from the man-city and its snarling roar. Bardwell, in a
way, started it by quoting from Thoreau; but it was old Trefethan, bald-
headed and dewlapped, who took up the quotation and for an hour to
come was Romance incarnate" (*Night,* 3–4).

At this point, the angle of narration shifts to Trefethan, whose unusual name is, like Bardwell's, symbolic.[14]

> "Well, look at me now. . . . That's what the Goldstead did to me—God
> knows how many millions, but nothing left in my soul . . . nor in my
> veins. The good red blood is gone. I am a jellyfish, a huge, gross mass of
> oscillating protoplasm, a—a . . ."
>
> But language failed him, and he drew solace from the long glass.
>
> "Women looked at me . . . then; and turned their heads a second
> time. Strange that I never married. But the girl. That's what I started to
> tell you about. I met her a thousand miles from anywhere, and then
> some. And she quoted to me those very words of Thoreau that Bardwell
> quoted a moment ago—the ones about the day-born gods and the night-
> born." (*Night,* 5)

The Thoreau quote is the following passage from *A Week on the Concord
and Merrimac Rivers,* which "the girl," Lucy, has clipped from a newspaper and carries, like precious gold dust, in a small buckskin pouch.[15]

> *The young pines springing up in the cornfields from year to year are to me a
> refreshing fact. We talk of civilizing the Indian, but that is not the name for his
> improvement. By the wary independence and aloofness of his dim forest life he pre-
> serves his intercourse with his native gods and is admitted from time to time to a*

rare and peculiar society with nature. He has glances of starry recognition, to which our saloons are strangers. The steady illumination of his genius, dim only because distant, is like the faint but satisfying light of the stars compared with the dazzling but ineffectual and short-lived blaze of candles. The Society-Islanders had their day-born gods, but they were not supposed to be of equal antiquity with the . . . night-born gods. (Night, 16)

Trefethan tells his story of finding this magnificent woman, "a regular She-Who-Must-Be-Obeyed,"[16] ruling a tribe of Indians, deep in the uncharted heart of the Northland wilderness while he was questing for gold:

It was a noble valley, now shut in by high canyon walls, and again opening out into beautiful stretches, wide and long with pasture shoulder-high in the bottoms, meadows dotted with flowers, and with clumps of timber—virgin and magnificent. . . . It was late fall, but the way those flowers persisted surprised me. I was supposed to be in sub-arctic America, and high up among the buttresses of the Rockies, and yet there was that everlasting spread of flowers. (*Night,* 6–7).

The prelapsarian implications are apparent, but Trefethan's materialistic lust blinds him to them. Like Billy Roberts's, his astigmatic vision comprehends Eden as no more than a new field for commercial exploitation: "Some day the white settlers will be in there and growing wheat down all that valley," he predicts, still unenlightened to the full significance of what he has missed.

Of course he can scarcely be unaware that the Woman he rejected is someone—or something—extraordinary. The Indians lead him to her tent, where he encounters her on a fresh mound of spruce boughs and furs: "and on top of all was a robe of swan-skins—white swan-skins—I have never seen anything like that robe. And on top of it, sitting cross-legged, was Lucy. She was nut-brown. I have called her a girl. But she was not. She was a woman, . . . a full-blooded, full-bodied woman, and royal ripe. And her eyes were blue" (*Night,* 7–8). Trefethan takes note of the remarkable robe upon which Lucy is enthroned but misses its deeper meanings, just as he misses what her name stands for: light, which is also vision. As J. E. Cirlot has remarked, "in poetry and literature," the white swan, sacred to Venus, "is an image of naked woman of chaste nudity and immaculate whiteness" (Cirlot, 306). During her own subsequent narrative, Lucy confesses that as a girl, before escaping to the wilderness, she had often yearned to run through the moonlit pastures "like a wild thing . . . to run white and naked in the darkness that I knew must feel like cool velvet . . ." (*Night,* 12). Cirlot suggests, furthermore, that the white swan is an androgynous symbol, "the mystic Centre and the union of opposites" (*Night,* 306). This latter meaning is apparent in Trefethan's description of Lucy's remarkable eyes: "That's what took me off my feet—her eyes—blue, not China blue, but deep blue, like the sea and sky all melted into one, and very wise. . . . They were a woman's eyes, a proper woman's eyes. You know what that means. Can I say more? Also, in those blue eyes were, at the same time, a wild unrest, a wistful yearning, and a repose, an absolute repose, a sort of all-wise and philosophical calm" (*Night,* 8).

A third frame is added to London's narrative when Lucy tells Trefethan her story: Having known nothing but hardship and work as the daughter of poor frontier parents, she tried to escape at age 18 by marrying a man who was going to Juneau to start a restaurant. But she unhappily discovered that she had merely traded one kind of drudgery for another; for her husband—"the Ox," she calls him—had married her not for love but to avoid paying wages to a cook and waitress. "'There was no meaning in anything,' she said, 'What was it all about? Why was I born? Was that all the meaning of life—just to work and work and be always tired?—to go to bed tired and wake up tired, with every day like every other day unless it was harder?'" But she clung desperately to her dreams of a better life:

> "'Sometimes,' she said, "when I was that dizzy from the heat of the cooking that if I didn't take a breath of fresh air I'd faint, I'd stick my head out of the kitchen window and close my eyes and see most wonderful things. All of a sudden I'd be traveling down a country road, and everything clean and quiet, no dust, no dirt; just streams ripplin' down sweet meadows, and lambs playing, breezes blowing the breath of flowers, and soft sunshine over everything; and lovely cows lazying knee-deep in quiet pools, and young girls bathing in a curve of stream all white and slim and natural. . . . And then I'd open my eyes, and the heat of the cooking range would strike on me, and I'd hear Jake sayin'—he was my husband—I'd hear Jake sayin', 'Why ain't you served them beans?'"" . . .
> (*Night,* 14–15)

Then it is she happens across the statement from Thoreau in the newspaper: "It was only a scrap of newspaper. But that Thoreau was a wise man. I wish I knew more about him. . . . I could have made him a good wife" (*Night,* 17). She is not destined to meet—or mate with—a

Thoreau, nor is she destined to remain a galley-slave for Jake the Ox: "I, who had lived all my life with the day-born, was a night-born . . . that was why I had hankered to run naked in the moonlight. And I knew that this dirty little Juneau hash-joint was no place for me. And right there and then I said I quit" (*Night* 17–18). When her husband tries to stop her, she pulls a .44 Colt pistol on him and leaves for the wilderness, traveling with three families of Indians in a canoe for Dyea.

But her escape—her individuation process, as it were—is neither simple nor easy. Only through a long night-journey, symbolic death and rebirth, does she win to the treasure of selfhood: "Romance! I got it the next day. We had to cross a big arm of the ocean—twelve or fifteen miles, at least; and it came on to blow when we were in the middle. That night I was along on the shore, with one wolf-dog, and I was the only one left alive" (*Night,* 20). She manages to survive by clinging to the dog's tail, and after wandering two days in the wilderness, she discovers an abandoned miner's shack and outside, still tied to trees, the skeletons of eight horses, each laden with a 150-pound moosehide sack filled with gold dust and nuggets. She caches all but 30 pounds of the gold, returns to the trading post at Dyea, outfits herself properly for Northland travel, and heads back into the wilderness. "She wandered several years over that country and on in to where I met her," explains Trefethan. "She hooked up with the Indians, doctored them, gained their confidence, and gradually took them in charge. She had only left that country once, and then, with a bunch of the young bucks, she went over Chilcoot, cleaned up her gold-cache, and brought it back with her" (*Night,* 23).

Now she only wants a fitting mate: ". . . the funny thing is," she confesses, "though I'm night-born in everything else, I'm not when it comes to mating. I reckon that kind likes its own kind best. That's the way it is with me, anyway, and has been all these years" (*Night,* 25). She proposes marriage to Trefethan, who—driven by a more insidious lust—puts her off with the lie that he is already married. "If I give the word, you stay on," she tells him, "But I ain't going to give it. I wouldn't want you if you didn't want to be wanted . . . and if you didn't want me" (*Night,* 27). Anima-figure that she is, she cannot force herself on the man who needs her; to be saved, he himself must make the commitment to the spiritual vitality she represents. Trefethan admits that he was half in love with her—but real commitment is not possible in halfway measures; it must be total or not at all. Trefethan consequently fails in his individuation, remaining a partial human being and a slave to his materialistic compulsions. Opting for the fool's gold of civilization, he has missed the true gold of self-fulfillment:

> The brawl of the streets came up to us like a distant surf. A steward, moving noiselessly, brought fresh siphons. And in the silence Trefethan's voice fell like a funeral bell:
>
> "It would have been better had I stayed. Look at me."
>
> We saw his grizzled mustache, the bald spot on his head, the puff-sacks under his eyes, the sagging cheeks, the heavy dewlap, the general tiredness and staleness and fatness, all the collapse and ruin of a man who had once been strong but who had lived too easily and too well. (*Night,* 28)

Even so, Trefethan's poetic conscience is not completely dead: "'It's not too late, old man,' Bardwell said, almost in a whisper." But it is too late—it has been too late since the moment of spiritual cowardice and self-betrayal when Trefethan rejected Lucy and all that she signified 12 years earlier.

> "By God! I wish I were n't a coward!" was Trefethan's answering cry. "I could go back to her. She's there, now. I could shape up and live many a long year . . . with her . . . up there. To remain here is to commit suicide. But I am an old man—forty-seven—look at me. The trouble is," he lifted his glass and glanced at it, "the trouble is that suicide of this sort is so easy. I am soft and tender. The thought of the long day's travel with the dogs appals me; the thought of the keen frost in the morning and of the frozen sled-lashings frightens me—"
>
> Automatically the glass was creeping toward his lips. With a swift surge of anger he made as if to crash it down upon the floor. Next came hesitancy and second thought. The glass moved upward to his lips and paused. He laughed harshly and bitterly, but his words were solemn: "Well, here's to the Night-Born. She *was* a wonder." (*Night,* 28–29)

Indeed, Lucy—as quintessential anima-figure, soul-mate, the source of spiritual vitality—was, and *is,* a wonder. And her rejection is devastating, physically as well as spiritually. Jung remarks that the permanent loss of the anima after the middle of life "means a diminution of vitality, of flexibility, and of human kindness" (in other words, as London puts it, a capitulation to "the grotesque sordidness and rottenness of man-hate and man-meanness"), resulting in "resignation, weariness, sloppiness, irresponsibility, and finally a childish *ramollissement* [or 'softening'] with a tendency to alcohol" (Jung, 1968, 71).

In the sharp contrast between Lucy and Trefethan, London presents a remarkable paradigm of a twentieth-century man's psychic and spiritual predicament, anticipating by more than a decade T. S. Eliot's symbolic treatment of this problem in *The Waste Land* and *The Hollow Men.* With its complex structure and manifold theme—civilization versus wilderness, the age-old human quest for Romance and Eternal Youth (Eden), the symbolic equation of sexual and spiritual commitment, the Jungian process of individuation, woman's liberation—with all these layers of meaning, "The Night-Born" is one of London's richest stories.

Comparable in theme but radically different in setting is "The Red One," written six years after "The Night-Born."[17] This story appeared posthumously in the October 1918 issue of *Cosmopolitan* and shortly thereafter appeared as the title story in a volume of London's tales published by Macmillan—a volume now distinguished as one of the scarcest and most valuable of Jack London first editions. Like the mysterious sphere that lies in its center, the story remained virtually undiscovered by the critics until 1972, when Thomas Clareson reprinted it with a brief afterword in *A Spectrum of Worlds,* where he praises its originality and remarks that London's "treatment of his theme anticipates the science fiction of mid-century. . . ."[18] Since then, however, the "The Red One" has been praised by every critic who has encountered it.

The plot of the story is as follows: An English scientist named Bassett, who has come to the Solomon Islands in quest of a rare giant butterfly, finds himself at the mercy of nature at her infernal worst after his party has been ambushed by headhunters. Through luck and grit he alone manages to survive the attack, only to suffer the lethal agonies of insect bites and tropical fevers as he wanders toward the interior of the island, often delirious and half-conscious, following the distant unearthly sound of some bell or gong:

> There it was! The abrupt liberation of sound, as he timed it with his watch, Bassett likened to the trump of an archangel. Walls of cities, he meditated, might well fall down before so vast and compelling a summons. For the thousandth time vainly he tried to analyze the tone-quality of that enormous peal that dominated the land far into the strongholds of the surrounding tribes. The mountain gorge which was its source rang to the rising tide of it until it brimmed over and flooded earth and sky and air. With the wantonness of a sick man's fancy, he likened it to the mighty cry of some Titan of the Elder World vexed with misery or wrath. Higher and higher it arose, challenging and demanding in such pro-

founds of volume that it seemed intended for ears beyond the narrow confines of the solar system. . . .[19]

After several days of wandering in quest for the source of this unearthly sound, on the verge of death from exhaustion, thirst, and fever, Bassett is rescued by a jungle damsel named Balatta, surely one of the most unforgettable princesses ever to rescue a knight in distress:

> She had been as innocent of garb as Eve before the fig-leaf adventure. Squat and lean at the same time, asymmetrically limbed, string-muscled as if with lengths of cordage, dirt-caked from infancy save for casual showers, she was as unbeautiful a prototype of woman as he, with a scientist's eye, had ever gazed upon. Her breasts advertised at the one time her maturity and youth; and, if by nothing else, her sex was advertised by the one article of finery with which she was adorned, namely a pig's tale, thrust through a hole in her left earlobe. So lately had the tail been severed, that its raw end still oozed blood that dried upon her shoulder like so much candle-droppings. And her face! A twisted and wizened complex of apish features, perforated by upturned, sky-open, Mongolian nostrils, by a mouth that sagged from a huge upper lip and faded precipitately into a retreating chin, and by peering querulous eyes that blinked as blink the eyes of denizens of monkey-cages. (*Curious*, 203–4)

Bassett is saved by this Melanesian Beatrice and carried to her village, where he impresses the bushmen with the power of his 10-gauge shotgun and the magic of compass, watch, burning glass, and matches: "At the last, with due emphasis of solemnity and awfulness, he had killed a young pig with his shotgun and promptly fainted" (*Curious*, 205). Though wasting away from fever, he is determined to survive until he can solve the mystery of great distant sound that emanates from what the natives variously call "The Thunderer," "The God-Voiced," "The Sun Singer," "The Star-Born," and "The Red One." About this mystery, however, they are ominously reticent, revealing only that it is the god of a dozen allied villages and that "it extends back into old history carried down by word of mouth through the generations" (*Curious*, 206). Bassett becomes the companion of old Ngurn, the village priest who is patiently waiting for his head to add to the tribal collection in "the devil-devil house." Bassett attempts to strike up a bargain: he proposes that he'll give Ngurn his head to cure when he dies if first Ngurn takes him to look upon the Red One. But Ngurn counters, "I will have your head anyway when you are dead," adding, with brutal frankness, "Besides, you have not long to live. You are almost a dead man now" (*Curious,* 208). Unable to counter this kind of dead reckoning, Bassett turns to the woman who symbolizes his primitive anima:

> Bassett was a fastidious man. He had never recovered from the initial horror caused by Balatta's female awfulness. Back in England, even at best, the charm of woman, to him, had never been robust. Yet now, resolutely, as only a man can do who is capable of martyring himself for the cause of science, he proceeded to violate all the fineness and delicacy of his nature by making love to the unthinkably disgusting bushwoman. (*Curious,* 208–9)

Bassett's scheme works: Balatta finally succumbs, risking unspeakable tortures and death to guide him in his quest of the Red One. This object is discovered to be a giant sphere, 200 feet in diameter, nestling in a tremendous pit upon a vast plateau within the heart of the island, surrounded by human bones, obscene totemic figures, and, strangely, helmeted figures. Ignoring Balatta's terrified gibberings, the scientist approaches the gigantic red pearl itself, gently touching the iridescent surface, which trembles and vibrates with sound as if a living thing. Then he sees the cause of the great haunting sound that had lured him through the jungles: it is a huge king post, 50 feet long and elaborately carved with helmeted gods, suspended from a tripod to serve as a battering ram against the great hollow sphere. What is the significance of this sphere?

> Here was where Ngurn officiated and functioned religiously for himself and the twelve tribes under him. Bassett laughed aloud, almost with madness, at the thought of this wonderful messenger, winged with intelligence across space, to fall into a bushman stronghold and be worshipped by apelike, man-eating headhunting savages. It was as if God's Word had fallen into the muck mire of the abyss underlying the bottom of hell; as if Jehovah's Commandments had been presented on carved stone to the monkeys of the monkey cage at the Zoo; as if the Sermon on the Mount had been preached in a roaring bedlam of lunatics. (*Curious,* 213)

And what is the meaning of this Word? It is conveyed only through a glass darkly as we follow Bassett to his dying epiphany. Bassett resolves to return to civilization with the news of this great discovery: "Then he would lead an expedition back, and, although the entire population of Guadalcanal be destroyed, extract from the heart of the Red One the message of the world from other worlds" (*Curious*, 215). But he is destined never to leave the island. He grows progressively more feeble as fevers ravage his wasting body. At the end he persuades old Ngurn to take him to the Red One so that he may be ritually beheaded while the archangelic tones of the great sphere are still ringing in his ears. He experiences a profound if momentary insight even as the priest's axe descends.

> And for that instant, ere the end, there fell upon Bassett the shadow of the Unknown, a sense of impending marvel of the rending of walls before the imaginable. Almost, when he knew the blow had started and just ere the edge of steel bit the flesh and nerves, it seemed that he gazed upon the serene face of the Medusa, Truth—And, simultaneous with the bite of the steel on the onrush of the dark, in a flashing instant of fancy, he saw the vision of his head turning slowly, always turning, in the devil-devil house beside the breadfruit tree. (*Curious*, 218)

So it would seem that, like Virginia Woolf's Lily Briscoe, Bassett has had his moment of vision. But what of the readers? Have we shared that illuminating moment? Feelingly, perhaps; knowingly, perhaps not. Certainly, critics' opinions on the ending differ greatly. Thomas Clareson concludes that Bassett's only answer is "the *cri de coeur* of a man appalled by a mechanistic universe governed by determinism." Billy Collins says that Bassett's final vision is that of "the heart of darkness." Andrew Sinclair, on the other hand, writes that Bassett's "final discovery is not that of Conrad's Kurtz, 'The horror! The horror!' It is [instead] another mystery." Ellen Brown places a quite positive construction upon Bassett's final vision, concluding that "The Red One does indeed contain the secrets of eternal life, and this is the revelation of Bassett at his death—he sees 'the serene face of the Medusa, Truth' and envisions the curing of his head in the devil-devil house. This is his moment of realization. He has been initiated [and] will be reborn."[20] The Medusa is indeed the key: Like Balatta and like the Red One itself, she is horrifying, she is female, and, for Bassett she is the Truth he has so assiduously avoided. Bassett is brought face-to-face at last with the mystery of the Feminine, and she is part of himself. For the rational twentieth-century materialist, this recognition is both "the horror" and the Pearl of Great Price.

On the broadest level, perhaps, *mystery* itself is an answer to the riddle posed by this great red interterrestrial sphinxlike sphere. Significantly, only a few months before London began writing "The Red One" he sent his most famous fan letter to Conrad: "I had just begun to write when I read your first early work," confessed London; "I have merely madly appreciated you and communicated my appreciation to my friends through all these years" (*Letters*, 1467).[21] Conrad's influence is pervasive in "The Red One," not only in the atmosphere, which is reminiscent of "Heart of Darkness," but also in the hero's quest for some glimpse of ultimate reality. An essential difference between the heroes, however, is that Bassett, who is described as "a scientist first, a humanist afterward," lacks the compassionate sensibility and the fine neural balance that make Marlow one of the great characters in modern literature. London might use Marlow's words to ask his reader, "Do you see him? Do you see the story? Do you see anything? It seems to me I am trying to tell you a dream—making a vain attempt, because no relation of a dream can convey the dream-sensation, that comingling of absurdity, surprise, and bewilderment in a tremor of struggling revolt, that notion of being captured by the incredible which is the very essence of dreams. . . ." Marlow's observation is startingly like that of Jung's discussion of the "visionary mode" in *Modern Man in Search of a Soul:* "It is a strange something that derives its existence from the hinterland of man's mind. . . . A great work of art is like a dream . . . it does not explain itself and is never unequivocal" (Jung 1933, 156, 171).

While "The Red One" does not explain itself, Jungian theory, especially the theory of archetypes, sheds significant light on London's mysterious work of art. Bassett represents consciousness in modern man—a consciousness characterized by disregard for the realm of the spirit and too much regard for the machine and scientific worlds—journeying into the jungle of the collective unconscious. He has come of his own volition, in search of the butterfly, a mandala symbol for the soul, and at last experiences the epiphany of the Great Round. This Great Round is the ouroboric, androgynous beginning and end, the repository of wisdom and rebirth.[22]

In a coincident interpretation, James Kirsch perceives the gigantic red sphere as a symbol of the Self—and as a projection of London's own quest for self-fulfillment.[23] Kirsch's perception reinforces Charmian London's inference linking the composition of "The Red One" with her husband's discovery of Jung. In this story "is evidenced the author's profound meditation upon the reaching out of the most primordial toward the most cosmic—all in stride with his study of race consciousness. Sometimes I wonder if it can be possible, in the ponderings of the dying scientist, Bassett, that Jack London revealed more of himself than he would be willing to admit—or else, who knows? more of himself than he himself realized" (*Book,* II, 336). It is likely that London did, indeed, reveal more of himself than he realized in "The Red One." He was himself a sick and dying man, like Bassett in this respect at least, when he composed the story; and like Bassett, London, too, was obsessed in his desire to reach out and to touch the great cosmic pearl of Truth—which for both of them manifests itself in what Walt Whitman celebrates in "Out of the Cradle Endlessly Rocking" as "the Word final, superior to all"—the word *Death.* But Kirsch also suggests that London's discovery transcends his personal quest for ultimate reality, concluding that "What Jack London observed in discovering the mysterious sphere, The Red One, was an event in the collective unconscious. [His story] is an accurate picture of American psychology and of Western man as a whole . . ." (Kirsch, 153–54).

Still further illumination may be shed on this story by examining the work of another of Jung's protégés: Erich Neumann's *The Great Mother.* Neumann underscores the transformative aspects of this complex archetype, corroborating the reading of "The Red One" as a story of individuation and spiritual rebirth. London's protagonist begins as a sterile, dehumanized man of science; the metonymy for his hypermasculine rationality is his phallic shotgun. As the Medusa figure and other female imagery in the story suggests, Bassett represents the pathologically over-conscious twentieth-century man who has not only rejected but who would willfully violate the vitalizing force of the unconscious, symbolized in the Great Round as feminine. This force has been universally symbolized in the complex image of the Great Mother, an archetype that variously manifests itself as anima-figure, Sophia figure, Good Mother, Earth Mother, and Terrible Mother. To Bassett the anima-figure is merely something to be used to advance his own scientific knowledge, even though it would mean her death. Thus abused, the Great Mother assumes her most terrifying aspect and Bassett progressively weakens. The following statement from Erich Neumann relates directly to Bassett's long, confused journey into the center of the island in his quest to find the source of the great sound that calls him: "The labyrinthine way is always the first part of the night sea voyage, the descent of the male following the sun into the devouring underworld, into the deathly womb of the Terrible Mother." And, even more telling, as we seek for the meaning of the last scene in London's story, is this comment by Neumann: "The petrifying gaze of Medusa belongs to the province of the Terrible Great Goddess, for to be rigid is to be dead. . . . The Gorgon is the counterpart of the life womb; she is the womb of death or the night sun."[24]

We should bear in mind, however, that "the serene face of the Medusa, Truth," is simultaneous with another image in Bassett's final moment: "the vision of his head turning slowly, always turning, in the devil-devil house beside the breadfruit tree" (*Curious,* 218), Counterpoised against the image of stasis and death is a rich cluster of dynamic symbols that connote affirmation. J. E. Cirlot notes that the head symbol "coalesces with that of the sphere as a symbol of Oneness," further suggesting that decapitation symbolizes "man's discovery of the independence of the spiritual principle, residing in the head, as opposed to the vital principle represented by the body as a whole." The house is equated with "the repository of all wisdom, that is, tradition itself." And "the symbolism of the tree denotes the life of the cosmos: its consistence, growth, proliferation, generative and regenerative processes. It stands for inexhaustible life, and is therefore equivalent to a symbol of immortality" (*Cirlot,* 134–35, 146, 328).

In view of these remarks, it would seem clear that through the force of the Great Mother and her priest, old Ngurn, Bassett has in truth been vitally transformed. The overrational scientist has been purged; the humanist remains. In the moment before he gives the signal for the axe to fall, it occurs to him that he might play one final grisly joke, depriving the old man of his precious head by simply blowing it off with the shotgun that lies beside him: "But why cheat him? Was Bassett's next thought. Headhunting, cannibal, beast of a human that was as much ape as human, nevertheless Old Ngurn had, according to his lights, played squarer than square. Ngurn was in himself a forerunner of ethics and contract, of consideration, and gentleness in man. No, Bassett decided; it would be a ghastly pity and an act of dishonor to cheat the old fellow at the last. His head was Ngurn's, and Ngurn's to cure it would be" (*Curious,* 218). Bassett has come a long way from his safe laboratory and from his willingness to sacrifice the entire population of Guadalcanal for the sake of scientific knowledge. His dramatic shift from contempt for the "savages" to dealing with them in a spirit of fair play is an example of London's own evolving attitudes toward "the other," whether of race or gender. The final scene is, consequently, not one of

despair but one of redemption. His head has indeed become Ngurn's—
and will be "cured" in a deeper spiritual sense.

"The Red One" is a treasure trove of symbolic riches; it also happens
to be an astonishingly prophetic work. Not only does it anticipate such
first-contact stories as Arthur C. Clarke's *2001,* but, by weird coincidence, it takes place on an island that would become the setting for one
of the bloodiest battles of World War II: Gaudalcanal. Moreover,
Bassett's own holocaustal attitude prefigures the horrors of Auschwitz
and Hiroshima. But most significantly, London's story—read as an
archetypal parable—subtly indicates the way by which modern man
may find his soul: by reconciling himself with the Great Mother, with his
true Self, and thereby with his fellow men and women. Thus the ultimate revelation of the "The Red One" is not "The horror! The horror!"
but, rather, "The wonder! The wonder!"

Four months after finishing "The Red One," London started to work
on "The Water Baby," the last of the seven Hawaiian stories that constitute his volume titled *On the Makaloa Mat,* and the last story he ever
wrote. This posthumously published volume contains some of London's
richest and narratively most complex stories. They are almost all dialogue, and voice is controlled by native Hawaiian and women speakers,
while the hearers are white newcomers to Hawaii. In this volume, in stories such as "On the Makaloa Mat," "When Alice Sold Her Soul," and
"Shin Bones," the personal psychological quest for wholeness goes forward as the voice of "the other" speaks for tolerance in the present-day
community as well as for connection with the community of the mystic
past. "The Water Baby" is the best of these tales. If *The Acorn-Planter*
may be called the last will and testament to London's agrarian vision,
then "The Water Baby" should be recognized as the final testament to
his spiritual as well as communal vision. This is another of his most
unusual stories—again totally unlike anything he had written before. It
is also one of the most revealing pieces of fiction he ever created.

The setting or "frame" for this narrative is a two-man fishing excursion; however, there is virtually no physical action in the story proper—
only one incident, in fact, when one of the two characters—an intrepid
Hawaiian native, past 70 years old—nonchalantly dives to a depth of 40
feet to overcome a nine-foot devilfish with his bare hands (and teeth!).
The essential action is a dialogue between the young man who narrates
the story, named John Lakana (Jack London's Hawaiian name), and the
old native fisherman, named Kohokumu (whose name connotes "tree of
knowledge").[25] The old man has evidently spent the previous night in

revelry at a funeral celebration and shows no ill effects whatsoever, while his younger companion is suffering from a terrible headache. Imperturbably, Kohokumu persists in baiting his world-weary companion with his "interminable chanting of the deeds and adventures of Maui," the Promethean demigod of Polynesia—until Lakana can endure it no longer and changes the subject:

> "You were disgraceful last night at the funeral," I headed him off. "I heard all about it. You made much noise. You sang till everybody else was deaf. You insulted the son of the widow. You drank swipes like a pig. Swipes are not good for your extreme age. Some day you will wake up dead. You ought to be a wreck to-day—"
>
> "Ha!" he chuckled. "And you, who drank no swipes, who was a babe unborn when I was already an old man, who went to bed last night with the sun and the chickens—this day you are a wreck. Explain me that. My ears are as thirsty to listen as was my throat thirsty last night. And here to-day, behold, I am, as that Englishman who came here in his yacht used to say I am in fine form, in devilish fine form. (*Makaloa*, 149)

Of course Lakana, London's persona for the logical positivist, cannot explain it and therefore resorts to ad hominem tactics:

> "Only one thing is clear, and that is that the devil doesn't want you. Report of your singing has gone before you."
>
> "No," he pondered the idea carefully. "It is not that. The devil will be glad for my coming, for I have some very fine songs for him, and scandals and old gossips of the high *aliis* that will make him scratch his sides. So let me explain to you the secret of my birth. The Sea is my mother. I was born in a double canoe, during a Kona gale, in the channel of Kahoolawe. From her, the Sea, my mother, I received my strength. Whenever I return to her arms, as for a breast clasp, as I have returned this day, I grow strong again and immediately. She, to me, is the milk giver, the life source—"
>
> "Shades of Antaeus!" thought I.
>
> "Some day," old Kohokumu rambled on, "when I am really old, I shall be reported of men as drowned in the sea. This will be an idle thought of men. In truth, I shall have returned into the arms of my mother, there to rest under the heart of her breast until the second birth of me, when I shall emerge into the sun a flashing youth of splendor like Maui himself when he was golden young."
>
> "A queer religion," I commented.
>
> "When I was younger I muddled my poor head over queerer religions," old Kohokumu retorted. "But listen, O Young Wise One, to my

elderly wisdom. This I know: as I grow old I seek less for the truth from
without me, and find more of the truth from within me. Why have I
thought this thought of my return to my mother and of my rebirth from
my mother into the sun? You do not know. I do not know, save that,
without whisper of man's voice or printed word, without prompting from
otherwhere, this thought has arisen from within me, from the deeps of
me that are as deep as the sea. . . . Is this thought that I have thought a
dream?"

    "Perhaps it is you that are a dream," I laughed. "And that I and
sky and sea and the iron-hard land are dreams, all dreams.". . .

    "There is much more in dreams than we know," he assured me
with great solemnity.

    "Dreams go deep, all the way down, maybe to before the begin-
ning. . . ." (*Makaloa,* 150–52)

Praising this story for its "artistic elegance" and its "simple, lyrical
beauty," James McClintock explains that in the dialogue between the
two principal characters, London explicitly links Kohokumu with the
oedipal myths—that of the sun (the hero and libido energy) setting
(dying) in the sea (the womb) and rising in the morning (being reborn),"
adding that the "process of returning to the earth for sustenance symbolizes periodic acts of introversion . . ." (McClintock, 162–63). Yet it is
a Jungian, not a Freudian model that best describes London's fiction.

The title for the story comes from a folk tale told by Kohokumu to
John Lakana, who insists that he likes the old man's "whoppers" better
than his godawful singing. "It is too bad you are sick, and you so
young," Kohokumu cheerily responds. "And I shall not sing any more. I
shall tell you something you do not know and have never heard; something that is no dream and no whopper, but is what I know to have happened" (153). His tale concerns an 11-year-old boy named Keikiwai
(meaning "Water Baby"), who outwits 40 sharks in catching lobsters for
the king's luau. The lagoon in which the finest lobsters can be found is
infested by 40 ferocious sharks; and several natives have been killed or
maimed in trying to fish there. However, Keikiwai, who knows the language of the sea creatures, says a prayer to Moku-halii, the shark-god,
then declares for all the sharks to hear: "I shall now dive for a lobster for
the king. And no hurt shall befall me, because the shark with the short-
est tail is my friend and will protect me" (*Makaloa,* 156). He then picks
up a large lava rock and tosses it into the water with a big splash. All the
sharks rush to the point of the splash; and while they are thus diverted,
Keikiwai dives in and catches a fat lobster for the king's feast. When

they realize they have been tricked, the sharks attack and devour the shortest-tailed member of their group. This procedure is repeated until only one very large shark is left—and the natives find him dead on the beach the next morning, burst open from overeating.

Before his skeptical companion can debunk his tale, Kohokumu continues:

> "Hold, O Lakana!" he checked the speech that rushed to my tongue. "I know what next you would say. You would say that with my own eyes I did not see this, and therefore that I do not know what I have been telling you. But I do know, and I can prove it. My father's father knew the grandson of the Water Baby's father's uncle. Also, there, on the rocky point to which I point my finger now, is where the Water Baby stood and dived. I have dived for lobsters there myself. It is a great place for lobsters. Also, and often, have I seen sharks there, on the bottom, as I should know, for I have counted them, are the thirty-nine lava rocks thrown in by the Water Baby as I described."
>
> "But—" I began.
>
> "Ha!" he baffled me. . . .
>
> "Of course I know. The thirty-nine lava rocks are still there. You can count them any day for yourself. Of course I know, and I know for a fact." (*Makaloa,* 159)

McClintock points out the precision with which London used the symbols Jung had identified with libido renewal and psychic maturing in his *Psychology of the Unconscious:* "The Water Baby (libido energy, since he speaks the fish language and 'the fish as a libido symbol') conquers the sharks (subconscious anxieties, an 'incest barrier' that denotes 'treasure guardian' and connotes death) and captures the lobster delicacies (the 'treasure difficult of attainment') and thus stays the wrath of the King (avoids destruction and reaffirms life)." However, because of Lakana's reluctance to swallow Kohokumu's fable hook, line, and sinker, McClintock concludes, "The implied tension between civilized skepticism and a natural affirmation of life remains unresolved" (*McClintock,* 163).

"The Water Baby" may also be described as dramatizing London's attempt to come to terms with two radically different modes of approaching the truth: what philosophers call "epistemological" knowledge (knowledge as an objective, single truth) in favor of "hermeneutics" (knowledge as an interpretation amongst other interpretations). His discovery of Jung's work appears to have furnished London with an artistic regeneration that was not so much a positivistic attempt to refute determinism as a deeper and more sophisticated sense of the ambiguity generated by a psychological approach to self-knowledge. At the end of "The Water Baby" the reader does not know whether the protagonist's mind has truly been changed, nor the limitations of his worldview transcended. The ambiguity appears to signal London's doubting of the undifferentiated "self" as he had earlier conceived it; and the doubt may mark the greatest contribution Jung made to London's work. Because Lakana's last word in the story is an ambiguous "But—," we cannot know for sure whether he has taken the old fisherman's wisdom to heart—yet this tentative ending further enhances the story's thematic emphasis upon the vital necessity of our embracing an open, hermeneutic knowledge (Reesman, 1988, 205).[26] We may contrast the communal, mythic weltanschauung represented by old Kohokumu not only with John Lakana's modern-day skepticism but also with the fatal epistemological individualism personified in the protagonists of "To Build a Fire" and *Martin Eden* (both of which, significantly, were composed after London had visited Hawaii in 1907 during the voyage of the *Snark*). On both the personal and social levels, "The Water Baby" embodies a Jungian insistence on the duality of self-knowledge in the process of the healthy individuation of the psyche; it suggests furthermore that if one side is dominant, it is the unconscious. When the unconscious is not addressed, it is perceived as ridiculous or even frightening, but when its place in the dialogue between consciousness and unconsciousness is admitted, this provides the psyche—individual or collective—with new energy and understanding of itself.

London completed "The Water Baby" on 2 October 1916, just a few weeks before his death. Charmian remarks his deep absorption in Jungian theory at this time: "Throughout Dr. Jung's chapter on 'Symbolism of Mother and Rebirth,' there are penciled indications of Jack's grasp of the meaning of folk-lore and mythology of recorded time. Also the comprehension of how to raise lower desires to higher expressions. He has underscored Jesus's challenge to Nicodemus, cited by Jung: 'Think not carnally or thou art carnal, but think symbolically and then thou art spirit'" (*Book*, II, 354). This is an extraordinary transition—*transformation* would be the better word, except that the process was not completed—for a writer who had prided himself throughout his career on being a materialistic monist and who had energetically disavowed any pretensions toward the spiritual. Yet, as we have consistently seen, London was moving in this direction all along—what one finds in "The Water Baby" is thus a culmination of his lifelong search for spirit in the physical world. Charmian also quotes the following passage from Beatrice Hinkle's Introduction to Jung's book, annotated by London, who made a point of repeating the final italicized statement to her astonished ears:

> The value of self-consciousness lies in the fact that man is enabled to reflect upon himself and learn to understand the true origin and significance of his actions and opinions, that he may adequately value the real level of his development and avoid being self-deceived and therefore inhibited from finding his biological adaptation. He need no longer be unconscious of the motives underlying his actions or hide himself behind a changed exterior, in other words, be merely a series of reactions to stimuli, as the mechanists have it, *but he may to a certain extent become a self-creating and self-determining being.* (*Book,* II, 357)

Clearly, far from being a burnt-out case, London was undergoing a creative and philosophical metamorphosis during the final months of his life. The evidence is unmistakable. Somehow in a profound way the influences of Jung and Hawaii synchronized to work a sea change into something rich and strange. Jack London the hardcore materialist was becoming Jack London the spiritual idealist. John Lakana merges into old Kohokumu, moving toward his rebirth into the sun from the Sea his Mother. Perhaps the greatest tragedy of London's career is that he could not have lived a few more years to complete this transformation and to write of further insights from his newfound world.

Chapter Six

A Man for Many Literary Seasons

In 1936, 20 years after Jack London's death, critic Arthur Hobson Quinn wrote what he thought would be London's literary epitaph: "It is almost certain that his vogue is passing, for there is something impermanent in the very nature of the literature of violence."[1] That much of the world's great literature was "literature of violence" had momentarily slipped Professor Quinn's mind. Critics of the succeeding generations— New Critics, they were called—were quite willing to see London buried and forgotten because they were attuned to the exquisite sensibility of Henry James, to the fine cerebral verse of T. S. Eliot, and to the psycholinguistic complexities of James Joyce. London seemed an insufferable boor. His name was therefore discreetly expunged from college textbooks, and he was reduced to a sentence or two in the literary histories. His radical Socialism and, perhaps, his later portrayals of cultural relativism—even feminist ideas—also contributed to his poor standing with traditional critics.

He might have been forgotten entirely, except for a couple of nagging reminders: Jack London titles kept selling on the popular market, and a handful of academic critics refused to subscribe to the New Critical gentility. Even during the 1950s, at the crest of the New Critical wave, while most sensible graduate students devoted their interpretive energies to established figures such as Crane, Hemingway, and Faulkner, a half-dozen critical apostates gave London the obscure immortality of *Dissertation Abstracts.*[2] But all of this began to change in the 1960s. King Hendricks published two important monographs at Utah State University: *Creator and Critic: A Controversy between Jack London and Philo M. Buck, Jr.* (1961), and *Jack London: Master Craftsman of the Short Story* (1966). Richard O'Connor's *Jack London: A Biography* (1964), though flawed both factually and interpretively, was widely reviewed and brought considerable attention to a writer who had been virtually forgotten by the literati. *Letters from Jack London,* edited by King Hendricks and Irving Shepard, provided not only further publicity the following year but also a reliable and accessible source of primary materials for London scholars. Two additional basic works were published in 1966: *Jack London and the Klondike* by distinguished scholar Franklin Walker and the monumental *Jack London: A Bibliography,* compiled by Hensley C. Woodbridge et al. In 1967, Professor Woodbridge also inaugurated *The Jack London Newsletter,* thus giving London scholars a ready and respectable forum—so that *American Literary Scholarship,* which had given Jack London less than a full sentence in its first issue (1963), was now devoting several full pages of each annual volume to scholarly and critical works about London.

As we noted in the preface, the London Revival ("nascence" might be the more accurate term) hit full stride in the 1970s. In addition to the works mentioned in our preface, many others from 1970 on have already become indispensable. Another basic reference tool, *The Fiction of Jack London: A Chronological Bibliography,* compiled by Dale Walker and James Sisson, appeared in 1972; and in 1973 Dale Walker published his pioneering monograph on London's fantasy fiction, *The Alien Worlds of Jack London.* A revised and enlarged edition of the Woodbridge bibliography appeared in 1973. The original edition of this Twayne U. S. Authors Series *Jack London,* in 1974, was the first book-length critical study of London's work. Nineteen seventy-six, the centennial of London's birth, was a banner year for London studies, highlighted by special issues of *Modern Fiction Studies, Western American Literature,* and *The Pacific Historian.* Also in 1976 London studies gained the added benefit of the creation of the Jack London Foundation with its informative newsletter and various activities promoting interest in London's life and works. The foundation's executive director, Russ Kingman, established a research center in Glen Ellen, and subsequently published *A Pictorial Life of Jack London.* During the following year three biographies appeared: Robert Barltrop's *Jack London: The Man, The Writer, the Rebel;* Irving Stone's *Jack London,* a revised and enlarged edition of *Sailor on Horseback;* and Andrew Sinclair's *Jack: A Biography of Jack London.* Joan Sherman published her reference guide and also organized London sessions for the 1978 and 1979 conferences of the Modern Language Association (MLA). Ray Wilson Ownbey's *Jack London: Essays in Criticism,* which appeared in 1978, confirmed the substantial scholarly work that had been published in the academic journals during the past decade. Further evidence of the viability of London scholarship was manifested the following year in the publication of Dale Walker's *No Mentor but Myself: A Collection of Articles, Essays, Reviews, and Letters, by Jack London, on Writing and Writers* and Richard Etulain's *Jack London on the Road: The Tramp Diary and Other Hobo Writings.*

London scholarship continued at a healthy pace in the 1980s. In 1981 *Sporting Blood: Selections from Jack London's Great Sports Writing,* edited with instructive commentaries by Howard Lachtman, gave new insight into another neglected facet of London's creativity. Donald Pizer's two-volume Library of America edition of London's works, published in 1982, furnished—at last—an accurate and readily available text for five novels, three books of nonfiction, 25 short stories, and four socialistic essays. Also in 1982 volume 12 of the *Dictionary of Literary Biography: American Realists and Naturalists,* edited by Pizer and Earl J. Harbert, granted major status to London, according him equal space with Howells, James, and Twain. In the same year the University of North Carolina Press issued Joan Hedrick's *Solitary Comrade: Jack London and His Work.* In 1983 appeared *Dearest Greek: Jack and Charmian London's Presentation Inscriptions to George Sterling,* edited with an introductory essay and notes by Stanley Wertheim and Sal Noto. Carolyn Johnston's study of London's Socialism, *Jack London—An American Radical?,* appeared in 1984, as did Gorman Beauchamp's monograph on London's science fiction and fantasy, *Jack London* (Starmont Reader's Guide 15); at the end of that year the MLA devoted three sessions to London's work featuring papers by such veteran scholars as Sam Baskett, Donald Pizer, and Earl Wilcox. London was also featured in sessions at other conferences, including the College English Association (CEA), the American Literature Association, and the Popular Culture Association.[3] On 11 January 1986 (the Saturday before London's birthday), at a special ceremony in Glen Ellen, California, the U.S. Postal Service issued a Jack London stamp in its Great American Series. Two years later, Clarice Stasz published her perceptive psychological study, *American Dreamers: Charmian and Jack London.*

Especially significant during this past decade has been the growing interest in London on the part of academic presses. In 1988 the Stanford University Press published the three-volume edition of *The Letters of Jack London,* and in the same year the University of Pennsylvania Press issued Bert Bender's *Sea Brothers: The Tradition of American Sea Fiction from "Moby-Dick" to the Present,* which includes an important chapter on London. London is becoming an essential part of broad studies of American literature; he is interestingly treated, for example, in Mark Seltzer's *Bodies and Machines* and June Howard's *Form and History in American Literary Naturalism.* London's growing reputation with literary critics is demonstrated not only by the way he is now included as a matter of course in these works and others (including, for example, Forrest G. Robinson's *Having It Both Ways: Self-Subversion in Western Popular Classics,* Alfred

Hornung's essay on London in a collection entitled *An American Empire: Expansionist Cultures and Policies, 1881–1917,* Eric Homberger's *American Writers and Radical Politics, 1900–39: Equivocal Commitments,* Lee Clark Mitchell's *Determined Fictions: American Literary Naturalism,* and Joseph A. Boone's essay in the collection *Gender Studies: New Directions in Feminist Criticism* and in his subsequent book *Tradition Counter Tradition*), but also by the greater *depth* of the analysis accorded to his works.[4]

The nineties have seen a burst of London scholarship. Macmillan has issued a new edition of 50 short stories; Oxford University Press has included several volumes of London's works in its World's Classics Series; and Stanford University Press has released a three-volume edition of London's complete short stories to complement its edition of the London letters. Scholarly tools such as Kingman's *Jack London: A Definitive Chronology* and James Williams's "The Composition of Jack London's Writings" (*American Literary Realism* 23, 2 [Winter 1991]: 64–86) have appeared. New editions of hard-to-find works such as *The Kempton-Wace Letters,* edited by Douglas Robillard (New College and University Press, 1990), are available. And critical studies continue to appear, including Mark E. Zamen's *Standing Room Only: Jack London's Controversial Career as a Public Speaker* and Tony Williams's *Jack London: The Movies,* as well as scholarly articles that reflect new critical and theoretical approaches, particularly narratological, feminist, psychoanalytic, and new historicist.

In 1990, the Jack London Society was formed as an international organization of scholars; the society publishes a newsletter, *The Call,* and sponsors panels at the American Literature Association Conference and elsewhere. It held its first Jack London Society International Symposium in the summer of 1992 in Sonoma, California, and its second in the fall of 1994 at the Huntington Library. Such noteworthy recognition would seem to confirm, at last, London's status as a major figure in American literary history.

His Significance

The Great World Author.   Notwithstanding the slowness of our own critical establishment to grant Jack London full literary status, he has long been regarded abroad as a major figure—even, according to some, as "America's Most Powerful Writer." We mention in our preface that *The Call of the Wild* may be fairly considered America's greatest world novel. But we should add that London's international appeal derives from more than this one masterpiece. New foreign editions of such

works as *The Sea-Wolf, White Fang, The Iron Heel, Martin Eden,* and selected
stories have continued to appear and to elicit critical praise for nearly three
generations. As early as 1914, for example, Danish scholar Georg Brandes
called London the best of the new twentieth-century American writers,
remarking particularly on his originality and his "singularly forcible" style,
"free from all affectation." During the 1920s, Anatole France asserted that
"London had that particular genius which perceives what is hidden from
the common herd, and possessed a special knowledge enabling him to
anticipate the future." Both George Orwell and the great Argentine
author Jorge Luis Borges have edited collections of London's stories,
Orwell citing his genius for "rousing pity and indignation" and Borges
noting the literary bond between London and Hemingway. More recently,
London's reputation has become securely established in Japan with the for-
mation of the Jack London Society of Japan under the leadership of Shinko
Yamazaki and Eiji Tsujii, translator of more than a half-dozen London masterpieces into Japanese. And during this same period London has received
significant scholarly attention in China. Beijing University Professor Li
Shuyan, who has recently translated and edited a collection of critical
essays on London, notes that "Whatever happens in the critical world,
London will go on enjoying the admiration of the Chinese readers. Martin
Eden and the many heroes of London's stories of the North will always be
an encouraging force to those who are fighting against adversities, and
who believe the worth of a man lies in doing, creating and achieving." In
Russia, London has long been the foreign writer most widely read—not so
much for his political ideas as for what his celebration of what Vil Bykov
calls "the man of noble spirit." Bykov has compared him favorably with
Tolstoy and Chekhov, adding that "London brought to the Russian reader
a world full of romanticism and vigor, and the reader came to love him."
This same "world full of romanticism and vigor" may account considerably
for London's universal popularity.[5]

The Social Crusader.   He was "a born protestant." Writing for the
working class directly from his own experiences, he spoke with authority about the "Submerged Tenth." He was the first writer to depict the
hobo with genuine understanding.[6] He also pioneered in the sympathetic, realistic treatment of the convict. Such works as *The People of the
Abyss* and *The Road* possess social and historical significance apart from
any literary considerations. The same may be said of much of London's
fantasy and "social science fiction"—for example, *The Iron Heel* and *The*

Star Rover. As often happens with dystopian fiction, London's apocalyptic prophecies may have been self-defeating in that many of the social ills he decried have been subsequently remedied—but the most fundamental have not. His protests against the enormities perpetrated by capitalist overlords may sound as foreign to modern America as the term proletarian itself; nevertheless, many of the social and economic inequities he attacked still plague our society—and his concerns with pollution, our penal system, and the demands of the The Third World are even more immediate. Finally, much of the critical attention he is enjoying today focuses on the timely cultural concerns of race, class, and gender so radically approached by London throughout his career.

The Folk Writer.   Jack London is the archetypal "kosmos" envisioned by Walt Whitman—the poet/seer embraced as lovingly by his people as he has embraced them. He has achieved a popularity so wide and so long-standing that he seems to have become a permanent legend in the American heritage. Other popular writers have become household words in the American common culture—for example, Horatio Alger, O. Henry, Zane Grey. But in the combining of a sustained popular appeal with serious literary merit and heroic personal stature Jack London is comparable to only one other figure in American literature—Mark Twain—and even that great writer did not excite the American yearnings for romantic adventure as profoundly as London—in short, theirs are complementary appeals. London's variations on the complex theme of the American Dream place much of his work in the mainstream of our cultural history. Martin Eden anticipates the disenchanted success novels of Theodore Dreiser, Sinclair Lewis, and Scott Fitzgerald. *Burning Daylight, The Valley of the Moon*, and *The Little Lady of the Big House* dramatize the archetypal tensions between civilization and the wilderness, the machine versus the garden, masculinity and feminity. For London as for Whitman, the artistic Self contains multitudes.

The Literary Craftsman.   No American writer has been more versatile or more audacious. The range of subjects treated in London's fiction is simply astonishing: agronomy, alcoholism, androgyny, animal training (and rights), astral projection, bull-fighting, leprosy, political corruption, psychology (animal as well as human), racial exploitation, revolution, spiritualism, surfing, war, and the writing game itself—to mention only a few of his more noteworthy topics. And no American writer has given sympathetic voice to so many different types of humanity: for example, the Native American (in *Children of the Frost* and other Northland tales), Polynesian (in "The Heathen" and in the Hawaiian stories), and Melanesian (in "Mauki" and other *South Sea Tales*); the displaced Chinese (in "The Chinago" and "Chun Ah Chun"); the revolutionist (in "The Mexican") the old boxer (in "A Piece of Steak"), and the New Woman (in *Burning Daylight* and *The Valley of the Moon*). Especially notable are dialogic voices London provided for his female characters, which, like the various types of community he strove to create in his fiction, speak to a new understanding of human diversity. Even at the height of his career, while magazine editors were clamoring for his manly adventure stories, he persisted in trying the new and the different in brilliant but virtually unmarketable pieces like "Samuel," "Told in the Drooling Ward," and "War." Guided by the principles of sincerity, functionalism, and imaginative Realism, London ushered in a new prose for the modern fictionist—clear, straightforward, uncluttered, imagistic—a style particularly well-suited to the short story and to the depiction of violence and physical action. He was a major force in establishing for fiction a respectable middle ground between the gutter and the drawing room, and his efforts prepared the way for the new generations of Hemingway, Ring Lardner, and Norman Mailer.[7] A consummate storyteller, he is gifted with the power to modulate narrative tempo so that his reader is often spellbound. While even his best work occasionally suffers from stylistic lapses, even his worst work is readable. If he is sometimes clumsy, he is seldom dull. He is capable of moments of great lyric intensity. He possesses, moreover, an exceptional feeling for irony, cosmic as well as dramatic. Such stories as "To Build a Fire," "The Night-Born," and "The Red One" are masterpieces of short fiction. And even such longer works as *The Sea-Wolf* and *White Fang* have become popular classics.

But London's ultimate greatness derives from his "primordial vision"—the mythopoeic force that animates his finest creations and to which we respond without fully understanding why. To echo the wisdom of old Kohokumu in "The Water Baby," we might remind ourselves that there is much more in dreams—and in great literary art—than we know. They truly "go deep, all the way down, maybe to before the beginning."

His Credo

If in the final analysis Jack London still eludes us, perhaps it is only fitting and proper. After all, he is one of our great folk heroes, and our avatars are traditionally invested with certain mysteries. Perhaps, also, he himself came closest to giving us the key to the Jack London legend when he wrote:

> I would rather be ashes than dust!
> I would rather that my spark should burn out
>   in a brilliant blaze than it should be
>   stifled by dry-rot.
> I would rather be a superb meteor, every atom
>   of me in magnificent glow, than a sleepy
>   and permanent planet.
> The proper function of man is to live, not to
>   exist.
> I shall not waste my days in trying to prolong
>   them.
> I shall use my time.[8]

Notes and References

Preface

    1. The 27 Jack London Scrapbooks in the Henry E. Huntington Library contain more than 5,000 pages of newspaper and magazine clippings about London.

    2. The number of languages into which London's books have been translated now exceeds 80, from Albanian to Ukranian. In 1992 Hensley Woodbridge compiled "A Survey of Book Length Translations of the Works of Jack London Based on the *Index Translationum,* 1975–1985," an unpublished monograph presented at the First Biennial Jack London Society Symposium, August 2–4, 1992, Sonoma, Calif. There one finds that London is still one of the most popular American writers in Europe, and some countries have far more of London's work in print than does the United States.

Chapter One

    1. Dixon Wecter, *The Hero in America* (Ann Arbor, Mich.: University of Michigan Press, 1963), 16.

    2. See Clell T. Peterson, "The Jack London Legend," *American Book Collector* 13 (January 1963):23–27; and Kenneth S. Lynn, *The Dream of Success* (Boston: Houghton Mifflin, 1955), 3–10, 75–118.

    3. Alfred Kazin, *On Native Grounds: An Interpretation of Modern American Prose Literature* (New York: Reynal & Hitchcock, 1942), 111.

    4. *The Letters of Jack London,* ed. Earle Labor, Robert C. Leitz III, and I. Milo Shepard, 3 vols. (Stanford: Stanford University Press, 1988), 26; hereafter cited in text as *Letters.* This letter is addressed to Mabel Applegarth, the refined young woman whom Jack had met in 1895. She became his first great love and was later used as the model for Ruth Morse in his autobiographical novel *Martin Eden.*

    5. Henry Steele Commager also observes: "On the one side lies an America predominately agricultural; concerned with domestic problems; conforming, intellectually at least, to the political, economic, and moral principles inherited from the seventeenth and eighteenth centuries—an America still in the making, physically and socially; an America on the whole self-confident, self-reliant, and conscious of its unique character and of a unique destiny. On the other side lies the modern America, predominantly urban and industrial; inextricably involved in world economy and politics; troubled with the problems that had long been thought peculiar to the Old World; experiencing profound changes in population, social institutions, economy, and technology; and

trying to accommodate its traditional institutions and habits of thought to conditions new and in part alien." *The American Mind: An Interpretation of American Thought and Character Since the 1880's* (New Haven, Conn.: Yale University Press, 1950), 41.

6. See also Frederick Jackson Turner, "The Significance of the Frontier in American History," *The Turner Thesis Concerning the Role of the Frontier in American History,* ed. George Rogers Taylor, rev. ed. (Boston: D. C. Heath, 1956), 17; hereafter cited in text.

7. See Sam S. Baskett, "Jack London's Heart of Darkness," *American Quarterly* 10 (Spring 1958):77: "Enmeshed as he was in the diverse forces making up the chaotic multiplicity of twentieth-century life, inevitably London described a spiritual wasteland not far removed from Marlow's, or Kurtz's—or even [T. S.] Eliot's."

8. See Franklin Walker, *Jack London and the Klondike: The Genesis of an American Writer* (San Marino, Calif.: Huntington Library, 1966), 12ff.; Fred Lewis Pattee, "The Prophet of the Last Frontier," in *Side-Lights on American Literature* (New York: Century, 1922), 98–160; and Howard Mumford Jones, *The Frontier in American Fiction: Four Lectures in the Relation of Landscape to Literature* (Jerusalem at the Magness Press: Hebrew University, 1956), 61.

9. See Roy W. Carlson, "Jack London's Heroes: A Study of Evolutionary Thought," Ph.D. Diss., University of New Mexico, 1961, 6–99; and Conway Zirkle, *Evolution, Marxian Biology, and the Social Scene* (Philadelphia: University of Pennsylvania Press, 1959), 318–87, who notes that London, "intellectually honest and logical . . . never discarded any idea of importance for the mere reason that it disturbed his tranquility or his philosophy. He was always able to change his philosophical concepts as his knowledge increased and, as long as he lived, he never ceased to grow" (320).

10. R. W. B. Lewis, *The American Adam: Innocence, Tragedy, and Tradition in the Nineteenth Century* (Chicago: University of Chicago Press, 1955), 5.

11. Joan London, in "W. H. Chaney: A Reappraisal," *American Book Collector,* 17 (November 1966), praises Chaney as "a man whom Jack London need not have been ashamed" (11): "Eccentric, yes, stubborn and hot-tempered, but his excellent mind was a generous one, and his dedication to the cause of humanity, and his devotion to his principles command admiration and respect" (13).

12. John London was actually left with nine children when his wife died. But only three—Eliza, Ida, and Charles—had come west with him. Charles had died 11 days after their arrival in California, and John had placed Eliza and Ida in the Protestant Orphan Asylum until he could make a proper home for them. See Russ Kingman, *A Pictorial Life of Jack London* (New York: Crown Publishers, 1979), 24–25.

13. *John Barleycorn* (New York: Century, 1913), 41; hereafter cited in text as *Barleycorn.*

14. "The Apostate." *When God Laughs and Other Stories* (New York: Macmillan, 1911), 57.

15. *The Valley of the Moon* (New York: Macmillan, 1913), 263–64; hereafter cited as *Valley.*

16. *Jack London's Tales of Adventure,* ed. Irving Shepard (Garden City, N.Y.: Doubleday, 1956), 54–55; hereafter cited in text.

17. *The Education of Henry Adams,* Modern Library Ed. (New York: Random House, 1931), 344.

18. See Samuel Eliot Morison and Henry Steele Commager, *The Growth of the American Republic,* 3d ed. (New York: Oxford University Press, 1942), 331.

19. *The Road* (New York, Macmillan, 1907), 152; hereafter cited in text as *Road.*

20. "How I Became a Socialist," *War of the Classes* (New York: Macmillan, 1905), 277–78; hereafter cited in text as *War.*

21. Quoted in Charmian London, *The Book of Jack London* (New York: Century, 1921), I, 210–11; hereafter cited in text as *Book.*

22. Pierre Berton, *The Klondike Fever: The Life and Death of the Last Great Gold Rush* (New York: Alfred A. Knopf, 1958), 100.

23. "The Gold Hunters of the North," *Revolution and Other Essays* (New York: Macmillan, 1912), 200; hereafter cited in text as *Revolution.*

24. Henry James, "The Art of Fiction," in *Selected Literary Criticism,* ed. Morris Shapira, pref. by F. R. Leavis (Harmondsworth, Middlesex, England: Penguin, 1963), 86–87.

25. Compare this lyrical account of his trip with the matter-of-fact jottings in London's notebook (*Book,* I, 247–57).

Chapter Two

1. Mary Johnston, *To Have and To Hold,* ch. 31 "In Which an Indian Forgives and Forgets," *The Atlantic Monthly* 85 (January 1900): 54; in this same issue appeared London's "An Odyssey of the North."

2. Kenneth S. Lynn, "Disturber of Gentility" (review of Richard O'Connor's *Jack London* [Boston: Little, Brown, 1964]), *New York Times Book Review,* 14 February 1965, 20.

3. This editorial decision is more comprehensible in view of the following comment in Georgia Loring Bamford's *The Mystery of Jack London: Some of His Friends, Also a Few Letters—A Reminiscence* (Oakland, Calif.: Piedmont Press, 1931): "By this time there were thousands of people back from the Klondike, most of them 'busted' and, apparently, all with the feeling that they could write printable, desirable 'stuff' about the Gold Rush that would set the world on fire. Every editorial table in San Francisco was overburdened with articles and people were willing to sell them for anything they could get" (111). As Clell T. Peterson observes in "Jack London's Alaskan Stories,"

American Book Collector 9 (April 1959): "It is largely true that London rose to success because of the public interest in Alaska, but he had to become a first-rate writer to do it" (17).

4. Quoted by London in his 6 December 1898 letter to Mabel Applegarth (*Letters,* 29). The difficulty he had in collecting his $5 is dramatized in chapter 33 of *Martin Eden.*

5. King Hendricks, "Determination and Courage." *The Eleusis of Chi Omega* 66 (May 1964):306. Also see *Jack London Reports: War Correspondence, Sports Articles, and Miscellaneous Writings,* ed. King Hendricks and Irving Shepard (Garden City, N. Y.: Doubleday, 1970), xii–xvi; hereafter cited in text as *Reports.*

6. *The Son of the Wolf, Tales of the Far North* (Boston: Houghton Mifflin, 1900), 190; hereafter cited in text as *Wolf.*

7. In *Jack London and His Times* (New York: Doubleday, 1939), Joan London notes that while he was still developing his style, London spent days actually copying Kipling in longhand (170); hereafter cited in text as *Times.* London's defense of Kipling's art and ideas is strongly voiced in "These Bones Shall Rise Again," *Revolution* 219–34.

8. *The Development of the American Short Story* (New York: Harper, 1923), 347–53.

9. Maxwell Geismar, *Rebels and Ancestors: The American Novel, 1890–1915* (Boston: Houghton Mifflin, 1953), 186; hereafter cited in text.

10. C. G. Jung, *Modern Man in Search of a Soul,* trans. W. S. Dell and Cary F. Baynes, Harvest Books (New York: Harcourt, Brace & World, n.d., first publ. 1933), 171–72; hereafter cited in text.

11. See C. G. Jung, *The Archetypes and the Collective Unconscious,* trans. R. F. C. Hull, 2d ed. Bollingen Series XX (Princeton, N.J.: Princeton University Press, 1968), passim; hereafter cited in text.

12. *Children of the Frost* (New York: Macmillan, 1902), 3. This entire volume of short stories is keyed to the theme of the vanishing Northland Indian; the sympathetic mood of these tales contrasts with *The God of His Fathers,* published the year before and dedicated "To the Daughters of the Wolf [the conquering Anglo-Saxon] Who Have Bred and Suckled a Race of Men."

13. Mircea Eliade, *Myth and Reality,* trans. William R. Trask (New York: Harper & Row, 1963), 199.

14. Jack London, "Where the Trail Forks," in *The God of His Fathers* (New York: McClure, Phillips & Co., 1901), 191; hereafter cited in text as *God.*

15. Herman Melville, *Moby-Dick,* ed. and introd., Charles Feidelson, Jr. (Indianapolis: Bobbs-Merrill, 1964), 263–64.

16. James Baird, *Ishmael: A Study of the Symbolic Mode in Primitivism,* Harper Torchbook Ed. (New York: Harper & Brothers, 1960), 334, 17–18.

17. Baird mentions London several times in *Ishmael,* but always as an "exoticist" whose narratives "provide suitable examples of the Pacific voyage

without the appearance of primitive feeling" (123) and whose fiction is artistically inferior to that of the genuine primitivist (37, 207). Baird rightly designates *A Son of the Sun* as a minor Nietzschean allegory; except for the first-rate story "The Pearls of Parlay," these "David Grief" stories are among London's poorest (significantly, they were the inspiration for a Hollywood television series in the late 1950s). But he wrongly classifies this book as a "Polynesian novel": neither "Polynesian" nor "novel," it is a collection of separate, unrelated episodes set in Melanesia. In London's Polynesian and Northland fictions (none of which Baird mentions), the characteristics of authentic primitivism are clearly evident.

18.   Jack London, *White Fang* (New York: Macmillan, 1906), 3; hereafter cited in text as *White.*

19.   London first published the story in *The Youth's Companion* in 1902 and then rewrote it for *Century* magazine in 1908. The transition from a tale for boys to a tale for adults is marked by the tremendous depth of the 1908 version, as opposed to a moralistic simplicity displayed in the earlier version. Our analysis is of the 1908 story, which is the standard version. A full recounting of the actual episode that inspired London's story is given by Franklin Walker in *Jack London and the Klondike,* 255–60.

20.   *Lost Face* (New York: Macmillan, 1910), 63–64; hereafter cited in text as *Lost.* The holograph manuscript of this story, on file in the Huntington Library, reveals that London began by naming his protagonist "John Collins," changed to "the man" in his third paragraph, then revised his earlier references to read "the man."

21.   An unpublished computer analysis by Professor Donald Danvers, Centenary College of Louisiana, yields the following key word counts in the story: *cold,* 31; *freeze{ing},* 28; *frost,* 10; *ice,* 19; *snow,* 35; *heat,* 1; *hot,* 2; *warmth,* 4.

22.   For other notable commentaries on this story, see Clell T. Peterson, "The Theme of Jack London's 'To Build a Fire,'" *American Book Collector,* 17 (November 1966): 15–18; Earle Labor and King Hendricks, "Jack London's Twice-Told Tale," *Studies in Short Fiction,* 4 (Summer 1967): 334–47 (including reprint of first version, published in *Youth's Companion,* 29 May 1902); James K. Bowen, "Jack London's 'To Build a Fire': Epistemology and the White Wilderness," *Western American Literature,* 5 (Winter 1971): 287–89; and Lee Clark Mitchell, *Determined Fictions: American Literary Naturalism* (New York: Columbia University Press, 1989), 34–54.

23.   Charles Child Walcutt, *American Literary Naturalism: A Divided Stream* (Minneapolis: University of Minnesota Press, 1956), 97–98.

24.   Aldous Huxley, *Point Counter Point* (New York: Doubleday, Doran, 1928), 295.

25.   The failure of *Hearts of Three* (London: Mills & Boon, 1918; New York: Macmillan, 1920) was caused in part by its being conceived as a motion-picture novel written in collaboration with the famous creator of *The*

Perils of Pauline, Charles Goddard, who provided London with scenario notes. Even Charmian, often excessive in her praise, admits that the result "should be viewed as something of a joke" (see *Book,* II, 316–19).

26. In contrast with these fables, *Michael Brother of Jerry* (New York: Macmillan, 1917) is truly an animal story in that London wrote it as a protest against the cruelties inflicted upon animals in training them for performance on stage. (It is also a pioneering indictment of the inhumanity and ignorance of the treatment of lepers, especially in the United States.)

27. Alfred S. Shivers, in "The Romantic in Jack London," *Alaska Review* 1 (Winter 1963), suggests that from one point of view "the story may be taken as a misanthropic allegory in the form of a beast fable. . . . In the canine he could penetrate to the uttermost reaches of primitiveness, a goal toward which he seemed to be repeatedly striving" (44). Also see Donald Pizer, "Jack London: The Problem of Form," *Studies in the Literary Imagination* 16 (Fall 1983):108.

28. *The Faith of Men and Other Stories* (New York: Macmillan, 1904), 203. James Sisson has brought to our attention the German translation of "Bâtard" as "Zwei Teufel" ("Two Devils") and also the plural in the Latvian translation (see Hensley C. Woodbridge, John London, and George H. Tweney, *Jack London: A Bibliography* [Georgetown, Calif.: Talisman Press, 1966], 215, Item 628).

29. See also C. G. Jung's explanation of the "primordial vision" as "an experience . . . which cannot be accepted by the conscious outlook" in *Modern Man in Search of a Soul,* 159.

30. Charles G. D. Roberts, *The Kindred of the Wild* (Boston: Page, 1902), 29.

31. See Simon O. Lesser, *Fiction and the Unconscious* (Boston: Beacon Press, 1957), 113.

32. Maxwell Geismar, ed., "Introduction," *Jack London: Short Stories,* American Century Series (New York: Hill & Wang, 1960), ix–x.

33. See Joseph Campbell, *The Hero with a Thousand Faces,* Meridian Ed. (New York: Meridian, 1956), 34–46.

34. Richard Chase, *The American Novel and Its Tradition,* Anchor Ed. (Garden City, N.Y.: Doubleday, 1957), 13.

35. *The Call of the Wild* (New York: Macmillan, 1903), 26; hereafter cited in text as *Call.*

36. See J. E. Cirlot, *A Dictionary of Symbols,* trans. Jack Sage (New York: Philosophical Library, 1962), 223; hereafter cited in text.

37. Quoted by George Wharton James in "Jack London, Cub of the Slums, Hero of Adventure, Literary Master, and Social Philosopher," *National Magazine* 37 (December 1912): 489–90; also quoted by Charmian London in *Book,* II, 49–50. See James R. Giles, "Thematic Significance of the

Jim Hall Incident in *White Fang,*" *Jack London Newsletter* 2 (May–August 1969): 49–50.

38.   Eliseo Vivas, *The Artistic Transaction* (Columbus, Ohio, 1963), 10, 30–31.

Chapter Three

1.   Granville Hicks, *The Great Tradition: An Interpretation of American Literature Since the Civil War,* rev. ed. (New York: Macmillan, 1935), 193.

2.   Winifred Blatchford, "In the Library," *The Clarion* (London), No. 1304, 1 December 1916, 2.

3.   "Getting into Print," *The Editor* 17 (March 1903): 82.

4.   Sources in sequence: *Martin Eden* (New York: Macmillan, 1909), 232, hereafter cited in text as *Martin;* "These Bones Shall Rise Again," *Revolution,* 224; "The Terrible and Tragic in Fiction," *The Critic* 42 (June 1903): 542, reprinted in *Reports,* 334; *Revolution,* 231, 224; *Letters,* 335.

5.   "What Communities Lose by the Competitive System," in *Jack London: American Rebel,* ed. Philip Foner (New York: Citadel, 1947), 429; originally published in *Cosmopolitan* (November 1900).

6.   "The Phenomena of Literary Evolution," *Bookman* 12 (October 1900):150.

7.   "The House Beautiful," *Revolution,* 170.

8.   See Jack London, *No Mentor but Myself; A Collection of Articles, Essays, Reviews and Letters,* ed. Dale L. Walker (Port Washington, N.Y.: Kennikat, 1979).

9.   "On the Writer's Philosophy of Life," *The Occident* 70 (December 1916): 147, originally published in *The Editor,* October 1899.

10.   "The Material Side," *The Occident* 70 (December 1916): 144; hereafter cited in text as "Material."

11.   Porter Garnett, "Jack London—His Relation to Literary Art," *Pacific Monthly* 17 (April 1907): 453.

12.   Anna Strunsky Walling, "Memoirs of Jack London," *The Masses* 9 (July 1917): 13.

13.   Rose Wilder Lane quoted in Richard O'Connor, *Jack London: A Biography* (Boston: Little Brown, 1964), 139.

14.   *The Kempton-Wace Letters* (New York: Macmillan, 1903), 87, 89, 170; hereafter cited in text as *Kempton.*

15.   *The People of the Abyss* (New York: Macmillan, 1903), 274–75; hereafter cited in text as *People.* See James R. Giles, "Jack London 'Down and Out' in England: The Relevance of the Sociological Study *People of the Abyss* to London's Fiction," *Jack London Newsletter* 2 (September–December 1969): 79–83.

16.   Roy W. Carlson, Jr., makes a strong case in support of his assertion

that *The Sea-Wolf* was London's "most ambitious novel" (152ff). Over a half million copies of this novel have been sold in the hardcover edition by Macmillan—not including the countless paperback sales see O'Connor, 198), and it has been made into eight motion pictures. See Woodbridge's *Bibliography,* 282–87 and Tony Williams, *Jack London—The Movies* (Middletown, Calif.: Rejl, 1992), 69–85, passim.

17. Quoted in Foner, 61–62.

18. Robert E. Spiller, "Toward Naturalism in Fiction," *Literary History of the United States,* ed. Spiller et al. (New York: Macmillan, 1955), 1036; Gordon Mills, "Jack London's Quest for Salvation," *American Quarterly* 7 (Spring 1955):5. In *The Novels of Jack London: A Reappraisal* (Madison: University of Wisconsin Press, 1983), Charles N. Watson, Jr., says that Larsen "belongs, surely, among the great hero-villains of American fiction, serving as a link between Ahab's metaphysical rebellion and the amoral striving of Faulkner's Thomas Sutpen" (78).

19. *The Sea-Wolf* (New York: Macmillan, 1904), 73–74; hereafter cited in text as *Sea-Wolf.*

20. James Ellis interprets Larsen's headaches as a symbol of the tension between the animal and the human in his character, and between materialism and idealism in his philosophy; see "A New Reading of *The Sea-Wolf,*" *Western American Literature* 2 (Summer 1967): 129–31.

21. Zirkle, 331. See Van Weyden's comments about Larsen as an anachronism in *The Sea-Wolf,* 75; see also the title story in *The Strength of the Strong* (New York: Macmillan, 1914), 1–33; volume hereafter cited in text as *Strength.*

22. Sam S. Baskett, "Sea Change in *The Sea-Wolf,*" *American Literary Realism* 24, 2 (Winter 1992):5–22; hereafter cited in text. See also Forrest G. Robinson, "The Eyes Have It: an Essay on Jack London's *The Sea-Wolf.*" *American Literary Realism* 18 (Spring and Autumn 1985):178–95; rpt. in Forrest G. Robinson, *Having It Both Ways: Self-Subversion in Western Popular Classics* (Albuquerque: University of New Mexico Press, 1993), 55–78, for a view of Maud as actually in control of sexuality among the characters.

23. Quoted in Foner, 61.

24. Robert Brainard Pearsall suggests that "such people may be willing to die for love [but the] notion of slipping into bed for love would not necessarily occur to them"—in "Elizabeth Barrett Meets Wolf Larsen," *Western American Literature* 4 (Spring 1969):12.

25. See "Jack London to Yale Men," *Yale Alumni Weekly* 15 (31 January 1906):344 [our thanks to James Sisson for this reference]; also see Joan London, 301, for a slightly different version of London's Yale speech, and 308–9 for his speech to New Yorkers.

26. Joseph Blotner, *The Modern American Political Novel, 1900–1960* (Austin: University of Texas Press, 1966), 150–51.

27. *The Iron Heel* (New York: Macmillan, 1908), 83–84; hereafter cited in text as *Iron*.

28. Letter to "Dear Comrade Harris," 26 October 1914 (Huntington Library file).

29. See London's review of this book in *War in the Classes*, 197–206.

30. Irving Stone, *Sailor on Horseback: The Biography of Jack London* (Cambridge, Mass.: Houghton, Mifflin, 1938), 229; hereafter cited in text.

31. Spiller, 1037; Foner, 97; Geismar, 1953, 163; Walter Rideout, *The Radical Novel in the United States, 1900–1954* (Cambridge, Mass.: Harvard University Press, 1956), 42; Max Lerner, "Introduction," *The Iron Heel*, American Century Series (New York: Sagamore Press, 1957), xi. See also Charles N. Watson Jr.'s, helpful commentary on *The Iron Heel* in his *The Novels of Jack London*, 99–122; and Gorman Beauchamp's comparison of *The Iron Heel* with the story "Goliah" in his "Jack London's Utopian Dystopia and Dystopian Utopia," in *America as Utopia*, ed. Kenneth M. Roemer (New York: Burt Franklin, 1981), 91–107.

32. Geismar, 186. In fact, at least two attempts to psychoanalyze London antedate Geismar's: Wilfrid Lay, "John Barleycorn under Psychoanalysis," *Bookman* 14 (March 1917):47–54; and "Ms. Notes [on] Jung's *Psychology of the Unconscious* Compiled by Mary Wilshire lately direct from Jung in Zurich" (Huntington Library). Charmian used the latter, along with Jack's marked copy of C. G. Jung's *Psychology of the Unconscious*, ed. Beatrice M. Hinkle (New York: Moffat, Yard, 1916), in writing *The Book of Jack London* (II, 320–24, 334, 353–59). Especially noteworthy is the perceptive analysis by Dr. James Kirsch, founder and former president of the Society of Jungian Analysts of Southern California: "Jack London's Quest: 'The Red One,'" *Psychological Perspectives* 11 (Fall 1980):137–54.

33. *Before Adam* (New York: Macmillan, 1907), 1; hereafter cited in text as *Before*. In writing this novel, London was influenced by the "germ plasm theory of heredity" formulated by the German biologist August Weismann; for an instructive discussion of this and related ideas, see Hamilton Cravens and John C. Burnham, "Psychology and Evolutionary Naturalism in American Thought, 1890–1940," *American Quarterly* 23 (December 1971):635–57.

34. *The Scarlet Plague* (New York: Macmillan, 1915), 73–75. This novel was first serialized in *London Magazine* 28 (June 1912):513–40; hereafter cited in text as *Scarlet*.

35. Ed. Morrell, *The Twenty-Fifth Man* (Montclair, N.J.: New Era, 1924), 367–68. See also Charmian's record of Jack's response to the evidence of Morrell's ordeal, *Book*, II, 226. London used Morrell's own story as a frame, and many of the prison episodes in *The Star Rover* are virtually identical to those depicted as fact in Morrell's book.

36. *The Star Rover* (New York: Macmillan, 1915), 122; hereafter cited in text as *Star*.

37. Letter to Earle Labor from William F. Almand, Jr., 13 February 1962. For another personal testimonial to the moving power of this novel, see Jonathan

Yardley, "Reconsideration: Jack London," *The New Republic* (2 June 1973):31–33.

38.   Franklin Walker, "Jack London: *Martin Eden*," in *The American Novel from James Fenimore Cooper to William Faulkner*, ed. Wallace Stegner (New York: Basic Books, 1965), 133. Charles N. Watson, Jr., notes: "London himself declared that Martin Eden was his best novel, and I believe it is that and more: it is the central document of his life as an artist. Having re-created in Martin the intensity of his own early artistic ambition, he then unsparingly portrays the spiritual desolation that follows when such ambition is lost. But the loss was Martin's, not London's. By purging his despair—by making Martin his scapegoat—London enabled his own creative impulse to survive" (164).

39.   The *Mariposa* was the name of the ship London himself had sailed on when he interrupted his *Snark* cruise in 1908 to return home to straighten out his financial affairs.

40.   See Watson (156) for an excellent commentary on the mythic significance of Martin's death.

41.   London allegedly took the hero's given name from Martin Johnson, the young cook and handyman aboard the *Snark* who later became a world-famous explorer, but Anders Kruskopf, in "Martin Eden in Sonoma," *American-Scandinavian Review* 31 (Winter 1943):347–48, points out that Martin Eden was the name of one of London's neighbors.

42.   A cogent refutation of the suicide theory is Alfred S. Shivers, "Jack London: Not a Suicide," *The Dalhousie Review* 49 (Spring 1969):43–57. An expert in pharmacology, Shivers explains the futility of attempting to calculate exact lethal dosages of morphine (the alleged evidence Irving Stone used in *Sailor on Horseback* as the basis for his inference that London deliberately took his own life). Russ Kingman has persuasively argued that London died from a stroke and heart failure.

Chapter Four

1.   Charmian Kittredge London, *The Log of the Snark* (New York: Macmillan, 1915), vii.

2.   The actual size of his crew was six: "Uncle" Roscoe Eames, Herbert Stolz, Martin Johnson, Tochigi, Jack, and Charmian. Of the original six, only half—Martin, Jack, and Charmian—were together at the end of the voyage.

3.   See chapter 2 of London's *The Cruise of the Snark* (New York: Macmillan, 1911), 16–35; hereafter cited in text as *Cruise*. See chapter 2 of Martin Johnson's *Through the South Seas with Jack London* (New York: Dodd, Mead, 1913), "The Building of the 'Snark,'" 13–48.

4.   "Shin Bones," *On the Makaloa Mat* (New York: Macmillan, 1919), 141; hereafter cited in text as *Makaloa*.

5. "From 'My Hawaiian Aloha,'" *Stories of Hawaii by Jack London,* ed. A. Grove Day (New York: Appleton-Century, 1965), 282.

6. *The House of Pride* (New York: Macmillan, 1912), 47–48, 57; hereafter cited in text as *House.* This story was based on an episode in Hawaiian history in which Deputy Sheriff Louis H. Stolz (father of *Snark* crewman Bert Stolz) was killed; see A. Grove Day's "Introduction," *Stories of Hawaii,* 11, and Day's *Jack London in the South Seas* (New York: Four Winds Press, 1971), 80–81.

7. See Day, *Stories of Hawaii,* 9–12.

8. "The Terrible Solomons," *South Sea Tales* (New York: Macmillan, 1911), 199; hereafter cited in text as *South.*

9. *A Son of the Sun* (Garden City, N.Y.: Doubleday, Page, 1911), 17–19; hereafter cited in text as *Sun.*

10. See especially Ernest Hemingway's *In Our Time* (New York: Scribner's, 1958; first publ. 1925), 11–12, 33, 43. For Conrad's influence, see Sam S. Baskett, "Jack London's Heart of Darkness," *American Quarterly* 10 (Spring 1958): 66–77.

11. For additional examples of this double-edged irony, see "Chun Ah Chun," *The House of Pride,* 151–89, and "The Chinago," *When God Laughs and Other Stories* (New York, 1911), 153–85; also see Steven T. Dhondt, "Jack London's *When God Laughs:* Overman, Underdog, and Satire," *Jack London Newsletter* 2 (May–August, 1969): 51–57.

12. Leo Marx, *The Machine in the Garden,* Galaxy Ed. (New York: Oxford University Press, 1967), 71, 228; hereafter cited in text.

13. Roderick Nash, *Wilderness and the American Mind* (New Haven, Conn.: Yale University Press), xii; also see ch. 9, "The Wilderness Cult," 141–60; and *The Call of the Wild (1900–1916),* ed. Roderick Nash (New York: George Braziller, 1970), 1–15.

14. *Moon-Face and Other Stories* (New York: Macmillan, 1906), 149–52; hereafter cited in text as *Moon.*

15. For discussion of the "Sleepy Hollow" motif, see Marx, 11–33.

16. Charmian London diary (Huntington Library).

17. Associate Editor, *Pacific Rural Press,* 15 November 1913. For equally high praise of London's ranch, see Bailey Millard, "Jack London's Valley of the Moon Ranch," *Orchard and Farm* 38 (October 1916): 8.

18. Luther Burbank, *The Harvest of Years* (Boston: Houghton Mifflin, 1927), 225.

19. Howard Lachtman, "Another Look at 'The Valley of the Moon,'" in "This World," *San Francisco Chronicle* (20 July 1975).

20. Peter J. Schmitt, *Back to Nature: The Arcadian Myth in Urban America* (New York: Oxford University Press, 1969), 136.

21. *Burning Daylight* (New York: Macmillan, 1910), 151. For an exceptionally informed reading of this novel, see ch. 8 of Charles N. Watson, Jr., *The Novels of Jack London* (Madison: University of Wisconsin Press, 1983), 165–86.

22. Quoted by Charmian London in *Book,* II, 226.

23. Leroy Armstrong, "The Man Who Came Back: Two Twentieth Century Pilgrims and Where They Landed," *The Saturday Evening Post* (12, November 1910): 42. For the London articles and annotations, see Jack London, "Notes and annotations for *The Valley of the Moon*," Jack London Collection, MS. 1369, Huntington Library.

24. See Clarice Stasz, "Androgyny in the Novels of Jack London," *Western American Literature* 11 (Summer 1976): 128. In the same issue also see Earle Labor, "From 'All Gold Canyon' to *The Acorn Planter:* Jack London's Agrarian Vision," 99–100. In *American Dreamers: Charmian and Jack London* (New York: St. Martin's Press, 1988), Stasz suggests that *The Little Lady of the Big House* upsets modern male critics because it "cuts to the quick of masculine values, digs at their worth, and questions the purity of the Arcadian dream, the strive for perfection" (260).

25. For a full treatment of Saxon's role in *The Valley of the Moon*, see Jeanne Campbell Reesman, "Jack London's New Woman in a New World: Saxon Brown Roberts' Journey into the Valley of the Moon," *American Literary Realism* 24, 2 (Winter 1992):40–54.

26. Clell T. Peterson, "Jack London's Sonoma Novels," *American Book Collector* 9 (October 1958):15.

27. *The Little Lady of the Big House* (New York: Macmillan, 1916), 84–85; hereafter cited in text as *Little*.

28. See particularly chapter 7 of Kevin Starr's *Americans and the California Dream 1850–1915* (New York: Oxford University Press, 1973), 210–38: "The Sonoma Finale of Jack London, Rancher; hereafter referred to in text." And see counterstatements by Howard Lachtman, "The Curious Case of Kevin Starr, Critic," *Jack London Newsletter* 6 (September–December 1973): 155, and Earle Labor, "Jack London's Agrarian Vision," 85–92.

29. See the provocative analysis of the significance of this novel by Watson in *The Novels of Jack London*, 211–34. Watson concludes that "for all its imperfections, what London actually wrote is a more sober, more mature performance than any of his earlier novels, including his best ones. In earlier works London might have taken Dick's posturing seriously; here the whole point of the novel is Dick's discovery of its ultimate futility" (234). For an extended treatment of the feminist ideas in the novel, see Jeanne Campbell Reesman, "Irony and Feminism in *The Little Lady of the Big House*," *Thalia: Studies in Literary Humor*, 12, 1 and 2 (1992): 33–46.

30. *The Acorn-Planter* (New York: Macmillan, 1916); hereafter cited in text as *Acorn*. The play was never produced by the Grove Players, evidently because of the difficulties involved in finding "Efficient Singers" and "Capable Orchestra." For a history of the Bohemian Club, see John van der Zee, *The Greatest Men's Party on Earth* (New York: Harcourt Brace Jovanovich, 1974).

31. Kevin Starr has used this phrase with reference to *The Little Lady of the Big House* in *Americans and the California Dream* (Starr, 220), apparently

unaware of the existence (or content) of *The Acorn-Planter*—possibly because of the scarcity of this play (Macmillan printed a total of only 1,350 copies, and the play has never been reprinted).

32. "Let us not wantonly destroy these wonderful machines . . . that produce efficiently and cheaply," insisted London. "Let us control them. Let us profit by their efficiency and cheapness" (*Book*, II, 294).

Chapter Five

1. In *American Dreamers*, Clarice Stasz notes that London first became familiar with Freud "when he received a copy of *Selected Papers on Hysteria* in 1912. In 1916 he added the recently translated *Three Contributions to the Theory of Sex* and Edwin Holt's commentary *The Freudian Wish and Its Place in Ethics*" (303). For a perceptive analysis of his semiautobiographical Freudian story "The Kanaka Surf," in which a suspicious husband tests his wife's fidelity by pretending to drown (and nearly drowning both of them), see Howard Lachtman, "Man and Superwoman in Jack London's 'The Kanaka Surf,' *Western American Literature* 7 (Summer 1972):101–10. Lachtman notes that ". . . the linkage of physical action and psychological drama reveals London's ambitious experiment to internalize the adventure story in order to explore the more unknown frontier of the human psyche. . . . Save for its happy ending, the domestic conflict in 'The Kanaka Surf' is a replica in a miniature of that in Jack London's last novel [*The Little Lady of the Big House*]. But the fact that the second version of essentially the same story *does* end happily is an indication of how London was willing to rework his material so that, in transplanting a dark romance from Sonoma to Waikiki, he could move from negation to affirmation" (109–10). London had also mentioned Freud a year before writing "Kanaka Surf," on 19 August 1915, in a Preface to Osias L. Schwarz's *General Types of Superior Men: A Philosophico-Psychological Study of Genius, Talent and Philistinism in Their Bearings upon Human Society and Its Struggle for a Better Social Order* (Boston: Richard G. Badger, 1916), 6.

2. C. G. Jung, *Psychology of the Unconscious: A Study of the Transformation and Symbolisms of the Libido, A Contribution to the History of the Evolution of Thought*, authorized translation, with Introduction, by Beatrice M. Hinkle, M.D., of the Neurological Department of Cornell University Medical School and of the New York Post Graduate Medical School (New York: Moffat, Yard, 1916).

3. In a letter to Leo Mihan, 24 October 1916, London wrote: "I have quite a few books on psychoanalysis, which you would have access to any time you are visiting us. Also, I have just recently subscribed to the *Psychoanalytic Review*, which is a quarterly. Doctor Jung's book is a very remarkable book to me, and I do not hesitate to assert that you are no more excited about it than am I" (*Letters* 1598).

4. See David Mike Hamilton, *"Tools of My Trade": The Annotated Books in Jack London's Library* (Seattle: University of Washington Press, 1986).

London's personal library comprised "some fifteen thousand volumes . . . on almost every conceivable subject: evolution, biology, psychology, economics, political economy, travel, navigation, and philosophy, as well as drama, poetry, and fiction" (1). Hamilton says that Jung's book "marks the culmination of London's study of psychology—a study which had tremendous impact on London's thinking and especially on his writing" (43).

5. See Leslie Fiedler, "Archetype and Signature," in *No! in Thunder: Essays on Myth and Literature* (Boston: Beacon Press, 1960), 309–28.

6. James I. McClintock, *White Logic: Jack London's Short Stories* (Grand Rapids, Mich.: Wolf House Books, 1975), 132. In addition to "Samuel," "The Night-Born," "The Red One," and "The Water Baby," which are discussed at length in this chapter, the following stories, all composed during the period of London's alleged decline, are especially noteworthy for their artistic quality: "The Sea Farmer" (1912, the story of a sailing master's agrarian dream), "A Piece of Steak" (1909, a story of prizefighting that transcends that brutal world to become a classic parable of youth versus age), "War" (1911, a compact parable reminiscent of Ambrose Bierce's "An Occurrence at Owl Creek Bridge"), "Told in the Drooling Ward" (1914, a startlingly original, humorous, and compassionate first-person narrative of a mentally retarded man), and, as noted in the text, "The Madness of John Harned" (1910) and "The Mexican" (1911).

7. See note 6 above. The novel was *Adventure,* serialized in *Popular Magazine,* October–December 1910, and published by Macmillan the following year. Shortly before sailing from Australia, London had completed two notable socialist tales, "The Strength of the Strong" (29 January 1909; *Hampton's Magazine,* March 1911; *The Strength of the Strong,* 1914) and "South of the Slot" (6 February 1909; *The Saturday Evening Post,* 22 May 1909; *The Strength of the Strong*). See Carolyn Johnston, *Jack London—An American Radical?* (Westport, Conn.: Greenwood Press, 1984): "'South of the Slot' is a kind of Dr. Jekyll and Mr. Hyde tale" about a professor of sociology at the University of California who crosses the dividing line marked by the trolley's slot, which separates the lower and upper classes of San Francisco. One of his finest socialist tales, "The Strength of the Strong" is "a parable celebrating collectivism as a means of survival in a prehistoric setting" (132–33).

8. In addition to the archetypal characters discussed in this chapter, especially noteworthy are London's Indian women. See Alfred S. Shivers, "Jack London's Mate-Women," *American Book Collector* 15 (October 1967): 17–21; Clarice Stasz, "Androgyny in the Novels of Jack London," *Western American Literature* 11 (Summer 1976): 121–33; and Jacqueline M. Courbin, "Jack London's Portrayal of the Natives in His First Four Collections of Arctic Tales," *Jack London Newsletter,* 10:3 (1977): 127–37.

9. Charmian London calls this one of Jack's "most thoughtful stories" (*Book* II, 176). See London's 26 May 1910 letter to John S. Phillips, editor of *American Magazine*: "Why, the material in the story of 'Samuel' cost me at

least $250 hard cash to acquire, and 43 days at sea between land and land, on a coal-laden tramp-steamer. Also, it took me two weeks to write. And my wife threw in 43 days of her time helping me in making a study of the vernacular, and in writing it down and classifying it" (*Letters*, 895; see also 1023, 1205).

10. *The Interpreter's Dictionary of the Bible*, 4 vols. (New York: Abingdon Press, 1962), IV, 201.

11. See E. G. Withycombe, *The Oxford Dictionary of English Christian Names* (New York: Oxford University Press, 1947), 96: "[Margaret] was one of the most popular medieval saints, largely, perhaps, because her last words were reported to be: 'Hearken to my prayer, O God, and grant to every man who shall write my life or relate my works, or shall hear or read them, that His name be written in the book of eternal life, and whosoever shall build a church in my name, do not bring him to thy remembrance to punish him for his wrong-doing.'"

12. Clell T. Peterson, "Jack London's Alaskan Stories," *American Book Collector* 9 (April 1959): 22.

13. Jack London, *The Night-Born* (New York: Century, 1913), 3; hereafter cited in text as Night.

14. *Webster's Third International Dictionary* defines "tref" (*trefa*) as "ritually unclean or unfit." "Ethan" is associated with "prophet" or "sage"; see *Encyclopaedia Judaica Jerusalem* (New York: Macmillan, 1971), VI, 921.

15. The source for London's story was an article titled "California Girl's Wild Ghost Dance" by Lillian Ferguson in the San Francisco *Sunday Examiner Magazine*, 15 July 1900. Ferguson tells of a young woman named Annie Mitchell, who at age 16 left her parents' home in California to live with relatives in Oklahoma but who was so mistreated that she fled to live with a tribe of Ponca Indians and married the chief. When a group of white spectators intruded on one of the sacred tribal dances, Annie was unjustly arrested as being indirectly responsible for the ensuing near riot. The Thoreau quote, varying slightly from the original, appears in the newspaper article and in the story under the title "Thoreau's Cry of the Human." The newspaper clipping, with London's scribbled marginalia, is on file in the Huntington Library.

16. A reference to the anima-figure (as Terrible Mother) in H. Rider Haggard's novel *She*, which C. G. Jung ranked alongside Melville's *Moby-Dick* as one of the great works of archetypal fiction. See *Modern Man in Search of a Soul*, 154–58; and Jung, 1968, 71.

17. According to London's magazine sales record, "The Red One" was finished 20 May 1916. London's original title for this story was "The Message."

18. Thomas D. Clareson, ed., *A Spectrum of Worlds* (Garden City, N. Y.: Doubleday, 1972), 87. Dale L. Walker includes a commentary on "The Red One" in *The Alien Worlds of Jack London*, concluding that this story "gives proof that London could indeed rise up in his latter days to write with stunning effect." In *Curious Fragments: Jack London's Tales of Fantasy Fiction*, Walker calls it a "fantasy

story of shuddering impact. . . . By far the best and most significant of London's stories in [the science fiction] category. In his foreword to the same volume, Philip José Farmer writes, "'The Red One,' my favorite, conceals beneath its blood-sweat-dirt-beauty tale of South Seas adventure the 'impenetrable,' the unconquerable mystery of things beyond man's ken" (Walker, viii). Farmer—one of the most highly respected American science-fictionists—testifies to London's influence upon such other major figures as Isaac Asimov, Arthur C. Clarke, and Robert Heinlein, adding, "It is no exaggeration to say that every time I write, London, to some effect, is guiding my pen" (Walker, vii). Andrew Sinclair calls it "the most haunting of [London's] final stories," *Jack: A Biography of Jack London* (New York: Harper & Row, 1977), 231. In "Science-Fictionizing the Paradox of Living: Jack London's 'The Red One' and the Ecstasy of Regression," *The Dolphin* [Publications of the University of Aarhus, Denmark] 11 (April 1985): 39, Per Serritslev Petersen observes that "with 'The Red One' London finally found his science fictional 'objective correlative,' the formula through which his unique psychological reality, his structure of feeling, could most effectively be evoked." Similarly, Gorman Beauchamp remarks that the story is "a fitting coda to London's career," in *Jack London* (Mercer Island, Wash.: Starmont House, 1984), 85.

19.   "The Red One," Walker, 198–99. Because of the relative inaccessibility of the original edition of this work, we have used Walker's edition as our text.

20.   Clareson, 90; Billy Collins, "Jack London's 'The Red One': Journey to a Lost Heart," *Jack London Newsletter* 10 (January–April 1977): 6; Sinclair, 231; Ellen Brown, "A Perfect Sphere: Jack London's 'The Red One,'" *Jack London Newsletter* 11 (May–December 1978): 85.

21.   London wrote to praise Conrad's *Victory*. He ended his letter: "Aloha (which is a sweet word of greeting, the Hawaiian greeting, meaning 'my love be with you')" (*Letters*, 1467–68). Conrad responded, obviously touched and pleased by London's admiration, and called London "a true brother in letters—of whose personality and art I have been intensely aware for many years. . . ." He goes on to praise "the vehemence of your strength and the delicacy of your perception." After a description of wartime events (including seeing a "Zep" pass overhead the night before bound for an air raid on London), Conrad signs off, begging London to "keep me in your kind memory and accept a grateful and cordial hand grasp" (Huntington Library).

22.   See Jeanne Campbell, "Falling Stars: Myth in 'The Red One,'" *Jack London Newsletter* 11 (May–December 1978): 87.

23.   James Kirsch, "Jack London's Quest: 'The Red One,'" *Psychological Perspectives* 11 (Fall 1980): 137–54; hereafter cited in text. Dr. Kirsch, founder of the C. G. Jung Institute of Los Angeles and founder and former president of the Society of Jungian Analysts of Southern California, first delivered this essay

as a lecture given 11 March 1955 to the Analytical Psychology Club of Los Angeles. We are indebted to Mrs. Nathan J. Bender for providing us with a copy of Kirsch's original paper.

24.   Erich Neumann, *The Great Mother: An Analysis of the Archetype*, trans. Ralph Manheim (Princeton, N.J.: Princeton University Press, 1955), 177–78. For further remarks concerning relevant symbols in this story (e.g., head, helmet, skull, pig, and "the blood red one"), see Neumann, 45–46, 74–77, 150–52, 161, 191.

25.   Jeanne Campbell Reesman, "The Problem of Knowledge in Jack London's 'The Water Baby,'" *Western American Literature* 23 (Fall 1988): 213; hereafter cited in text. "Lakana," in addition to being the Hawaiian version of "London," is also a variant of "lantana," a California shrub that when imported to Hawaii developed uncharacteristically lush and widespread foliage.

26.   Reesman also notes: "The voracious shark literally bursting with its proof is a brilliant symbol for the futility of relying only on epistemology" (Reesman, 1988, 212).

Chapter Six

1.   Arthur Hobson Quinn, *American Fiction: An Historical and Critical Survey* (New York: D. Appleton-Century, 1936), 542.

2.   Sam S. Baskett, "Jack London's Fiction: Its Social Milieu," Ph.D. Diss., University of California, 1951; Elsie Edmondson, "The Writer as Hero in Important American Fiction since Howells," Ph.D. Diss., University of Wisconsin, 1952; Abraham Rothberg, "The House that Jack Built: A Study of Jack London: The Man, His Times, and His Works," Ph.D. Diss., Columbia University, 1952; Anne Marie Springer, "Jack London and Upton Sinclair," in "The American Novel in Germany: A Study of the Critical Reception of Eight American Novelists Between the Two World Wars," Ph.D. Diss., University of Pennsylvania, 1959; Thomas Daniel Young, "Jack London and the Era of Social Protest," Ph.D. Diss., Vanderbilt University, 1950. Also during the 1950s, a few noteworthy essays on London appeared in scholarly publications: Sam S. Baskett, "Jack London and the Oakland Waterfront," *American Literature* 27 (November 1955): 363–71, and "Jack London's Heart of Darkness," *American Quarterly* 10 (Spring 1958): 66–77; Gordon Mills, "Jack London's Quest for Salvation," *American Quarterly* 7 (Spring 1955): 3–14, and "The Symbolic Wilderness," *Nineteenth-Century Fiction* 13 (March 1959): 329–40; and Charles Child Walcutt, "Jack London: Blond Beasts and Supermen," *American Literary Naturalism: A Divided Stream* (Minneapolis: University of Minnesota, 1956), 87–113.

3.   The CEA session, chaired by Sam S. Baskett, included papers by Donald D. Kummings, Earle Labor, Jeanne Campbell Reesman, and James

Williams; the papers were subsequently published in the *Jack London Newsletter* 19 (September–December 1986): 89–108.

4.   Sources cited in order: Mark Seltzer, *Bodies and Machines* (New York: Routledge, 1992), 12–16, 166–72; June Howard, *Form and History in American Literary Naturalism* (Chapel Hill: University of North Carolina Press, 1985), 111–14, 51–62, 93–95, 152–57, passim; Forrest G. Robinson, *Having It Both Ways: Self-Subversion in Western Popular Classics* (Albuquerque: University of New Mexico Press, 1993), 55–78; Alfred Hornung, "Evolution and Expansion in Jack London's Personal Accounts: *The Road* and *John Barleycorn*," in *An American Empire: Expansionist Cultures and Policies, 1881–1917*, ed. Serge Ricard (Aix-en-Provence: Université de Provence [Groupe de Recherche et d'études Nord-Américaines], 1990), 197–213; Eric Homberger, *American Writers and Radical Politics, 1900–39: Equivocal Commitments* (New York: St. Martin's Press, 1986), 1–33; Lee Clark Mitchell, *Determined Fictions: American Literary Naturalism* (New York: Columbia University Press, 1989), 34–54; Joseph A. Boone, "Male Independence and the American Quest Genre: Hidden Sexual Politics in the All-Male Worlds of Melville, Twain and London," in *Gender Studies: New Directions in Feminist Criticism,* ed. Judith Spector (Bowling Green, Ohio: Bowling Green State University Popular Press, 1986), 187–217 [rpt. Joseph Allen Boone, *Tradition Counter Tradition: Love and the Form of Fiction,* Women in Culture and Society Series, Catherine R. Stimpson, gen. ed. (Chicago: University of Chicago Press, 1987), 226–77].

5.   Sources cited in order: Bernard D. Kaplan, "Greatest American Author? Europe for Jack London," *San Francisco Sunday Examiner and Chronicle,* 8 February 1976, sec. A, p. 20; *New York Tribune,* 22 May 1914, and Emil Opffer, "Georg Brandes, the 'Danish Carlyle,' Defends the American Woman," unidentified and undated clipping in "Jack London Scrapbook," vol. 12, p. 389, Huntington Library; Anatole France, introduction to *The Iron Heel* (New York: McKinlay, Stone & Mackenzie, 1924), xiii; George Orwell, introduction to *Love of Life and Other Stories by Jack London* (London: Paul Elek, 1946), 14 [for London's influence on Orwell, also see Victor R. S. Tambling, "Jack London and George Orwell: A Literary Kinship," in *George Orwell,* ed. Courtney T. Wemyss and Alexej Ugrinsky (New York: Greenwood Press, 1987), 171–5]; Jorge Luis Borges, "Prólogo," *Las muertes concéntricas Jack London* (Buenos Aires: Librería La Ciudad, 1979), 9–10; Eiji Tsujii, "To Make Jack London More Popular in Japan," *Jack London Newsletter* 19 (January–April 1986): 42–46; Shuyan, Li, "Jack London in China," *Jack London Newsletter* 19 (January-April 1976): 42–46; Vil Bykov, "Jack London in the Soviet Union," *The Book Club of California Quarterly Newsletter* 24 (Summer 1959): 55–56. Also see Hensley C. Woodbridge, "Jack London's Current Reputation Abroad," *Pacific Historian* 21 (Summer 1977): 166–77.

6.   See Frederick Feied, *No Pie in the Sky: The Hobo as American Cultural Hero in the Works of Jack London, John Dos Passos, and Jack Kerouac* (New York:

Citadel Press, 1964); and Richard W. Etulain, ed., *Jack London on the Road: The Tramp Diary and Other Hobo Writings* (Logan: Utah State University Press, 1979).

7.   London virtually invented the modern prizefight story. *The Game* (New York: 1905), in which the hero is killed in the ring, is alleged to have prompted Heavyweight Champion Gene Tunney's retirement from boxing when he read London's short novel in the late 1920s. Compare London's series on the Jeffries-Johnson bout (*Jack London Reports,* 264–301) with Norman Mailer's coverage of the Frazier-Ali fight in *Life* magazine, 70 (19 March 1971): 18–36.

8.   Shepard, vii.

Bibliography

PRIMARY SOURCES
Original Materials

More than 60,000 items related to Jack London (letters, notes, manuscripts, diaries, scrapbooks, business and ranch records, and more than 6,000 volumes from London's personal library) are on file at the Henry E. Huntington Library in San Marino, California. The second largest collection of Londoniana is held by the Merrill Library at Utah State University in Logan. Other important collections are located at the Bancroft Library, University of California, Berkeley; the Special Collections Department of the University of California at Los Angeles; the Cresmer Collection at the University of Southern California; the Stanford University Library; the Stuart Library of Western Americana at the University of the Pacific; the Oakland Public Library; the Special Collections Library at the University of Virginia; the Jack London Foundation Research Center in Glen Ellen, California; the Jack London State Park in Glen Ellen; and the Jack London Research Center at Centenary College of Louisiana.

Books

At least three Jack London collected editions were published in the former Soviet Union; 17 volumes of the *Obras completas* have been issued in Portugal; four volumes of the Bodley Head Jack London have been released in England; Horizon Press has published a dozen volumes edited by I. O. Evans and printed in Great Britain; Macmillan has reissued a half-dozen hardbound titles enhanced by handsome illustrations and introductory essays; the Library of America has included a number of London's major works in its two-volume Jack London edition; a Japanese publisher, Hon-no-Tomasha, has released a 25-volume selected English edition with a copy of Russ Kingman's biography; and the paperback publishers have struck a bonanza as title after title has dropped out of copyright. Stanford University Press has published the complete stories in three volumes. But the scholar must sometimes rely on cheap, sometimes inaccurate reprints or on Interlibrary Loans, realizing that some items (e.g., London's plays) are virtually inaccessible. The following list of first editions, while a source of delight to the secondhand book dealer, often represents frustration for the serious London scholar.

The Son of the Wolf [stories]. Boston: Houghton Mifflin, 1900.
The God of His Fathers [stories]. New York: Century, 1901.
Children of the Frost [stories]. New York: Century, 1902.
The Cruise of the Dazzler [juvenilia]. New York: Century, 1902.
A Daughter of the Snows [novel]. Philadelphia: J.B. Lippincott, 1902.
The Kempton-Wace Letters [with Anna Strunsky]. New York: Macmillan, 1903.
The Call of the Wild [novella]. New York: Macmillan, 1903.
The People of the Abyss [sociological study]. New York: Macmillan, 1903.
The Faith of Men [stories]. New York: Macmillan, 1904.
The Sea-Wolf [novel]. New York: Macmillan, 1904.
War of the Classes [essays]. New York: Macmillan, 1905.
The Game [novella]. New York: Macmillan, 1905.
Tales of the Fish Patrol. New York: Macmillan, 1905.
Moon-Face and Other Stories. New York: Macmillan, 1906.
White Fang [novel]. New York: Macmillan, 1906.
Scorn of Women [play]. New York: Macmillan, 1906.
Before Adam [novel]. New York: Macmillan, 1907.
Love of Life and Other Stories. New York: Macmillan, 1907.
The Road [tramping reminiscences]. New York: Macmillan, 1907.
The Iron Heel [novel]. New York: Macmillan, 1908.
Martin Eden [novel]. New York: Macmillan, 1909.
Lost Face [stories]. New York: Macmillan, 1910.
Revolution and Other Essays. New York: Macmillan, 1910.
Burning Daylight [novel]. New York: Macmillan, 1910.
Theft: A Play in Four Acts. New York: Macmillan, 1910.
When God Laughs and Other Stories. New York: Macmillan, 1911.
Adventure [novel]. New York: Macmillan, 1911.
The Cruise of the Snark [travel sketches]. New York: Macmillan, 1911.
South Sea Tales. New York: Macmillan, 1911.
The House of Pride and Other Tales of Hawaii. New York: Macmillan, 1912.
A Son of the Sun [stories]. Garden City, N.Y.: Doubleday, Page & Company
    1912.
Smoke Bellew [stories]. New York: Century, 1912.
The Night-Born [stories]. New York: Century, 1913.
The Abysmal Brute [novella]. New York: Century, 1913.
John Barleycorn [semiautobiographical prohibition treatise]. New York: Century,
    1913.
The Valley of the Moon [novel]. New York: Macmillan, 1913.
The Strength of the Strong [stories]. New York: Macmillan, 1914.

The Mutiny of the Elsinore [novel]. New York: Macmillan, 1914.

The Scarlet Plague [novella]. New York: Macmillan, 1915.

The Star Rover [novel]. New York: Macmillan, 1915.

The Acorn-Planter: A California Forest Play. New York: Macmillan, 1916.

The Little Lady of the Big House [novel]. New York: Macmillan, 1916.

The Turtles of Tasman [stories]. New York: Macmillan, 1916.

The Human Drift [miscellany]. New York: Macmillan, 1917.

Jerry of the Islands [novel]. New York: Macmillan, 1917.

Michael Brother of Jerry [novel]. New York: Macmillan, 1917.

The Red One [stories]. New York: Macmillan, 1918.

On the Makaloa Mat [stories]. New York: Macmillan, 1919.

Hearts of Three [novel]. New York: Macmillan, 1920.

Dutch Courage and Other Stories. New York: Macmillan, 1922.

The Assassination Bureau, Ltd. [novel completed by Robert L. Fish]. New York: McGraw-Hill, 1963.

Letters from Jack London, edited by King Hendricks and Irving Shepard. New York: Odyssey, 1965.

Jack London Reports [essays and newspaper articles], edited by King Hendricks and Irving Shepard. New York: Doubleday, 1970.

Daughters of the Rich [curtain raiser written by Hilda Gilbert but published under London's name with his permission], edited by James E. Sisson. Oakland, Calif.: Holmes Book Co., 1971.

Gold [three-act play written by Herbert Heron, based upon two London stories, "A Day's Lodging" and "The Man on the Other Bank," published under the names of Heron and London as joint authors], edited by James E. Sisson, Oakland, Calif.: Holmes Book Co., 1972.

Jack London on the Road: The Tramp Diary and Other Hobo Writings, edited by Richard W. Etulain. Logan: Utah State University Press, 1979.

No Mentor but Myself: A Collection of Articles, Essays, Reviews, and Letters, by Jack London, on Writing and Writers, edited by Dale L. Walker. Port Washington, N.Y.: Kennikat, 1979.

A Klondike Trilogy: Three Uncollected Stories, edited by Earle Labor. Santa Barbara, Calif.: Neville, 1983.

Dearest Greek: Jack and Charmian London's Presentation Inscriptions to George Sterling, edited by Stanley Wertheim and Sal Noto. Cupertino, Calif.: Eureka Publications, 1983.

With a Heart Full of Love: Jack London's Presentation Inscriptions to the Women in His Life, edited by Sal Noto. Berkeley, Calif.: Twowindows Press, 1986.

The Letters of Jack London, edited by Earle Labor, Robert C. Leitz III, and I. Milo Shepard. 3 vols. Stanford, Calif.: Stanford University Press, 1988.

The Complete Short Stories of Jack London, edited by Earle Labor, Robert C. Leitz III, and I. Milo Shepard. 3 vols. Stanford, Calif.: Stanford University Press, 1993.

Parts of Books

Umbstaetter, H. D., ed. *The Red Hot Dollar and Other Stories from* The Black Cat, with an Introduction by Jack London. Boston: Page, 1911.

Sinclair, Upton, ed. *The Cry for Justice: An Anthology of the Literature of Social Protest,* with an Introduction by Jack London. Philadelphia: John C. Winston, 1915.

Cox, Francis A. *What Do You Know About a Horse?,* with a Foreword by Jack London [Foreword written by Cox but published under London's name with his permission]. London: G. Bell & Sons, 1915.

Schwarz, Osias L. *General Types of Superior Men: A Philosophico-Psychological Study of Genius, Talent, and Philistinism in Their Bearings upon Human Society and Its Struggles for a Better Social Order,* with a Preface by Jack London [Preface written by Schwarz but published under London's name with his permission]. Boston: R. G. Badger, 1916.

SECONDARY SOURCES

Bibliography

Bubka, Tony. "A Jack London Bibliography: A Selection of Reports Printed in the San Francisco Bay Area Newspapers: 1896–1967." Master's thesis, San Jose State College, 1968.

Hamilton, David Mike. *"Tools of My Trade": The Annotated Books in Jack London's Library.* Seattle: University of Washington Press, 1986. Detailed description of some 400 of the 15,000 volumes in London's personal library.

Harty, Kevin J. "Dissertations on Jack London, 1936–1987: Evidence for Canonicity." *Jack London Newsletter* 20 (May–December 1987): 58–62.

Lachtman, Howard. "Criticism of Jack London: A Selected Checklist." *Modern Fiction Studies* 22 (Spring 1976): 107–25.

McMillan, Marilyn Johnson. "Jack London's Reputation as a Novelist: An Annotated Bibliography." Master's thesis, Sacramento State College, 1967. London's contemporaries "were favorable towards the works that were concerned with adventure and romance and hostile towards the philosophical socialism expressed in others."

Sherman, Joan. *Jack London: A Reference Guide.* Boston: G. K. Hall, 1977. Comprehensive annotated bibliography of works about London, compiled chronologically.

Sisson, James E. "Jack London's Plays: A Chronological Bibliography." Included in *Daughters of the Rich.* See also Russ Kingman, "Jack London, Playwright," *Pacific Historian* 24 (1980): 135–40; and Keith Newlin,

"Portrait of a Professional: The Plays of Jack London," *American Literary Realism 1870–1910* 20 (Winter 1988): 65–84.

———. "Jack London's Published Poems: A Chronological Bibliography." *The London Collector* 1 (July 1970): 20–21.

Tavernier-Courbin, Jacqueline. "Bibliographical Update." In *Critical Essays on Jack London,* edited by Jacqueline Tavernier-Courbin. Boston: G. K. Hall, 1983, 281–91.

Walker, Dale L. "Jack London (1876–1916)." *American Literary Realism 1870–1910* 1 (Fall 1967): 71–78. Selective listing of works about London, indicating areas of needed scholarly study. See also Earle Labor, "Jack London: An Addendum." *American Literary Realism 1870–1910* 2 (Spring 1968): 91–93.

Walker, Dale L., and James E. Sisson III. *The Fiction of Jack London: A Chronological Bibliography.* El Paso: Texas Western Press, 1972. Annotated, with photographs.

Woodbridge, Hensley C., John London, and George H. Tweney. *Jack London: A Bibliography.* Georgetown, Calif.: Talisman Press, 1966. Enlarged edition, Millwood, N.Y.: Kraus Reprint Corp., 1973. This comprehensive work, containing more than 4,000 entries, lists London's publications, including motion pictures based upon his works, with reprints and translations, as well as writings about London in English and foreign languages. Professor Woodbridge has periodically listed addenda to this bibliography in the *Jack London Newsletter.* Additional bibliographical items are published in *What's New About London, Jack?* (David H. Schlottmann, ed., 929 South Bay Rd., Olympia, WA 98506).

Biography

Of the many books and pamphlets published about London's life, none can be called definitive, but the following are the most significant.

Bamford, Georgia Loring. *The Mystery of Jack London: Some of His Friends, Also a Few Letters—A Reminiscence.* Oakland, Calif.: Georgia Loring Bamford— Piedmont Press, 1931. Valuable source of firsthand information about London's early years and his friendship with Frederick Irons Bamford.

Etulain, Richard. "The Lives of Jack London." *Western American Literature* 11 (Summer 1976): 149–64. Balanced scholarly assessment of major London biographies.

Fleming, Becky London. "Memories of My Father, Jack London." *The Pacific Historian* 18 (Fall 1974): 5–10. Brief, affectionate reminiscence by London's late second daughter. Also see her columns 'From My Mailbox' in back issues of *Jack London Echoes,* and her interview with Lailee von Dillen, published as "Becky London: The Quiet Survivor Talks About Her Father," *The Californians* 9, 4 (January–February 1992): 34–39.

Haughey, Homer L., and Connie Kale Johnson. *Jack London Ranch Album*. Stockton, Calif.: Heritage, 1985. Useful, attractive photographic record of the history of Beauty Ranch. Published in cooperation with the Valley of the Moon Natural/History Association and the California Department of Parks and Recreation.

————. *Jack London Homes Album*. Stockton, Calif.: Heritage, 1987. Companion volume to *Ranch Album*.

Kingman, Russ. *Jack London: A Definitive Chronology*. Middletown, Calif.: Rejl, 1992. The most detailed resource on London's life available.

————. *A Pictorial Life of Jack London*. New York: Crown, 1979. Reprint. Middletown, Calif.: Rejl, 1992. The most reliable biography published to date.

London, Charmian Kittredge. *The Log of the* Snark. New York: Macmillan, 1915. Day-to-day account of the Londons' voyage; useful complement to *The Cruise of the* Snark.

————. *Our Hawaii*. New York: Macmillan, 1917. New and revised ed., 1922. Detailed, substantial record of the London's visits to Hawaii. Illustrated. For index, see Andrew Flink, *Jack London Newsletter* 18 (January–April 1985): 1–35.

————. *The Book of Jack London*, 2 vols. New York: Century, 1921. Sentimental, poorly organized, and badly written; mostly a pastiche of her husband's own letters, notes, and quotes—nevertheless an invaluable source of information about London's life. For index, see Charles N. Watson, Jr., *Jack London Newsletter*, 16 (May–August 1983): 47–95.

London, Joan. *Jack London and His Daughters*. Intro. by Bart Abbott. Berkeley: Heyday Books, 1990. An account that suffers from personal bitterness and lack of scholarly apparatus.

————. *Jack London and His Times*. New York: Doubleday, 1939. Reissued with a new introduction by the author. Seattle: University of Washington Press, 1968. This carefully written and well-organized biography by London's daughter complements Charmian's work; much of the book relates, however, to the milieu rather than to the man.

Noel, Joseph. *Footloose in Arcadia: A Personal Record of Jack London, George Sterling, Ambrose Bierce*. New York: Carrick & Evans, 1940. Gossipy, maliciously distorted account by the Rufus Griswold of Londoniana. See Etulain above.

O'Connor, Richard. *Jack London: A Biography*. Boston: Little, Brown, 1964. Uneven and highly prejudicial, particularly in treatment of Charmian London.

Sinclair, Andrew. *Jack: A Biography of Jack London*. New York: Harper & Row, 1977. Facile but misleading account of London's life and personality with obsessive emphasis upon his medical problems. See Dale L. Walker, "The Exhumation of Jack: Andrew Sinclair's Patho-Biography," *Jack London Newsletter* 10 (September–December 1977): 119–26.

Starr, Kevin. "The Sonoma Finale of Jack London, Rancher." In his *Americans and the California Dream,* 210–38. New York: Oxford University Press, 1973. See Howard Lachtman, "The Curious Case of Kevin Starr, Critic," *Jack London Newsletter* 6 (September–December 1973): 154–60. Starr's account of London's later years "is the embodiment of everything that can go wrong when a historian fails to recognize the depth and scope of his topic, and substitutes sensationalism for the true art of revelation." For further corrections of Starr's errors, see Earle Labor, "From All Gold Canyon to *The Acorn-Planter:* Jack London's Agrarian Vision," *Western American Literature* 11 (Summer 1976): 83–101.

Stasz, Clarice. "The Social Construction of Biography: The Case for Jack London." *Modern Fiction Studies* 22 (Spring 1976): 51–71. Perceptive comparative analysis of seven biographical studies. "Jack London is perhaps one of the most difficult subjects of biography because his rich personality encompassed so many paradoxical qualities."

————. *American Dreamers: Charmian and Jack London.* New York: St. Martin's Press, 1988. Particularly valuable for its depiction of Charmian as a prototype for the New Woman and a much stronger and more influential wife than London's biographers have generally recognized.

Stone, Irving. *Sailor on Horseback: The Biography of Jack London.* Cambridge, Mass.: Houghton Mifflin, 1938. Allegedly "corrected and updated," this book was reissued with 28 London stories as *Irving Stone's Jack London* (Garden City, N.Y.: Doubleday, 1977). Though unreliable, this "Biographical Novel," as it was subtitled after reviewers discovered numerous passages plagiarized from London's own writings, has probably done more to popularize London than any other book not written entirely by London himself. It has appeared in a score of foreign editions, in Braille, and in more than a dozen paperback reprintings. For analysis of Stone's scholarly deficiencies, see Earle Labor, "An Open Letter to Irving Stone," *Jack London Newsletter* 2 (September–December 1969): 114–16, and Winifred M. Middaugh, "'Jack London, Sailor on Horseback': Biography or Fiction?" *Jack London Newsletter* 15 (September–December 1982): 132–57.

Walker, Franklin. *Jack London and the Klondike: The Genesis of an American Writer.* San Marino, Calif.: Huntington Library, 1966. Scholarly and articulate—an indispensable guide to London's Northland experience and writings.

Walling, Anna Strunsky. "Memoirs of Jack London." *The Masses,* 9 (July 1917): 13–17.

Williams, James. "The Composition of Jack London's Writings." *American Literary Realism* 23, 2 (Winter 1991): 64–86. Chronological listing of 406 of London's works by date composed, with introductory essay stressing London's diversity of subject, experimentation with form, and volume.

Books and Monographs

Beauchamp, Gorman. *Jack London.* Starmont Reader's Guide 15. Mercer Island, Wash.: Starmont House, 1984. Biographically erratic but critically astute commentary on London's fantasy and science-fiction writings.

Feied, Frederick. *No Pie in the Sky: The Hobo as American Cultural Hero in the Works of Jack London, John Dos Passos, and Jack Kerouac.* New York: Citadel Press, 1964. "Jack London was the first American writer of any significance to speak of the tramp or hobo from intimate knowledge and understanding."

Foner, Philip S., ed. *Jack London: American Rebel—A Collection of His Social Writings Together with an Extensive Study of the Man and His Times.* New York: Citadel Press, 1947. Includes substantial introductory essay with strong Socialistic bias.

Hedrick, Joan D. *Solitary Comrade: Jack London and His Work.* Chapel Hill: University of North Carolina Press, 1982. Problematic psychological analysis of London's career from his early work through *Martin Eden;* gives "scant attention to the [last] third of London's active career" because it does not fit the book's view of London's "life and art [as] essentially a two-part scheme, with his working-class experiences on one side and his middle-class experiences on the other, and the 'long sickness' as the watershed between them."

Hendricks, King, ed. *Creator and Critic: A Controversy between Jack London and Philo M. Buck, Jr.* Logan: Utah State University Press, 1961. Contains six letters exchanged between author and critic following the publication of Buck's essay "The American Barbarian"; also includes a substantial Introduction by Hendricks, to whom Buck had given London's letters.

————. *Jack London: Master Craftsman of the Short Story.* Logan: Utah State University, 1966. Cites three major characteristics of London's writing: ability to create a narrative, to create atmosphere, and to use irony; "To Build a Fire," "Love of Life," "The Law of Life," and "The Chinago" are discussed as exemplifying these qualities.

Johnston, Carolyn. *Jack London—An American Radical?* Westport, Conn.: Greenwood, 1984. Sensible, well-researched study of London's Socialism.

Lundquist, James. *Jack London: Adventures, Ideas, and Fiction.* New York: Ungar, 1987. Succinct, useful introduction to London's life and works, despite occasional factual and typographical errors.

Martin, Stoddard. *California Writers: Jack London, John Steinbeck, The Tough Guys.* New York: St. Martin's, 1983. Original and perceptive, especially in discussions of music, racism, and women in London's novels. Asserts that London "represents the beginning of serious California literature."

McClintock, James I. *White Logic: Jack London's Short Stories.* Grand Rapids, Mich.: Wolf House Books, 1975. Close analysis of the major body of London's short fiction, especially strong in treatment of Jung's influence on the late Hawaiian tales. For index, see Keith Kroll, *Jack London Newsletter* 19 (May–August 1986): 47–54.

Nakada, Sachiko. *Jack London and the Japanese: An Interplay between the West and the East.* Yamanashi-ken, Japan: The Central Institute, Jorinji Zen Monastery, 1986. Despite stylistic problems (especially idiomatic), an informative history of London's Socialistic as well as literary impact on Japan; includes bibliography of Japanese translations of London's works and articles written about London by Japanese scholars.

Ownbey, Ray Wilson, ed. *Jack London: Essays in Criticism.* Santa Barbara, Calif.: Peregrine Smith, 1978. Contains 10 essays on major themes in London's work.

Tavernier-Courbin, Jacqueline, ed. *Critical Essays on Jack London.* Boston: G. K. Hall, 1983. Comprehensive collection with 23 essays on London, including important selections by H. L. Mencken, Carl Sandburg, Anatole France, and Katherine Mansfield, along with useful pieces by contemporary academic critics and a substantial introductory essay on London as a professional writer. Also contains "Bibliographical Update" of Sherman's *Reference Guide.*

Walcutt, Charles Child. *Jack London.* Minneapolis: University of Minnesota, 1967. Hastily written pamphlet by a leading authority of American literary Naturalism. Reprint. *Seven Novelists in the American Naturalist Tradition: An Introduction.* Minneapolis: University of Minnesota Press, 1974, 131–67.

Walker, Dale L. *The Alien Worlds of Jack London.* Grand Rapids, Mich.: Wolf House Books, 1973. Concise, pioneering study of London's "fantasy fiction."

Watson, Charles N., Jr. *The Novels of Jack London: A Reappraisal.* Madison: University of Wisconsin Press, 1983. Intelligent, painstakingly researched analysis of nine of London's most important novels.

Wilcox, Earl J., ed. *The Call of the Wild by Jack London: A Casebook with Text, Background Sources, Reviews, Critical Essays, and Bibliography.* Chicago: Nelson Hall, 1980. An excellent book for scholars and teachers dealing with London's masterpiece. Also includes the story "Bâtard" and nine London letters.

Williams, Tony. *Jack London—The Movies.* Middletown, Calif.: Rejl, 1992. As the first comprehensive study of its subject, the volume covers all film and television adaptations of London works from 1913 to the present, including domestic and foreign productions. Bibliography, filmography, 21 stills, and other pictures.

Woodward, Robert H. *Jack London and the Amateur Press.* Grand Rapids, Mich.: Wolf House Books, 1983. Documents London's relationship to the amateur press (mainly as patron rather than participant). Reprints hitherto inaccessible early prose pieces by London and by Anna Strunsky, including her review of London's first book, *The Son of the Wolf.*

Zamen, Mark E. *Standing Room Only: Jack London's Controversial Career as a Public Speaker.* Foreword by Earle Labor. New York: Peter Lang, 1990. Study of London as lecturer. Useful discussions of both well-known and little-known speeches.

Essays and Chapters

The following list is selective; many of the works cited in chapter notes are not repeated here.

Ahearn, Marie L. "*The People of the Abyss:* Jack London as New Journalist." *Modern Fiction Studies* 22 (Spring 1976): 73–83. As "a creative fiction/nonfiction that treats a true situation with all the skills of the novelist-as-reporter," London's first-person account of his experience in the slums of the East End "ought to be set alongside Norman Mailer's *The Armies of the Night,* Truman Capote's *In Cold Blood,* and Tom Wolfe's *The Pump House Gang* and *The Electric Kool-Aid Acid Test.*"

Baskett, Sam S. "Jack London's Heart of Darkness," *American Quarterly,* 10 (Spring 1958): 66–77.

———. "*Martin Eden:* Jack London's Poem of the Mind." *Modern Fiction Studies* 22 (Spring 1976): 23–36. Autobiographical characterization of London's protagonist.

———. "*Martin Eden:* Jack London's Splendid Dream." *Western American Literature* 12 (Fall 1977): 199–214. Compares London's intensely personal story of the failure of the imagination in the materialistic world with *The Education of Henry Adams, Adventures of Huckleberry Finn,* and *The Great Gatsby.*

———. "Sea Change in *The Sea-Wolf.*" *American Literary Realism,* 24, 2 (Winter 1992): 5–22.

Bender, Bert. "Jack London in the Tradition of American Sea Fiction." *The American Neptune* 46 (Summer 1986): 188–99. Discusses London's sea novels in depth, ranking him alongside such other "great figures in our tradition of sea literature [as] Freneau, Cooper, Dana, Melville, Stephen Crane, Joshua Slocum, O'Neill, Hemingway, and Peter Matthiessen." Reprinted in Bender's *Sea-Brothers: The Tradition of American Sea Fiction from "Moby-Dick" to the Present.* Philadelphia: University of Pennsylvania Press, 1988, 83–98.

Berkove, Lawrence I. "A Parallax Connection in London's 'The Unparalleled Invasion.'" *American Literary Realism* 24, 2 (Winter 1992): 33–39. Cogent reassessment of London's view of race in this apocalyptic story of war with China.

Birchard, Robert S. "Jack London and the Movies." *Film History: An International Journal* 1 (1987): 15–37. Meticulously researched illustrated narrative of London's losing war with exploitive early film makers.

Boone, Joseph A. "Male Independence and the American Quest Genre: Hidden Sexual Politics in the All-Male Worlds of Melville, Twain and London." In *Gender Studies: New Directions in Feminist Criticism,* edited by Judith Spector. Bowling Green, Ohio: Bowling Green State University Popular Press, 1986, 187–217. Reprinted in Joseph Allen Boone, *Tradition Counter Tradition: Love and the Form of Fiction.* Women in Culture and Society Series, general editor, Catharine R. Stimpson. Chicago: University of Chicago Press, 1987, 226–77.

Brown, Deming. "Jack London and O. Henry." *Soviet Attitudes Toward American Writing.* Princeton, N.J.: Princeton University, 1962. Despite London's loss of ideological respectability, he continued as the most popular American writer in Soviet Russia because of his forthrightness, largeness of heart, hardihood, and optimism (*cf.* Bykov, below).

Brown, Ellen. "A Perfect Sphere: Jack London's 'The Red One.'" *Jack London Newsletter* 11 (May–December 1978): 81–85.

Bruccoli, Matthew J. "Introduction." *The Sea-Wolf.* Riverside Ed. Boston: Houghton Mifflin, 1964. Definitive text of the novel that is "perhaps [London's] best;" the ocean functions as moral catalyst.

Bykov, Vil. "Jack London in the Soviet Union." *The Book Club of California Quarterly News Letter* 24 (Summer, 1959): 52–58. The leading Jack London scholar in the former Soviet Union says that because of narrative clarity, life-assertive force, and presentation of "noble" man, London's "fiction is more popular in the U.S.S.R. than that of any other foreign author."

Calder-Marshall, Arthur. "Introduction." *The Bodley Head Jack London.* 4 vols. London: Bodley Head, 1963, 1964, 1965, 1966. Each volume is introduced by a critical essay dealing with the titles in that volume. London is depicted as "the New Twentieth Century Man."

Campbell, Jeanne. "'Falling Stars': Myth in 'The Red One.'" *Jack London Newsletter* 11 (May–December 1978) 87–101.

Cooper, James Glennon. "The Womb of Time: Archetypal Patterns in the Novels of Jack London." *Jack London Newsletter* 8 (January–April 1975): 1–5; 9 (January–April 1976): 16–28; 12 (January–April 1979): 12–23. Detailed analysis of characters in London's novels as "neither demigods nor individuals but symbols of unconscious 'characters' in the collective psyche." Special emphasis on the Myth of the Hero.

———. "The Summit and the Abyss: Jack London's Moral Philosophy." *Jack London Newsletter* 12 (1979): 24–27. Suggests that in addition to the universal myths underlying London's works is the private myth "that human consciousness exists as a thrust toward enlightened moral freedom."

Courbin, Jacqueline M. "Jack London's Portrayal of the Natives in His First Four Collections of Arctic Tales." *Jack London Newsletter* 10 (September–December 1977): 127–37. Perceptive reevaluation of London's paradoxical vision of Indian life, concluding that, while he sometimes oversimplified their characters, "London has succeeded in depicting the Indians and Eskimos as real people."

Day, A. Grove. Introduction to *Stories of Hawaii* by Jack London. Honolulu: Mutual Publishing Co., 1985, 3–20. Helpful contextualizing of some of London's best tales.

———. "Jack London's 'Heart of Darkness.'" In his *Mad About Islands: Novelists of a Vanished Pacific.* Honolulu: Mutual Publishing Co., 1987, 162–72. Brief but compelling account of the *Snark*'s adventures in the South Seas.

Dhondt, Steven T. "Jack London's Satire in *When God Laughs.*" Master's thesis, Utah State University, 1967. Treats a neglected but important facet on London's work: his keen sense of irony as it related to his class consciousness.

———. "Jack London's *When God Laughs:* Overman, Underdog, and Satire." *Jack London Newsletter* 2 (May–August 1969): 51–57.

———. "'There Is a Good Time Coming': Jack London's Spirit of Proletarian Revolt." *Jack London Newsletter* 3 (January–April 1970): 25–34. Interprets "A Curious Fragment" as "satire on ignorance" and "The Apostate" as prophecy of proletarian hope in education and spirit of revolt.

Flink, Andrew. "*Call of the Wild:* Jack London's Catharsis." *Jack London Newsletter* 11 (January–April 1981): 12–19. Notes symbolic and psychological parallels between Buck's plight and London's experiences in the Erie County Penitentiary.

Fusco, Richard. "On Primitivism in *The Call of the Wild.*" *American Literary Realism* 20, 1 (Fall 1987): 76–80. Sources in Jean-Jacques Rousseau's *Discours sur l'inégalité.*

Giles, James R. "Jack London 'Down and Out' in England: The Relevance of the Sociological Study *People of the Abyss* to London's Fiction," *Jack London Newsletter* 2 (September–December 1969): 79–83.

Hensley, Dennis E. "Jack London's Use of the Linguistic Style of the King James Bible." *Jack London Echoes* 3 (July 1983): 4–11. "London read the Bible regularly . . . as an exercise in expanding his literary frontiers"; the influence of this reading is evident in his style as well as his plots.

Homberger, Eric. *American Writers and Radical Politics, 1900–39: Equivocal Commitments.* New York: St. Martin's Press, 1986, 1–33.

Hornung, Alfred. "Evolution and Expansion in Jack London's Personal Accounts: *The Road* and *John Barleycorn.*" In *An American Empire: Expansionist Cultures and Policies, 1881–1917,* edited by Serge Ricard. Aix-en-Provence: Université de Provence, Groupe de Recherche et d'études Nord-Américaines, 1990, 197–213.

Howard, June. *Form and History in American Literary Naturalism.* Chapel Hill:
    University of North Carolina Press, 1985. Scattered but provocative ref-
    erences to London's politics and literary style.
Jørgensen, Jens Peter. "'The Red One': A Freudian Approach." *Jack London
    Newsletter* 8 (September–December 1975): 101–3. Suggests that Bassett's
    "curiously sublimated sexual behavior" is the result of a
    Christian–Victorian upbringing" and that his "death is an orgiastic one,
    as was Kurtz's life in the heart of darkness."
Kirsch, James. "Jack London's Quest: 'The Red One.'" *Psychological Perspectives*
    11 (Fall 1980): 137–54.
Labor, Earle. "The Archetypal Woman as 'Martyr to Truth': Jack London's
    'Samuel.'" *American Literary Realism* 24, 2 (Winter 1992): 23–32. One of
    London's least-known and most unusual tales, "Samuel" is an uncanny
    tribute to "the indomitableness of the human spirit."
———. "From 'All Gold Canyon' to *The Acorn-Planter:* Jack London's Agrarian
    Vision." *Western American Literature* 11 (Summer 1976): 83–102.
    Definitive view of London's hopes for the promise of the land, especially
    in the latter years of his career.
———. "Jack London." In *A Literary History of the American West,* edited by
    Thomas J. Lyon et al. Sponsored by the Western Literature Association.
    Fort Worth: Texas Christian University Press, 1987: 381–97. "Unlike
    Twain's, . . . London's nihilistic moods were more transitory than chronic;
    and his predominant attitude was vigorously life-assertive. This charac-
    teristic optimism is nowhere more evident than in his writings about the
    American West, a region he envisioned progressively in symbolic and,
    ultimately, mythic terms."
———. "Jack London's *Mondo Cane:* 'Bâtard,' *The Call of the Wild,* and *White
    Fang.*" In Tavernier-Courbin's *Critical Essays on Jack London:* 114–30.
    Comparative analysis of London's three best "dog fables," indicating the
    thematic and structural factors that account for their perennial and uni-
    versal appeal.
———. "Jack London's 'Planchette': The Road Not Taken." *The Pacific
    Historian* 21 (Summer 1977): 138–46. Though an artistic failure, this
    weird tale obliquely reflects one of London's most crucial personal resolu-
    tions: his decision to marry Charmian Kittredge and move to the Valley
    of the Moon.
——— and King Hendricks. "Jack London's Twice-Told Tale." *Studies in Short
    Fiction,* 4 (Summer 1967): 334–47. Includes reprint of the first version of
    "To Build a Fire" from *Youth's Companion,* 29 May 1902.
———. "The Making of a Major Author: Jack London and the Politics of
    Literary Reputation." *Jack London Newsletter* 19 (September–December
    1986): 100–4. Discusses five criteria for an author's canonization, demon-
    strating why London—despite his international reputation as a great
    American author—failed to achieve this recognition at home.

Lacassin, Francis. "Jack London Between the Challenge of the Supernatural and the Last Judgment." Translated by Jack Hockett and annotated by Hensley C. Woodbridge. *Jack London Newsletter* 8 (May–August 1975): 59–65. Translation of leading French scholar's preface to *Histoires des siècles futurs* (Paris, 1974): [I]f the author of 'The Scarlet Plague' deserves to be classed among the forerunners of this literary genre, it isn't in the branch represented by Edgar Rice Burroughs and the 'fantastic heroic'; rather, he belongs to that genre which links H. G. Wells to the great utopians of the seventeenth and eighteenth centuries. . . ."

Lachtman, Howard. "Four Horses, a Wife, and a Valet: Up the California Coast with Jack London." *The Pacific Historian* 21 (Summer 1977): 103–34. Detailed account of London's highly publicized 1911 odyssey from the Valley of the Moon to Oregon, which provided an opportunity to celebrate his agrarian vision. Lachtman's essay also provides important insights into London's writing discipline.

———. "Revisiting Jack London's Valley of the Moon." *The Pacific Historian* 24 (Summer 1980): 141–56. A perceptive assessment of "London's little-known career as an agricultural architect, conservationist, and ecologist." Incisive critical comments about London's agrarian writings, particularly *The Valley of the Moon.*

———. "Introduction." *Sporting Blood: Selections from Jack London's Greatest Sports Writing.* Novato, Calif.: Presidio Press, 1981. "Jack London was our first celebrity sportswriter."

Lampkin, Loretta. "Jack London and the Reluctant Reader—Another Dimension." *Jack London Newsletter* 10 (September–December 1977): 146–50. Prescribes the teaching of London's works as means of breaking down student resistance to reading literature.

Li, Shuyan. "Jack London in China." *Jack London Newsletter* 19 (January–April 1986): 42–46. Informative survey by Beijing University professor, concluding that "Whatever happens in the critical world, London will go on enjoying the admiration of the Chinese readers."

Littel, Katherine M. "The 'Nietzschean' and the Individualist in Jack London's Socialist Writings." *Jack London Newsletter* 15 (May–August 1982): 76–91. Important, closely documented essay explaining that while London was influenced by both Nietzsche and Marx, "[i]t is more productive to consider these contradictory tendencies in dialectical terms, as stages in London's development, which he subsequently synthesized in a philosophical perspective beyond both polarities, than to view these intellectual deviations as mutually self-exclusive and irreconcilable."

Martin, Jay. *Harvest of Change: American Literature, 1965–1914.* Englewood Cliffs, N.J.: Prentice-Hall, 1967, 62, 208, 234–37. London was a "philosophical" rather than a "literary" fictionist, himself a "demonstration of the multiplicity of the modern mind" he predicted.

McClintock, James I. "Jack London: Finding the Proper Trend of Literary Art." *The CEA Critic* 39 (May 1972): 25–28. The magazine debate over Romance versus Realism shaped London's theory of art.

Mills, Gordon. "Jack London's Quest for Salvation." *American Quarterly* 7 (Spring 1955): 3–14. London's work was "in large measure simply an expression of the age-old problem of the unbridled will and the brotherhood of man, but presented in the vocabulary of materialistic thought."

Mitchell, Lee Clark. *Determined Fictions: American Literary Naturalism.* New York: Columbia University Press, 1989, 34–54.

Mohan, Chandra. "Jack London's Humanism." *Jack London Newsletter* 8 (May–August 1975): 40–49. Succinct, thoughtful essay by an Indian scholar, indicating some of the reasons for London's worldwide appeal, including his "inexhaustible love for human life," "notion that man is an evolutionary product of the great Nature of which he is a part," and his far-reaching ideas on social programs "that stand for the establishment of a just society through the democratic processes."

Moreland, David A. "The Author as Hero: Jack London's *The Cruise of the Snark.*" *Jack London Newsletter* 15 (January–April 1982): 57–75. Useful critical study of London's account of his most famous voyage: "Like kaleidoscopic fragments of colored glass, London's chaotic, eclectic beliefs take on a semblance of order when viewed from the perspective of his romantic egotism."

———. "Violence in the South Sea Fiction of Jack London." *Jack London Newsletter* 16 (January–April 1983): 1–35. Substantial. "When at his best Jack London utilized violence to dramatize his basic naturalistic vision of life as struggle in a world dominated by predatory individuals and races, while paradoxically maintaining and conveying his recognition of individual moral responsibility. Although there was much confusion in his attitudes toward race, usually London calls upon the reader to condemn the exploitation of the South Sea Islanders."

———. "The Quest That Failed: Jack London's Last Tales of the South Seas." *Pacific Studies* 8 (Fall 1984): 48–70. Interprets last tales as "an affecting literary record of [London's] unsuccessful search for the means to break [the] spell" of Naturalistic determinism.

Moreland, Kim. The Attack on the Nineteenth-Century Heroine Reconsidered: Women in Jack London's *Martin Eden.*" *The Markham Review* 13 (1983–84): 16–20. Though it confuses London with his character Martin Eden, the article casts light on an important literary context for Ruth Morse.

Oriad, Michael. "Jack London: The Father of American Sports Fiction." *Jack London Newsletter* 11 (January–April 1978): 1–11. London "probed the meaning of American sport, isolating the fundamental American myths and obsessions that are central to sport's importance in American life."

Pattee, Fred Lewis. *The Development of the American Short Story.* New York: Harper, 1923, chapter 15, "The Journalization of the Short Story," 347–53. Contains best short critique of London's contribution to this genre.

Peterson, Clell T. "The Jack London Legend." *American Collector* 9 (April 1959): 15–22. Significant analysis of the civilization versus wilderness theme in London's work: concludes that the tension was never resolved but worsened during his last years.

Pizer, Donald. "Jack London: The Problem of Form." *Studies in the Literary Imagination* 16 (Fall 1983): 107–115. Reprinted in Pizer, *Realism and Naturalism in Nineteenth-Century American Literature.* Carbondale: Southern Illinois University Press, 1984, 166–79. Instructive study of London's "ability to rely unconsciously yet with great success on the underlying characteristics of the fable/parable."

Qualtiere, Michael. "Nietzschean Psychology in London's *The Sea-Wolf.*" *Western American Literature* 16 (Winter 1982): 262–78. Carefully researched essay demonstrating that "the complex mental life of Wolf Larsen . . . was expressly designed to reflect Nietzche's personal psychological history."

Reesman, Jeanne Campbell. "Irony and Feminism in *The Little Lady of the Big House.*" *Thalia: Studies in Literary Humor* 12, 1 and 2 (1992): 33–46. Irony is crucial to reading this difficult work as feminist in effect.

———. "Jack London's New Woman in a New World: Saxon Brown Roberts' Journey Into the Valley of the Moon." *American Literary Realism* 24, 2 (Winter 1992): 40–54. "The woman is the key," as London said, to reading this pastoral tale of renewal and reaffirmation of marriage, home, and vocation.

———. "Jack London's Popular and Political Masks." *Jack London Newsletter* 20 (May–December 1987): 63–71. Analysis of conflicts between personal and authorial identity and values of individualism and socialism in *Martin Eden.*

———. "Knowledge and Identity in London's Pacific Fiction." *Jack London Newsletter* 19 (September–December 1986): 91–95. Survey of Hawaiian stories of *The House of Pride* and *On the Makaloa Mat,* with emphasis upon how race and gender issues are treated as part of London's communal themes.

———. "The Problem of Knowledge in Jack London's 'The Water Baby.'" *Western American Literature* 23 (Fall 1988): 201–15. Exploration of narrative dialogics and Jungian elements of London's last story.

Riber, Jørgen. "Archetypal Patterns in 'The Red One.'" *Jack London Newsletter* 8 (September–December 1975): 104–6. Identifies the central image in London's story as a complex manifestation of the Great Mother.

Robinson, Forrest G. "The Eyes Have It: An Essay on Jack London's *The Sea-Wolf.*" *American Literary Realism* 18 (Spring and Autumn 1985): 178–95.

Reprinted in Forrest G. Robinson, *Having It Both Ways: Self-Subversion in Western Popular Classics.* Albuquerque: University of New Mexico Press, 1993, 55–78. Persuasive construction of Maud Brewster as a source of power—both sexual and ironic—in *The Sea-Wolf*. Marred only by a curious lapse in the last pages of the book version: Robinson concludes his analysis with the notion that London could not have meant to portray Maud as such a strong woman (because London obviously identifies with Wolf); her "assertiveness and ascendency" are "inadvertent features of London's design propelled by the culture" instead of by London's artistry.

Shivers, Alfred S. "Jack London: Author in Search of a Biographer." *American Book Collector* 12 (March 1962): 25–27. Points out deficiencies in major biographies and in London's own autobiographical writings.

———. "Jack London: Not a Suicide." *The Dalhousie Review* 49 (Spring 1969): 43–57. An expert in pharmacology effectively disputes the suicide theory.

———. "Jack London's Mate-Women." *American Book Collector* 15 (October 1964): 17–21. London's "typical heroine is a varying composite made up of four women in the author's life: Bess Maddern[,] Charmian Kittredge, . . . Mabel Applegarth, [and] Anna Strunsky."

Schriber, Mary Sue. "London in France, 1905–1939." *American Literary Realism 1870–1910* 9 (Spring 1976): 171–77. Brief descriptive survey, including notes and checklist of French periodical criticism of London's works.

Simpson, Claude M., Jr. "Jack London: Proletarian or Plutocrat?" *Stanford Today,* Series 1, No. 13 (July 1965): 2–6. Concludes that "this paradoxical man is neither proletarian nor plutocrat," but the unstable and self-destructive mixture of both.

Stasz, Clarice. "Androgyny in the Novels of Jack London." *Western American Literature* 11 (Summer 1976): 121–33. Helpful study of male-female roles in London's fiction, concluding that, contrary to popular misconceptions of his ultramasculinity, "Jack London is no feminist's dream, but he is a male chauvinist's nightmare."

———. "Sarcasm, Irony, and Social Darwinism in Jack London's *Adventure*." *Thalia: Studies in Literary Humor,* 12, 1 and 2 (1992): 82–89. Important reassessment of this problematic novel.

———. "Introduction." *John Barleycorn: or, Alcoholic Memoirs by Jack London.* New York: Signet, 1990, 5–13. Insightful and informative.

Tavernier-Courbin, Jacqueline. "California and After: Jack London's Quest for the West." *Jack London Newsletter* 13 (May–August 1980): 41–54. "Jack London is perhaps the American writer whose life and work embodied most clearly and fascinatingly the psychology of the Frontier spirit."

———. *The Call of the Wild: A Naturalistic Romance.* New York: Twayne, 1994.

———. "Jack London's Science Fiction." *Jack London Newsletter* 17 (September–December 1984): 71–78. Points out that in much of his science fiction London depicts the terrifying extremes to which "scientific knowledge and power not allied with humanistic virtues and sound moral principles can lead the individual and society."

―――. "The Many Facets of Jack London's Humor." *Thalia: Studies in Literary Humor* 2, 1 (1979): 3–9. Reprinted in Tavernier-Courbin's *Critical Essays on Jack London,* 89–101: "An examination of Jack London's papers and private correspondence reveals that he conceived of much of his work as humorous, or, at least, as containing humorous elements. . . . Humor is by definition life-affirming, for it resides in the ability to perceive the comic, the pleasant or the incongruous in a reality which may be desperately somber. Jack London had that ability in the highest degree, not only in his work, but also in his life."

Tietze, Thomas R., and Gary Riedl. "'Saints in Slime': The Ironic Use of Racism in Jack London's *South Sea Tales.*" *Thalia: Studies in Literary Humor* 12, 1 and 2 (1992): 59–66. Broad coverage of the issue of race in London's Pacific works.

Walker, Dale L. "Jack London's War." *Jack London Echoes* 3 (October 1983): 22–33. Discussion of London's journalistic role in the Russo-Japanese War, concluding that "London had been present for the curtain falling on the Golden Age of war correspondence," that London's dispatches "proved to be the best reportage of the war," and that his courageous exploits "added greatly not only to the London legend but to the entire saga of war correspondence."

Walker, Franklin. "Ideas and Action in Jack London's Fiction." In *Essays on American Literature in Honor of Jay B. Hubbell,* edited by Clarence Gohdes. Durham, N.C.: Duke University Press, 1967. Fresh, perceptive assessment of London as a folk hero.

―――. "Jack London: *Martin Eden.*" In *The American Novel from James Fenimore Cooper to William Faulkner,* edited by Wallace Stegner. New York: Basic Books, 1965. Intelligent appreciation of a novel which retains its vital appeal despite its artistic unevenness.

Ward, Susan. "Jack London's Women: Civilization vs. The Frontier." *Jack London Newsletter* 9 (May–August 1976): 81–85: ". . . London accorded his dance-hall girls and Indian squaws a sneaking admiration which he did not bestow on their general [white] sisters."

―――. "Jack London and the Blue Pencil: London's Correspondence with Popular Editors." *American Literary Realism 1870–1910* 14 (Spring 1981): 16–25. London's ability lay in satisfying the public and always more beyond their demands.

―――. "Social Philosophy as Best-Seller: Jack London's *The Sea-Wolf.*" *Western American Literature* 17 (Winter 1983): 321–32. London successfully amalgamated two popular plots—the education story and the love story.

Watson, Charles N., Jr. "Jack London's Yokohama Swim and His First Tall Tale." *Studies in American Humor* 3 (1976): 84–95. Comparative analysis of two versions of story based upon one of London's personal adventures as a young seaman, noting influence of frontier humor on London's fiction, and the revealing of "a constant purpose of his later, more serious fiction—a determination to venture below the surface of polite literature and show life as it is."

————. "Jack London: Up from Spiritualism." In *The Haunted Dusk: American Supernatural Fiction, 1820–1920,* edited by Howard Kerr, John W. Crowley, and Charles L. Crow. Athens: University of Georgia Press, 1982. Examination of London's use of the supernatural: "Though he had no patience with the cruder varieties of nineteenth-century spiritualism, he often hedged his rejection of occultism while probing more receptively such alternative psychic phenomena as mystical transcendence, creative inspiration, and subconscious motivation."

Whalen-Bridge, John. "Dual Perspective in *The Iron Heel,*" *Thalia: Studies in Literary Humor* 12, 1 and 2 (1992): 67–76. Informative examination of London's most political novel, including, surprisingly, its humor.

Wilcox, Earl J. "'The Kipling of the Klondike': Naturalism in London's Early Fiction," *Jack London Newsletter* 6 (January–April 1973): 1–12. In his Northland stories "London asserts the Kiplingesque myth of the superior White Race, but he also adapts it to a naturalistic framework. For the survival thesis is clearly Darwinian in import."

————. "Overtures of Literary Naturalism in *The Son of the Wolf* and *The God of His Fathers.*" In Tavernier-Courbin's *Critical Essays on Jack London,* 105–13. Contends that London's "brand of realism and naturalism was distinctly his own," comprised as it is of "sociological and biological determinism; the survival of the fittest thesis; belief in the materialistic, primitivistic nature of man; accent on some reform and politically revolutionary themes; championing of anticapitalistic and prosocialistic concepts; use of the 'new woman' motif; and an implicit belief in determinism in all these forces."

Williams, Tony. "*Jerry of the Islands* and *Michael Brother of Jerry.*" *Jack London Newsletter* 17 (May–August 1984): 28–60. Extensive examination of London's last dog novels, suggesting need for further study of these neglected companion-pieces: "They are not merely entertainment works but encompass a broad spectrum of interests—socialism, animal rights, religious imagery, cosmological features, ecology—that run throughout all of his work. Indeed, they show the impossibility of compartmentalizing the writer either on the 'demeaning' level of juvenile fiction or separating the animal from the human condition."

———. "*The Mutiny of the Elsinore*—A Revaluation." *Jack London Newsletter* 19 (January–April 1986): 13–41. A defense of this critically denigrated novel as being far more thematically subtle and aesthetically complex than critics have generally recognized: "As a novel it reworks themes within *The Sea-Wolf* in the light of *The Iron Heel* to present London's anticipation of themes later presented in George Orwell's *1984*."

Wilson, Christopher P. "The Brain Worker: Jack London." In his *The Labor of Words: Literary Professionalism in the Progressive Era*. Athens: University of Georgia Press, 1985, 92–112. What could have been a useful study of an important topic—the effect of mass market sales on the author's notion of his art—instead slips too often into a glib version of London as a journalistic hack who created complex literary art despite himself.

Woodward, Servanne. "The Nature of the Beast in Jack London's Fiction." *Bestia* 1 (May 1989): 60–66. "London's sympathy for animals was part of a strong scientifico-political stance which clashed against homocentrism and which did not recognize the natural superiority of a class over another. . . . London's ideal humanity is endowed with individual beauty (and aesthetic feelings) allied with the strength of the beast as it is harnessed to the aesthetic ability, such as sports and dance."

Index

The Authors

Earle Labor is Wilson Professor of American Literature at Centenary College of Louisiana. In the summer of 1966 he was invited by King Hendricks to serve as guest professor at Utah State University, where he taught the first course on Jack London ever offered by an American university. In 1974, as a Fulbright lecturer at Aarhus University, Denmark, he presented the first course on Jack London in Western Europe. The original edition of this TUSAS volume was the first critical book on London to be published in this country. Labor has published more than 50 essays and reviews on London; in addition, he has edited *Great Short Works of Jack London* (1965, 1970), *Jack London: A Klondike Trilogy* (1983), and with Robert C. Leitz, III, and I. Milo Shepard, *The Letters of Jack London* (1988) and *The Complete Short Stories of Jack London* (1993). He is currently working on a major biography of Jack London.

Jeanne Campbell Reesman is Associate Professor of English at the University of Texas at San Antonio. She is the founder and executive coordinator of the Jack London Society and has published numerous articles on London and other American writers in *American Literary Realism, the CEA Critic,* the *Kenyon Review, Renascence, Thalia: Studies in Literary History, Western American Literature,* and elsewhere. She is also the author of *American Designs: The Late Novels of James and Faulkner* (1991) and a coauthor of *A Handbook of Critical Approaches to Literature* (1992).

The Editor

Nancy A. Walker is Director of Women's Studies and Professor of English at Vanderbilt University. A native of Louisiana, she received her B.A. from Louisiana State University and her M.A. from Tulane University. After receiving her Ph.D. from Kent State University in 1971, she taught American literature, American studies, and women's studies at Stephens College, where she also served as Assistant to the President and Chair of the Department of Languages and Literature.

A specialist in American women writers, Walker is the author of *A Very Serious Thing: Women's Humor and American Culture* (1988) and *Feminist Alternatives: Irony and Fantasy in the Contemporary Novel by Women* (1990), which won the first annual Eudora Welty Prize. She has published numerous articles in such journals as *American Quarterly, Tulsa Studies in Women's Literature, American Literature,* and *American Literary Realism,* and several essays on women's autobiography. With Zita Dresner, she edited *Redressing the Balance: American Women's Literary Humor from the Colonial Period to the 1980s* (1988).

Walker currently serves as general editor for the period 1800–1914 for Twayne's United States Authors Series and is editing a new critical edition of Kate Chopin's *The Awakening* for St. Martin's Press.